THE DETOUR

THE DETOUR

Towards Revising Catholicism

Robert Butterworth

GRACEWING

First published in 2005

Gracewing
2 Southern Avenue, Leominster
Herefordshire HR6 0QF

ISBN 0 85244 636 5

Typeset by
Action Publishing Technology Ltd, Gloucester GL1 5SR

Printed in England

Contents

Preface

Bob Butterworth and I have been friends now for many years. We were students together at Oxford and in Rome, and, for a few years, colleagues in London. So it is a pleasure to be invited to write a preface for this book. He states that it is not meant to be an autobiography. It could, perhaps, he says, be described as a sort of 'theological autobiography'. It tells the tale of how the author travelled through 'the barren uplands of the Catholic and Jesuit spirituality of a certain age which is perhaps now past'. He describes this journey as a lengthy detour that eventually brought him back to 'the sunny life of the lowlands' where he now finds himself. He describes the story as 'a joint product of accurate memory, hindsight and imagination' and this is a good description. He says he has written this book to clarify his own ideas about where he came from and how he got to where he now is. His method is one of narrative, an account of the different 'worlds' that he has lived in. So it is the story of how a young man can be drawn to religious life, become a priest, a university lecturer, head of department, and then abandon this way of life and return to what he terms 'the world of ordinary life'. It is a fascinating story told in a style that is lucid and elegant. It is critical of the Roman ecclesiastical system and provides an imaginative sketch of 'what might be the beginnings of an alternative approach to the religion of Catholicism'. Bob left the Jesuits after having been a member of the Society of Jesus for forty years, but his book is not an attack on the Jesuits. What he does criticize is what George Tyrrell called 'Jesuitism' – that is the wooden systematization of the original insights of Ignatius Loyola which took the Society over after its restoration in the nineteenth century.

He begins with the story of the day he was born and his mother died. This is beautifully told and very moving and in the words of an eyewitness who was present on that sad Christmas Eve 1930.

He goes on to recall happy memories of his childhood in Leyland, with his visits to the local shops, the butcher, the ironmonger, the toffee-shop, the greengrocer – all reminiscent of an age now swept away by our large supermarkets. He contrasts two worlds – the ordinary world of Leyland Towngate and another world, the religious world of the Catholicism of his local parish church. This religious world was destined to replace his ordinary world before he was out of his teens. He enjoyed the years he spent at Preston Catholic College where, for the first time, he encountered Jesuits. The teaching at the College he thought competent if uninspiring. In his final year he was very impressed by a sermon preached by Fr Bernard Basset, 'a highly intelligent, witty and imaginative Jesuit'. He says that he 'never before even imagined that anyone could be so coherently sincere, convinced and committed about Catholicism as he was'. He did well in his studies, though he was described by one headmaster as 'un peu difficile'. Towards the end of his final year he suddenly, out of the blue, decided to join the Jesuits. Just why he made this decision he cannot now remember. He was attracted by the way the Jesuits lived and when asked why he wanted to be a Jesuit, he was at a loss for words for a moment and replied that he couldn't think of a better way of spending his life. So in September 1948 he entered the Jesuit novitiate at Roehampton.

He goes on to describe the 'system' of Jesuit formation that he went through for the next fifteen years or so. He acknowledges that he is describing a system that is now a thing of the past, but he gives a clear and well-written account of the priestly formation that was universal throughout the Society of Jesus before the Second Vatican Council. This is a balanced and well-informed record of that system in which, as he says, both professors and students were trapped. His account of the 'social' life of the scholastics at Heythrop in the country is entertaining. It was another world – now only a memory. His years at Oxford were more colourful, with brilliant tutors such as Colin Hardie and Tom Stevens. Also he enjoyed his years in Rome, completing his doctorate under the supervision of the renowned Antonio Orbe S.J., and getting a chance to see Rome and the Vatican at close quarters.

When he returned to England he witnessed the crumbling of the short-lived Pontifical Athenaeum and played a key part in the transfer of Heythrop College from North Oxfordshire to the University of London. He describes in some detail how this came about, and how the teaching of philosophy and theology had at last to break free from the 'system' and be fitted into the syllabus of an English university. In some of the most interesting pages he tells how he was helped in re-interpreting theological language by Wittgenstein's *Philosophical Investigations* and H.-G. Gadamer's *Truth and Method*.

In conclusion he puts forward some tentative suggestions on how Catholicism might be re-interpreted in ways that would release it from the dead hand of the system and the excessive power of ecclesiastical authority. He considers himself a Catholic and does not in any way reject the Catholic system of beliefs and its credal and doctrinal tradition, but he thinks there is need for radical reinterpretation. He sketches out some imaginative and challenging 'rules' for such a process in which great stress is put on the humanity of Jesus. He draws an interesting distinction between Catholic faith and Catholic beliefs. A revision of Catholicsm, in his view, would have to stress the metaphorical nature of relgious language, and its beliefs should be taken as metaphorical and imaginative constructions. Without saying that I agree or disagree with him in all of this, I think he has raised points for reflection that are stimulating and refreshing. He presents a challenge to all concerned about Roman Catholic Christianity.

I have attempted here to communicate something of the flavour of this 'autobiography'. The whole book is an interesting tale, well-told, never dull and very readable. It is carefully crafted in a polished prose that is a delight to read. His memory is quite extraordinary and his clear and accurate account of the system of priestly formation during those years will be hard to match. He is not uncritical, but he has in fact succeeded in writing without bitterness. He is to be congratulated for providing the reader both with an interesting account of his own theological development and with a cracking good story.

Clarence Gallagher, S. J.
11 March 2005

Introduction

The book I have written is hard to categorize. It would be a species of 'theological autobiography', if such a genre existed. Perhaps the best way of introducing it, I think, is to try to say what it is not. For the rest, it is going to have to speak for itself.

I have not written an autobiography, at least in the accepted sense. I simply do not think that my life holds either the interest or the significance to deserve such grand treatment. But I have compiled a summary account of my life so far by way of helping me to discover how I have managed to get where I am from where I started religiously; and, more narrowly, how my later thinking about my native Catholicism relates, in my mind, to the version I was brought up on. The book is, if you like, an odd sort of traveller's tale: the tale of a route taken through the barren uplands of the Catholic and Jesuit spirituality of a certain age which is perhaps now past; a route taken by many better travellers than I, but which has rarely been described; a route taken which turned out, luckily for me, to be only a detour (but a long one) which eventually brought me back to the main road and the sunny life of the lowlands.

I have tried to write my tale *sine ira et studio* – without anger and spin. Far from angering me, my detour provided considerable enjoyment; but telling the story without putting some spin on it would have been pointless. I expect most readers to spot the spin, though I would like to think that I have been able to mix in the odd googly. The story itself is severely selective. I have pared down incident and anecdote to a minimum. Except where I have thought I should add a dash of colour or credibility here and there, or to indulge a personal affection, I have air-brushed most characters out, not because I do not appreciate their influence over me, or their personal kindnesses towards me, but because I thought that this kind of story did not require their formal presence. Their omission might also, I thought, spare them the unnec-

essary embarrassment which might arise from their being associated with conclusions with which they cannot possibly be
expected to agree. The story is a joint product of accurate
memory, hindsight and imagination – the best way I know of
expressing the kind of truth I had in mind when I began.

I have not written anything resembling a scholarly work:
indeed, after long familiarity with the mind-set and methods of
scholarship, I have deliberately avoided them in an effort to try
and say something original and imaginative, however rough it
has turned out to be. I have always tended to be an uncritical
admirer of scholars, without, I must admit, being much of one
myself. But I know enough about those who claim (sometimes
rightly) to be scholars to realize that what I have produced might
both annoy and alarm them. I should also add that I am enough
of a philosopher to know that I have not written a work of philosophical value; that I am familiar enough with scriptural exegetes
to know that my understanding of biblical texts is bound to be
considered sub-standard; and that I know enough of theology
and the particular *odium* it generates to know that many theologians will reject my views comprehensively. But I am also closely
enough acquainted with experts in these fields and with their
studied dislike of the imagination, their often craven pursuit of
political correctness and the academically fashionable, to feel
confident enough that any rejection of my chosen approach on
their part is not going to bother me in the slightest.

I have not written an attack on the Church, though I am critical
of the Roman religious and ecclesiastical system. Because I
believe it is simply too much to expect that the Roman, or any
other professionally entrenched system or institution, will ever
get round to reforming itself, I thought it better to get on with
sketching out what might be the beginnings of an alternative
approach to the religion of Catholicism in which the Church
could still have a role to play.

I have not written an attack on the Jesuits, either. I was forty
years in that distinguished Order, and the life and the work and
most of my colleagues I found congenial enough. I fancy there are
few human communities in which one is likely to encounter so
many high-minded and dedicated men. I left only after I had
found myself in an intolerable position. What I am criticizing,
however, is what Fr George Tyrrell (a religious genius who also
knew the Order well from inside) called 'Jesuitism' – that is, the
wooden systematization of the original insights of Ignatius
Loyola which took the Society over after its restoration in the

nineteenth century, and into whose procrustean mould we were still being forced halfway through the twentieth. About what, in the twenty-first century, may be happening in the Order well over fifty years after I joined, I have no idea. I have not lived in a Jesuit house for the last twenty-five years. I am still not entirely sure why I joined the Order in 1948, though I suggest a possible reason in the course of the book. I am still pondering the force of a passing remark which Professor Anthony Clare made in the context of his own choice of a medical career (*The Observer*, 29 July 1991): 'The Jesuits are interesting because they marry the notion of power with service – a potent mixture for a growing adolescent.' Perhaps so.

I have not written about religion in general, or about other Christian Churches or about non-Christian religions. I am unqualified to deal with such matters on so broad a front, and I have crippling doubts about the validity, let alone the use, of such an approach. I am writing only about what I know best, the traditional religion of the Roman Catholic Church, which, for simplicity's sake, I shall refer to throughout as 'Catholicism'. Likewise I refer to the Roman Catholic Church as 'the Church'. These two shorthand expressions I have adopted in order to make my life easier, and without any intention of offending those who might feel excluded thereby – just as I sometimes use 'he' when 'she' would do just as well, or even better.

I have not written an *Apologia pro Vita Mea*, for the simple reason that I do not feel I have any need or duty to defend or explain myself to anyone apart from myself.

I remain aware that my sketchy suggestion of a few new rules that might govern a revision of Catholicism as I experienced it is a product of my own creative imagination – but, I would hope, perhaps of the same kind of religious imagination (but at a far inferior level) that went into the construction of Catholicism in the first place. Inevitably, all this has led me to a thorough consideration of that most interesting of questions: what on earth do I personally mean by 'God'? But then 'God' is an idea which all serious persons ought to keep under constant review.

If I were to choose a motto for the work, a phrase to steer the reader through, it would be a sentence from Euripides (or perhaps a slightly later interpolator), *Hippolytus* 197:

'Stories are all we have to go on'.

Up to the time of writing this Introduction only three people had read what I have written. Two of them, John Ashton and Clarence Gallagher, old friends from Oxford, were wonderfully reticent in their criticisms of it, but were good enough to say they enjoyed the story. The third is my wife, Barbara, without whom there would be no story worth telling.

R.B.

Cowley, Uxbridge, 2004

[It will be clear that I owe much of what I say about my Lancashire home-town of Leyland to David Hunt's excellent *The History of Leyland and District* (Carnegie Press, 1990). I have his kind permission to make use of his work.]

Chapter 1

My Two Worlds

By 1930 the ancient village of Leyland, an inland settlement in that part of Lancashire which lies between the Ribble and the Mersey, had already lost much of whatever rural charm it may once have had. The old strip-farming of the flat surrounding fields had long gone, and the cottage textile industry of hand-loom weaving had given way to several busy cotton mills and bleach works. Other industries had then muscled in. Leyland Motors was already producing world-famous trucks and buses. The Leyland Paint and Varnish Company and the Leyland and Birmingham Rubber Company had brought more wealth, more dirt and ever more pungent smells to a fast growing industrial town. Leyland had, in fact, developed two faces. Its grim northern face looked out towards Preston, and it was here, where the main London, Midland and Scottish Railway line from London Euston to Glasgow had shaved off neighbouring Farington, that Leyland displayed its industrial strengths. From the railway station the road into town led down Station Brow, past the Police Station, and then on down Chapel Brow, at the bottom of which, and on the town's most prominent corner, stood the dirtiest and smelliest industrial plant of all – the Leyland and Farington Gas Works, an environmental horror which daily belched out smoke and fumes and heavy grit until the mid-1950s. But the town's softer face looked to the other compass-points: south, west and east into pleasant farmlands, across the flat 'mosses' towards Southport, and towards the moors of Anglezarke and Rivington beyond Chorley. Here is the Leyland of happy memory, where I was glad to be born and grow up. Over the past seventy years, in whatever worlds I have found myself living, I have looked to Leyland as their source and centre.

But one further establishment constituted an even more imposing element in my earliest world: the Leyland and Farington Co-operative Society Ltd.– 'grocers, drapers, boot and shoe dealers, bakers and confectioners, butchers, house furnishers, ladies and gents outfitters, and coal merchants', as Barrett's *Preston Directory* of 1932 lists the range of some of its comprehensive activities. With its many branches the Co-op was important, in those days, for the ways in which many working families managed their lives in this small town; and no branch was more important than the Drapery branch in Chapel Brow, all too near the Gas Works. Men's and women's clothes, hats and shoes (including repairs and bespoke clogs), soft furnishings (curtains of all kinds), haberdashery, kitchen hardware (pots and pans, crockery and cutlery), household furniture (beds, wardrobes, dressers, tables, chairs, three-piece suites, linoleum and carpets) – Chapel Brow Co-op Drapery had them all. My father, Henry Butterworth, was the manager, and it was he who had built it up into an efficient and profitable business.

The following account of what happened at the Co-op Drapery on the morning of Christmas Eve 1930 comes straight from the only surviving eye-witness. It was the last shopping day before Christmas, and it could be expected to be a very busy one. At a time when Christmas still began only a day or two before the feast and not several months in advance, Co-op customers would be keen to collect and spend their 'divi' – the ten per cent (2/- in the pound) they regularly earned on whatever they had spent at any branch of their local Co-op. On the Drapery doorstep three of my father's staff were standing – Molly Nelson, his second-in-command, a stylish blonde and a star performer in local light opera, and her two teenage assistants, Peg Marsden and – my eye-witness – Amy Morris. Amy, now an astonishingly active 90-plus-year-old, tells me that it was very unusual for my father to be late, since he was a stickler for all-round punctuality. Normally a pleasantly relaxed and mannerly person and well liked by everyone who knew him, he arrived, striding round the Gas Works corner, looking grim and ghastly. He did not speak to his waiting staff. They all knew, of course, that the arrival of his second child was imminent. He let the trio in, and then summoned Molly into his office. The other two took their coats off and stood huddled together, well aware by now that something must be dreadfully wrong. Eventually my father emerged and walked straight out of the shop again without acknowledging the young pair at all. Shortly afterwards Molly came out of his office, white as a sheet and in tears. Peg Marsden asked her if the expected baby was dead. 'No,' said Molly, 'it's not the baby – it's Minnie – Minnie's dead.' My father had just lost his wife, a great favourite with everyone who knew this happy couple. The staff trio collapsed in tears, and Amy remembers the day as one of the worst, if not the worst, of her long life. They had to spend it trying to cope with the Christmas rush. Whenever they had to explain my father's absence, they and the other assistants dissolved in tears again, and so did many of the customers.

Another duty my father did not neglect to do on that bleak day was to visit the local Registrar. In the Registration District of Chorley, in the Sub-district of Leyland, in the County of Lancaster, the Registrar on duty was Lavinia Seed, a name redolent of Spring and future growth. On that day she entered into her registers two closely connected events: the death of Wilhelmina Butterworth, formerly Tomlinson, and the birth of her second son, Robert – myself. On both of the certificates which she issued that same day she spelt Wilhelmina wrongly, as 'Wilhemina'. Perhaps nobody would have had the heart to correct her. Perhaps Dr C.M. Willmott L.R.C.P., the leading local doctor who had certified her death, had got it wrong first. Perhaps it was his doctor's handwriting. Wilhelmina had, in any case, always been called Minnie. On my birth certificate, however, Lavinia Seed got the date wrong as well. She wrote 'Twenty fourth December 1930'; but then she corrected it to 'Twenty Third', and carefully and very properly initialled the correction. I had been born very late on that day.

It is likely that what had happened was this: my mother Minnie, who was by this time thirty-six years old and had already given birth to my elder brother Harry almost five years before, apparently without problems, went into 'prolonged labour' early on 23 December 1930 at home, which was Holyoake, Towngate, Leyland. Before or when I was born much later that same day, severe complications set in. My mother haemorrhaged badly. Eventually – and by now it was 24 December – she suffered heart failure and died. I was once told that five hours had elapsed between my birth and her death. It seems likely that, had the confinement taken place in hospital rather than at home, much might have been done to avoid the problems that proved fatal. At any rate, there was no 'post mortem'. What is certain is that Christmas 1930 must have been an unspeakably hard time for the rest of the family. In the grim days after Christmas my mother was buried in the Roman Catholic section of Preston Cemetery – there was no Catholic cemetery in Leyland until the mid-1930s – and I was duly baptized into my parents' Roman Catholic faith by Dom Anselm Parker O.S.B. at St Mary's Church in Leyland.

My share in Minnie's legacy was rich in kind: an excellent
father and a solid Lancashire family background, reliable health,
adequate brains, a fair imagination – somewhat romantic,
perhaps, but normally disciplined – a buoyant enough temperament, a largely pragmatic attitude to life, overall common sense,
a useful sense of humour. Minnie, in other words, had left me a
more than fighting chance of becoming a viable human being in
whatever world I was going to have to live. What I have made of
that chance is strictly for me – and my God – to judge, though no
doubt others have their views. For my part, I would say that I
eventually turned out to be able to make my own rather clumsily
self-assertive way through life; to be able to make up my own
mind and to act on it; to be able to think radically, but within
reason; to be outspoken but fairly judiciously so; to be stubborn
but not altogether impossible; to be inclined to take myself seriously but not for too long; to be defensively over-sensitive but
only until I was sure I was not being got at; to be rather insensi-
tive of other people's feelings but only until I realized it; to be
fairly ambitious but not to bother putting myself out; to have
sufficient self-esteem but to be keen to keep it on the low, safe
side; to be able to work quite hard but usually in short bursts and
as and when it suited me; to admire the good things in life, but to
be dreamily indolent about getting them; to enjoy good company
but to be socially lazy and negligent and rather shy; to like
belonging to select groups but inclined to get bored with them; to
love recognition but to do as little as possible to deserve it – in
other words, I would say I turned out to be the middling sort of
person about whom it could be said, perhaps with a light sigh of
relief, that he did well enough but never really fulfilled his potential or promise. I hope I have not let Minnie down in becoming
the kind of person I think I have turned out to be.

But there was another, quite different part to Minnie's legacy,
and I have had to learn to cope with that as well. It is from her
that I inherited entry into another world altogether – the world of
Catholicism. How I have managed to work out how my very
ordinary world might relate to the more exotic world of
Catholicism is really what I have been moved to write about: how
true can I say I have been to the whole of Minnie's legacy? It is a
question that cannot be answered without reference to what
happened to me after my unpromising start in life; so whilst what
I have written has something of the form of an autobiography, its
real interest lies, at any rate as far as I am concerned, not so much
in the necessary details of an ordinary life as in the issues regard-

ing the world of Catholicism and the personal understanding of it which I was gradually led to develop as time and events went on.

I wish I had met my mother, or even learned more about her from those who knew her; but the habitual reserve of northern family life ensured, quite understandably, that unspeakable things were usually left unspoken. Oddly, I find myself regretting that I have never even seen her handwriting. I treasure a couple of excellent photographs of her. She looks such a thoughtful, kind, slightly dreamy person. I have visited her grave in Preston Cemetery, not without a certain disquiet. It has bothered me that there is no inscribed headstone, only a numbered stone stump among others. I can think of no reason for this apparent neglect. Perhaps my father could not bring himself to do anything about it, though that would be entirely untypical of him. Perhaps he was hoping to transfer her remains to a new Catholic cemetery in Leyland. I once thought I might do something about it myself. I viewed the scene carefully but decided to leave things just as they were. A magnificent beech tree shades her stone as well as the other anonymous markers, and I felt that nothing should be done to break the spell of what I found unforgettably understated.

The Butterworths Minnie had married into had long been a normal, nominal, Church of England family. In none of their lives, as far as I know, did religion or even church attendance play any significant part. Certainly I never heard any of them so much as mention such matters. The exception among them turned out to be my father, one of the many Henrys who regularly appear in every generation of his family over the last couple of centuries. He had converted to Catholicism before marrying Minnie. He stuck stoically to the practice of his new, rather ill-fitting religion for the rest of his life. Not that he ever expressed any religious views in my hearing; but then although he was a pleasantly affable man in his family and outside it, he was notably reserved when it came to any personal experience. Reserve seemed entirely natural to him, and I do not think it can have resulted simply from the trauma my mother's death must have inflicted on him. Not surprisingly, the rest of the family followed suit, and we hardly ever spoke about our feelings. I never saw my father angry or particularly moved. He never spoke about his past life, except for the occasional, and in time very familiar, jokey anecdote. He kept his distance, and never described his early life in Preston, his military service in the Loyal North Lancashire Regiment in the 1914–18 War, his very happy marriage to Minnie, and never, of course, her tragic death. Even when my brother and I would play with his bright-ribboned campaign medals and the heavy machine-gun bullet (was it still live?) which he kept as mementoes of his war service, he never expressed what they meant to him, or said where in France he had fought. He was a thoroughly good man: able, sensible, wise and kind. Occasionally he would sing old songs to himself. I cannot even begin to think what he had made of my mother's death. In the manner of those times, he lived in his own adult world.

He dutifully devoted his energies to constructing and main-taining our childhood world and a family life in which my brother and I could safely live and happily flourish. To this end he first imported his own mother and his deceased wife's sister, Gertie Tomlinson, into our home; and eventually he married again, and once more into a strongly Catholic family, the Dugdales of Coppull. To his two sons from his first marriage were added a daughter and another son; and my father continued to preside in his gentle way over a family which enjoyed a virtu-ally seamless and largely problem-free existence. As the poet Horace said: *Nil me paeniteat sanum patris huius* (Satires, I.6.89) – 'I would be mad not to be happy at being this man's son'.

My father had a brother and three sisters, all married and, except for one sister, all with children, our cousins. The family had lived in the same small area of central Lancashire in and around Preston from at least the end of the eighteenth century, though the Butterworth name was associated more with the Rochdale area in east Lancashire, where they had long been esquires. So Leyland, five or six miles from Preston, was consid-ered, I fancy, a bit off the beaten track, though one of my father's sisters also lived out on a limb in Blackburn. But we loyally and regularly exchanged Sunday visits with all of them. They were uniformly upright, cheerful and kindly folk, descended from hard-working, useful and undistinguished forebears: a cotton mill manager, a carter, an ostler and cab-driver, a baker and biscuit-maker, on the men's side; and from housekeepers and servants and grandly named 'power-loom operators' (mill-girls), on the women's. Minnie's Tomlinson forebears came from some miles further afield in the Fylde – from Lancaster, Kirkham and Wesham. Both sides of my family seem to have been wholly Lancastrian; and their family trees bud with solid English patronymics – Tomlinson, Higginson, Robinson, Wilson, Lawrenson.

But it was the Butterworth grandmother my father brought to live with us after my mother's death whose presence and influence I can first recall. Born Jane Robinson, daughter of a game-keeper in Cartmel, to the south of the Lake District and still in Lancashire in those days, she had married grandfather Henry Butterworth, the Preston baker and biscuit-maker. He was dead by the time his newly-converted son married Minnie Tomlinson at the English Martyrs Church in Preston in 1924; but Grandma Butterworth lived on into the 1940s. Anyone familiar with the Grandma in Giles' cartoons will already have a true image of Grandma Butterworth: diminutive, bespectacled, black-hatted and long black-coated, in buttoned boots, with a fox fur and umbrella. She was a splendid housekeeper, known especially for the incomparable recipes she passed down the family – Christmas cakes, mince pies, ginger wine, lemon cheese. She was also an excellent nursemaid. Nightly she sang me to sleep with the non-Catholic hymns of her Cartmel childhood. Our favourite was Sabine Baring-Gould's 'Now the day is ended' –

> Night is growing nigh,
> Shadows of the evening
> Steal across the sky.
> Now the darkness gathers,
> Stars begin to peep,
> Birds and beast and flowers
> Now have gone to sleep ...

It gave me my first look into a 'religious' world.

But that I was to be brought up a Catholic was ensured by Minnie and the Tomlinson connection, reinforced by my father's conversion. My Tomlinson grandparents, whom I never knew, were Catholics who had lived in Kirkham in the Fylde. My Tomlinson grandfather was a building contractor whose sizable business, I was told, folded at about the time of the 1914–18 War. He had built churches in his time; and he had undertaken to build superior bungalows in Lytham St Anne's, but the project failed, possibly because of the wartime shortage of labour. The Tomlinsons were a large family: ten children in all, although only seven stately daughters, of whom Minnie was the youngest, survived. When their father's business foundered, the girls had to leave the Holy Child Sisters' convent school in Preston where they had boarded, move into town from Kirkham, and go out to work and earn a living. Minnie found work in the Drapery branch of the Preston Co-operative Society, and it was there that she met my father, back from the army and employed as an assistant at the same branch. No doubt it was my father's promotion to Manager of the Co-op Drapery branch in Leyland – a job he kept for the next thirty years – that led to their getting married and moving to Leyland.

ॐ

You cannot be born in Leyland and not have your local pride constantly aroused wherever in the world you may encounter buses, trucks and vans. It was in the 1920s that Leyland had become a name of international renown in the world of motor transport. I recall my own immense pride at seeing, some years ago, an ageing truck with the 'Leyland' moulding on its radiator and a load of poncho'ed and woolly-hatted campesinos on its back, cruising along the Peruvian shore of Lake Titicaca down by Bolivia. On the same trip, on a visit to Arequipa, that delightful white-stoned city deep in southern Peru, I happened to be having dinner with a Dutch businessman who served (oddly, come to think of it) as Finnish Consul and ran a small factory which made rivets – 'for a truck factory in England', he explained. 'You won't have heard of it – it's called Leyland.' On a recent holiday in Malta it was a delight to find myself using the ancient Leyland buses – bulbous, battered, rattling articles, some more than half a century old – which make up much of the island's public transport. Nothing takes me back to my old roots more quickly than encounters such as these.

But ages before industry ever came to town, Leyland was an ancient settlement with a marked local identity and a dialect of its own. The earliest written evidence for the place and its Hundred – its name means fallow, unploughed land – is in the Domesday Book, 1086. There is mention of a priest, but none of a church, until shortly afterwards in 1100. In 1334 Pope John XXII entrusted the parish of St Andrew in Leyland to the care of the Benedictine Priory of Penwortham, on the south bank of the Ribble at Preston and a daughter house of the great Abbey of Evesham. So in pre-Reformation Leyland Benedictine monks were already a familiar presence. A fine old chalice, inscribed 'Restore mee to layland in Lankeshire' survived the Reformation and re-surfaced in Leyland in 1845, when the English Benedictines of Ampleforth Abbey in Yorkshire, already active in the Lancashire mission, set up the modern Catholic parish of Leyland St Mary's.

It is always difficult to assess, not least in the case of a small and remote place, the seriousness of the break with the old religion after Henry VIII suppressed Evesham and Penwortham in

1539, and Leyland St Andrew's officially passed over to the English form of Protestantism. The local squires, the Faringtons (or ffaringtons) – the last Squire ffarington died in 1947 when I was a schoolboy – had long patronized the parish church, and at first they cooperated with the reforms and did well out of them, whilst cagily hedging their bets. In the 1550s one Farington, Robert, left the priesthood and married into the Southworths of Samlesbury Hall, the family of St John Southworth, the English martyr. For this misdemeanour Robert found himself disinherited and imprisoned. Another Farington retained such strong Catholic sympathies that his house, Worden Hall, was duly marked with a cross by Lord Burghley on his famous map showing prominent and potentially hostile Lancashire Catholics. Samlesbury Hall was close to Leyland, as was Hoghton Tower, and both were Catholic safe houses visited by the Jesuit martyr St Edmund Campion. In Leyland itself, and only a few hundred yards from where we later lived in Balcarres Road, there stood what looked like an old farmhouse. This was Charnock Hall, where Robert Charnock, outwardly a landed gentleman but in fact a Lisbon-trained priest known as 'Mr Manley', kept on ministering to local Catholics until he died. His property, along with its alleged 'priests' holes', was later (in 1686) confiscated and granted 'to the poore vicar of Leyland' after it was judged to have been illegally conveyed in trust 'for the support and maintenance of priests of the Romish religion in the county of Lancashire'. It looks as though many local people round Leyland kept their heads down and hung on to their Catholicism without much interference from the authorities, who were inclined to be tolerant anyway. Leyland was a long way from the centres of power in the land, and it is unlikely that anti-Catholic legislation had widespread support, or that there was much of a will to enforce it, except perhaps to settle old scores.

Being a Catholic in Leyland certainly seemed entirely natural. We may not have attended the old, gloomy grey bulk of St Andrew's, with its squat, potent tower, its imposing clock and its fascinating graveyard; but we did have our own St Mary's close by it and near the town's ancient Cross. St Mary's was a serviceable brick barn of a church with a glittering marble and gold sanctuary, a hand-pumped organ in its choir-loft, and eventually its own peaceful cemetery, bought in the mid-1930s from the Farington Trust. Then there was the reassuring presence – in fact, the reappearance – of the Benedictines who devotedly ran the parish, and quietly but firmly maintained the contemporary forms of Tridentine Catholicism. They showed a great deal of initiative in the steady development, not only of the church buildings, but also of the excellent school which served a growing Catholic community. The full range of pre-Vatican II Catholicism was on generous offer: Masses, High, Low and *Cantatae* (all in Latin, of course), Confessions, Benediction of the Blessed Sacrament, annual *Quarant' Ore*, Holidays of Obligation, the Christmas Crib, the Holy Week ceremonies and the Easter celebrations, the great summer feasts and saints' days – Corpus Christi, Saints Peter and Paul, the Assumption of Our Lady – sometimes with a full-dress procession round the church grounds, and even out into Towngate itself. Nor were any of the other features that marked the Roman Catholicism of that time lacking: Lenten missions, Italianate devotions and novenas, pious guilds and confraternities for men and women and altar-boys, a wildly over-ambitious 'choir' which under the spirited guidance of Frank Jackson, an excellent dance-band pianist seated at the organ, wallowed in Father Faber's ultramontane hymns from 'The Westminster Hymnal', slaughtered plainchant and murdered the Masses of Lorenzo Perosi. All this went on, of course, in addition to the regular fare of baptisms, marriages, churchings and funerals.

There were normally three or four Ampleforth Benedictine monks on the parish staff. None was local, so they brought a wider, more cosmopolitan dimension into their parish than did the ordinary secular clergy of the Archdiocese of Liverpool who ran most of the surrounding parishes. The monks ranged from the charmingly eccentric to the outstandingly efficient – parish priests like Anselm Parker, Roger Lightbound and Edmund Fitzsimons. It was the last-named who, in the 1960s, built a completely new St Mary's, of revolutionary design and some artistic merit, to serve the by now four thousand Catholics who lived in what was still a small town, and to house the reformed liturgy of the Second Vatican Council. But I do not recall that Catholics, even back in the 1930s and 1940s, felt anything but thoroughly at home in Leyland. We did not feel like the minority we were. We did not feel left out of Leyland life, and still less did we feel any hostility either towards or from those who attended other churches. We Catholics were a strong tribe in our own right, and we were at home on our own ancestral territory, confident and well-led, buying our Friday fish from Carline's on Towngate, going to confession on a Saturday, and often attending church more than once on a Sunday.

᪇

It was into this tribe that I was born in the fine brick terraced house which, for no traceable reason, was called Holyoake. It stood in a busy part of Towngate, Leyland's old main street, about two hundred yards north of the town's ancient centre, Leyland Cross, and was rented from the Co-op, my father's employer. Our solid old house is no more. Some years ago, on one of my visits to Leyland, I was able to observe its demolition. The developers had already moved in and had started to rip it apart. It stood exposed to the elements, half torn down, most valuable or 'collectable' fixtures and fittings already removed and taken for recycling. I did not know it at the time, but this last sight of the old house furnished me with an image which, as will appear, came into its own many years later. Now, of course, the house has been completely demolished and some transient business – an Energy or a Travel Centre – occupies the characterless building erected in its place.

To the side of our house there was a gravelled square, open all along its front to Towngate itself. We called it what it was supposed to be – the car park: though there were few private cars in Leyland in the early 1930s, and I cannot remember anyone ever parking there. On the other side of the car park stood Leyland Public Hall, the headquarters of the Urban District Council, and along the back of the square was a high fence of old flaking railway sleepers which in summer smelled fragrantly of tar. The car park was our private playground, and it was from there outwards that my ordinary world began to grow as my life expanded and shaped itself into the adjacent areas. Behind our house was the entry to the 'backs' of Bradshaw Street, which had been built in the early nineteenth century as a row of 'step-houses' for handloom weaving, with a loomshop in the basement and a large window to catch as much natural light as possible. By our time Bradshaw Street had become a poor and deprived area, and later on the Council was moved to try to change its image – with some success – by knocking gaps in the terraces and renaming the street Spring Gardens. As Bradshaw Street, it remained a no-go area beyond the edge of my world. Even at our lowly level, class was made to count. My brother Harry was regularly sent round there, carrying large jugs of my Grandma's broth, usually to the McCormicks, a hard-pressed Irish Catholic family with a boy in Harry's class at school. We shopped at the Co-op Grocery just along Towngate, and we bought butter. People from Bradshaw Street shopped at Melia's, a cut-price, down-market store close by, and they bought something called margarine, which we never had in the house. Not that we could afford to be all that exclusive. Certain elect children from Spring Gardens were granted exemptions from their lowly lot and were reclassified as acceptable. They might come and play in our car park, but I still could not go there. Otherwise, of course, I would have had nobody of my own age to play with. Thus did I begin to import some simple social structures into my little world.

My brother Harry was an important part of that world. He must, of course, have remembered our mother, but once again the habitual family reserve prevented him from ever mentioning her. He was a pleasant, fair-haired, wiry boy with a good sense of humour and a surprising gift for dead-pan comedy which he certainly should have developed. He had a circle of young friends of his own, but I was never excluded, and the two of us played endless games together with one another's toys, kept in a large cupboard under the living room window. He once kept a rabbit and later owned a dog, but he displayed an early preference for model cars and ships – he had a large and powerful model of Donald Campbell's *Bluebird*, a tin submarine that submerged and surfaced in the bath, and a dashing miniature destroyer, H.M.S. *Grenville*. Later he turned to working steam engines, one of which drove a model motor-boat. All these were signs of things to come. I liked my big toy fort, and my soldiers defended it against the artillery barrage he would launch against it with a deadly scale-model howitzer. We spent much of our free time together, and I cannot recall that there was ever any friction between us. He loathed school, failed 'the scholarship' at the age of eleven, and left when he became fourteen. But he was very bright, and a brief outline of the rest of his distinguished career in engineering can be found in *Who's Who*. We lived in a happy world, and I fancy we were both spoilt because of what had happened to our mother. I have often wondered what link there might be between lacking a mother and the course of our later lives. That there is no connection would seem unlikely, perhaps incredible; but I cannot say that any clear causal chains have ever suggested themselves to me. Why did he turn out an outstanding engineer, whilst I took to classics and theology? Who knows the answers to such questions? What happens, just seems to happen. Or perhaps more constructively, *quisque suos patimur manis*, as Virgil (Aeneid 6.743) makes dead Anchises declare, with a famously nasty twist to the grammar – 'each one of us have to cope with their own ghosts'.

Harry was always somewhat closer than I was to our aunt,

Gertie Tomlinson, our mother's slightly older sister who lived with us and helped Grandma Butterworth to run the house. Gertie was a natural gem, and it was she who kept us all faithful to our Catholic practices. Once my mother's death was some years past, my widower father naturally became a possible partner in some second marriage. He was a handsome man, and several women, I have been told, were attracted to him; but he did not respond. I do not know whether Gertie ever entertained thoughts of marrying my bereaved father. After all, there had been a family precedent for it. One of the seven Tomlinson sisters had married my Uncle George Haslam, staunch Labour Councillor and later an Alderman of Bolton, but she died, still a young bride, in the serious 'flu epidemic of 1918; whereupon Uncle George promptly moved on to another Tomlinson sister, our Auntie Jo, and married her. In fact, Gertie never married in all her 80-odd years, but remained a strong and loyal support to our family until she died. She worked all her life in the local rubber factory, and during the war she was responsible for supervising the production of gas-masks. In the grimmest period of the war she was sent to Mansfield to continue this work, and never a week went by without her sending two letters – one for Harry and one for me – each with a half-crown stitched firmly to the top corner. None ever went astray, and this she attributed to her Catholic habit of writing 'S.A.G.' under the stamp – 'St Anthony, Guide'. She never lost her sense of humour, her friends or her Tomlinson dignity. After she moved out from our home to set up her own home in nearby Farington, she was always a delight to visit, and when you left, after the inevitable cup of tea (she drank over twenty cups a day), she would never leave her door until you disappeared with a final wave round the corner. She died on 22 December 1978 after a brief stay in an old folks' home in Penwortham. Sadly, I happened to be stuck in Jerusalem at the time. The next day, on my forty-eighth birthday, and almost the anniversary of her sister Minnie's death, there was a telegram waiting for me when I returned from a study-trip round the land of the Philistines and the Gaza Strip. I was able to celebrate the Christmas Mass for the repose of her generous soul in the Cave of St Jerome in Bethlehem, a few yards from the site of the Manger. Gertie was one of those people no one can recall without a fond smile. We were privileged to have been brought up with her in attendance.

My father also ensured that we kept in constant contact with his side of the family, and this enlarged my childhood world.

After Sunday dinner – at the northern hour of twelve – we would take an olive-green Fishwick's bus from Leyland Cross into Preston, and then a chocolate coloured Corporation bus, or even a tram, out to their houses in the suburbs. None of us owned cars or had telephones, but the postal service was excellent, and messages and invitations passed around all the time. One of my father's three married sisters, Eldey (not, apparently, an abbreviation, but a name otherwise unknown to me) lived on the Leyland side of Preston in South Meadow Lane, and we went there most often. From Eldey and Tom's house you could walk past Preston Cricket Club down to the River Ribble, and then go under the huge mainline railway bridge and viaduct with its massive pillars, its criss-cross cage of steel girders way up high in the sky, its ever-dripping drains which made deep puddles in the pathway, and the occasional heavy rumble and clank of a train, perhaps bound for faraway London or Scotland, perhaps even 'The Royal Scot' itself. It is still, to my mind, the bridge of all bridges. No other bridge, not even San Francisco's Golden Gate, has replaced it in significance. It struck deep awe mixed with dread into me as a small child, with its high, gloomy, cavernous spans and its monstrous feet in the dangerous, dark and dirty waters of the Ribble. It was always a relief to have passed it. Once under it, you moved into the bright municipal greenery of Miller and Avenham (pronounced 'Ane-am') Parks. If you walked on down the tree-lined river-bank, you could get as far as the Old Tram Bridge. Just where it joined the north bank you could look through sturdy iron railings on what was said to be a bottomless whirlpool. It had once swallowed a whole derailed tram, and, of course, all the passengers on board. The water certainly rolled and boiled a little under the bank, and it looked evil and threatening. You were being invited to believe that your world contained dark and hostile forces that could strike down the innocent. But then on your way back home to Eldey's for Sunday tea you would be cheered up again by the goldfish and carp in the park ponds, and by the large aviary which sheltered under the embankment of the railway that ran to Blackburn and beyond. There was always a whiff of the uncanny about visits to Eldey and Tom's – as there was about this rather quaint couple themselves. Braving the Scylla and Charybdis down at the river added to the effect. They had no children, but a nondescript sandy dog called Spark, the first animal I can remember. I recall vividly how he loved to swim in the Ribble, right under the dreadful bridge, ruddering himself through the fast-flowing water with his tail, but happily still a long way from the deadly whirlpool.

Back in Leyland, too, my little world, and the life that was being constructed in it, was beginning to expand and to be shaped and peopled by kind grown-ups from outside the family. We had good neighbours, the Dawbers, whose unmarried, grown-up daughters, Ethel and Bessie, were always ready to look after Harry and myself. I still visit their graves close to the church door at St Andrew's. Further along Towngate, a few doors away, were two shops, a butcher's and a toffee-shop (we never used 'sweet' as anything but an adjective). They were run, respectively, by Mr and Mrs Harry Shorrock. Harry Shorrock was a weighty member of the Leyland establishment, a Conservative and a Mason. He was, or he seemed to me, large, stout and squat, with brilliantined hair and a waxed moustache, dressed always in an open starched white coat, long apron, stiff white collar and a black tie, under which bulged his waistcoat with its heavy gold watch-chain. Thus vested he stood behind his counter, or behind his heavy wooden chopping-block, carving – almost peeling or shaving – wide flat steaks from a large haunch of beef with a long thin knife noisily steeled to razor-sharpness. Meat axes and other knives hung on a stainless steel rail in the window. At the back of the shop was a big, smelly, walk-in refrigerated room with a thick heavy door. Broad sides of beef and whole skinned and eviscerated sheep and pigs hung from large hooks in the ceiling. Mr Shorrock made his own sausages on what was surely a magic machine. I spent hours in his shop, no doubt making a thorough nuisance of myself – but I was even more often in Mrs Shorrock's shop next door.

She was as spindly thin as he was stout, with tightly bunned hair, spectacles, and a strong red nose. Her shop was lined with toffee jars. On the counter there were brass scales and weights and a special hammer for breaking up slabs of Everton and treacle toffee. Chocolate – Cadbury's, Fry's, Toblerone – was packaged, but little else was. Toffees had to be weighed out and slid into paper bags. The two shops were connected by a long dark living-room at the back, a room I well remember from years later, when I was about fourteen years old. Harry Shorrock had sadly died, and I was expected to call in and 'pay my respects', since they had always been so kind to me. But this was an altogether new venture for me, and I recall asking my father what I was expected to do or say. He told me to say that I was very sorry that Mr Shorrock had died, and if they asked me (as in fact they did) whether I wanted to see him in his coffin, I should simply say, 'No, thank you, I would rather remember him as he was.' In the event, it worked beautifully, and I was greatly relieved. I thought my father immensely wise. I knew I could never have worked it out for myself. I sat for a while in the long living-room with the family, including Billy and Florrie Shorrock, the adult son and daughter, all red-eyed at their loss. Then I said I had to go; but they were clearly pleased that I had come.

This ordinary world of mine was still a very rudimentary affair. At this distance from it, I can recall most of its spatial spread, but I have little sense of the time involved in its growth. I have found that the notion of 'world' has played an increasing part in the way I have come to understand life, and I need to try to be clear about how I use it. By 'world' I do not always mean the world at large in the ordinary geographical sense. I mean the set-up, the 'limited whole', the immediate circumstances, in which an individual finds himself having or choosing to live, to make what he can or wants of his existence. I am thinking of a 'world', not as '*the* world' considered as a wholly external or objective reality, but as a personal construct which involves and develops from an individual's 'reading' and understanding the reality that surrounds him – his own imaginative interpretation of it. A 'world' is what a person actually makes of their circumstances in order to facilitate living in them. People do more than passively accept what surrounds them – they take a hand in making it into their world. 'Worlds', to my mind, are not big affairs, but generally quite small ones – and, most importantly, are intensely individual. A 'world' is one's own particular and personal *cosmos*. We forget that in Greek *cosmos* does not entail size. It simply means the way things are ordered, arranged, constructed, set up, set out, made to look – as in 'cosmetics'. Thus everyone lives primarily in their own world, whilst remaining able, of course, to appreciate and share the different worlds of other people. Many move from world to world as their lives develop and their horizons expand – or contract. It has been said that when a person dies, a whole world dies with them. This seems to me to be true in the sense that the individual way in which that person lived their life, their individually achieved *modus vivendi* and approach to reality and to their experience of existing as a human being, is lost to the rest of us for ever. From childhood onwards, people's worlds are their own developing 'takes' on reality – as was the ordinary world I was beginning to live in myself.

One of the reasons I know this is that in a conversation some years ago with my elder brother, in which we swapped memories of Towngate, I came to realize how 'other' his world had been when we were young together – how much 'not-mine' it was. And yet we lived extremely close to one another, almost indistinguishably close, it might be said. The contents of our worlds overlapped, of course, but his world was much wider and deeper, more populated, and with a different shape and different people in it. I could be prompted to remember some of the dimensions and contents of his world, but familiar as they were, they had never been appropriated by me as mine. They had never formed a real part of whoever I was growing up to be. I was accruing a world of my own, and I enjoyed living in it, protected from harsh events, safe in a tall forest of kindly, undemonstrative grown-ups, a privileged member of a protected species.

Gradually, but very gradually, the fragmentary and scattered features of my ordinary Towngate world began to gather and interconnect, to fuse and form themselves into a world with an increasingly elaborate structure to it. Strings and trails of memory develop, connecting what where staccato events into something more like the setting for a personal life – even, it might be said, into something which gave rise to some sense of a personal identity or a self. Links appear, joining parts of local space and certain points of time. The links are like a snail's thick, old, haphazard tracks, knitted together over a garden rock and then hardened in the sun. I suppose I was now getting to the age of four or so. My little world widened, and I could begin to build the opposite side of Towngate into its structure. My memories become firmer and clearer, accommodating new features that had never been more than a cricket-pitch away. Holmes's Bakery comes into view, a traditional shop with a most enticing smell to it. It was there we bought bread and, our favourites, vanilla slices. We were not one of those traditional bread-baking families who were still quite common. Holmes' bread was white, beautifully textured and very crusty – large 2lb loaves, black-and-tan on their vaulted tops, and all soft within. This is the kind of bread that always brings me back to Thursday afternoons, when the Co-op, along with the other local shops, had its half-day. My father would be home for tea, and we would have his favourite apple pie and Lancashire cheese, and always lots of bread and jam. This special weekly treat has given all my Thursdays a holiday flavour which they retain even now. Thursday was never to be much of a working day.

More or less opposite Holyoake was old Mrs Crooks's shop,

another toffee-shop that was like a small dark cave, full of everything Mrs Shorrock had, but with the addition of perfect ice-cream. Two sizes of cornets were a ha'penny and a penny. Wafers were a penny and tuppence. The home-made ice-cream was dug out of a large, antique barrel with a narrow, thick lid. Still on the other side of Towngate was Carline's, our Friday fish shop. Grandma Butterworth was spared the chore of shopping. She employed a young girl called Annie Cardwell to run local errands for sixpence a week. Across Towngate there was also Tommy Ball's toy-shop, which we regularly patronized. Then there was Dick Holmes the greengrocer, with a shop full of dark bins of potatoes and other roots and tubers, with shelves lined with cabbages and the like. No doubt the range of vegetables was limited by the restricted northern tastes of those days; but there were always many different kinds of fruit, including the pomegranates we always had at Christmas. At the end of the row, just opposite Leyland Cross, was Heaton's ironmongery. Here we filled our gallon can with paraffin, essential for the daily lighting of fires along with newspaper and sticks or 'cops' – the spent cardboard bobbins from the cotton-mill. At Heaton's every describable item of domestic hardware was readily available, and in all sizes – nails, screws, washers, oil-cans, putty, paint, candles, bath-plugs, tops for hot water-bottles, all stocked in little drawers at the far side of two large counters. Larger household objects and garden tools – mangles, ironing boards, dolly-tubs, washboards, dustbins, spades, forks, even lawn-mowers – either hung from the ceiling or filled most of the floor space. The whole place smelled of oil and paraffin. The two shopkeepers, dry, taciturn men in brown overall coats who knew exactly where everything was, magicked anything you might ask for out of drawers and elsewhere and on to the counter. They seemed infallibly efficient. At a later age I might have been tempted to invent items and ask for them in order to test their seemingly endless resources.

I find myself surprised now by the extent to which my world was defined by small shops; but in Towngate, apart from the still light traffic, there was really little else going on. Perhaps visits to today's supermarkets and shopping malls define today's young lives in similar, or even more powerful ways. All my small Towngate shops are gone now, swept away by waves of marauding developers who have left only ugliness or emptiness. Our end of Towngate down to the Cross is currently (2004) a dead-end, and mainly given over to being the large car park of the vast new Tesco's which has risen from the ruins opposite what was once

Holyoake. Still, as we shall see, this was not the only world of mine that I was to see slowly demolished.

I have never been given to having experiences which could be thought to transcend what is on normal offer in the ordinary world. I can recall only two such episodes in my whole life, both when I was young, and both connected with Towngate as it was. One was an inexplicably heightened affair which I shall come to later; but the other just had to do with my being ill, and the setting for it was Holyoake and the little Towngate shops opposite. Nowadays it would be called an out-of-body experience. The memory of it remains with me as if it had happened yesterday. When I was still very young – I think I may have just started school – I contracted scarlet fever. I had to be taken to an isolation hospital at Charnock Richard (a place known to all who use the M6 motorway for its service station). I can recall being carried by an ambulance man out of Holyoake and down the short garden path to be put into the waiting ambulance. I was wrapped in a red blanket, but I was either asleep or unconscious. Nonetheless I retain a most vivid – and, I was later assured, accurate – memory of the event. I do so because I (whatever 'I' means in this context) was hovering just above the roof of Mrs Crooks's toffee-shop across the road from Holyoake. I recall looking down, quite consciously and with great interest, on the whole scene of my being taken to hospital. I can see it all in memory now, always from exactly the same elevated and remote point of view among the chimneys. I have never had any similar experience. I take it that it was just some odd effect of the fever on my brain, causing something like a concurrent dream in which I somehow imagined, though from a distance and accurately, what was actually happening to me. There was nothing at all spooky about it. I do not know whether I was close to death, though, come to think of it, I suppose I might have been. I have read somewhere that it is when the brain is being starved of oxygen that such experiences can occur. At any rate, I had to stay in hospital for quite some time, and I rather enjoyed it all. We sang songs in our ward and after a lengthy confinement to bed we all had to learn to walk again, and this involved much sliding across the shiny floors. My family visited regularly, but they were only allowed to wave to me from behind a hedge about twenty yards from the ward window. When at last I got back home to Holyoake, I was given a much-loved Hornby train, and this increased the repertoire of games which Harry and I could play together.

There were areas behind the shops on the other side of Towngate where I was not allowed to go on my own. But I could ride my red-and-white tricycle up and down the wide pavement on our side of the road, past Waring's Men's Outfitters and Baron's Ladies Gowns, provided I did not go further than Leyland Cross. By a strange coincidence I still have photographic proof that this is what I did from no less a source than an official postcard view of the Cross taken from Towngate in the mid-30s. In the corner of the photograph, obtruding into the scene, but perhaps intended to provide either scale or added interest, is myself on my tricycle. But the trip down the line of shops to the Cross evokes another memory, this time a darkly embarrassing one. Just beyond the Public Hall was a saddler's shop called Crozier's. Horses were part of everyday life, of course. Milk, coal, and other domestic and commercial deliveries were all commonly brought by horse-drawn carts. Crozier's window was full of fascinating horse tackle: leather straps and reins in endless variety, looped and strung together with shining metal rings, cruel-looking bits and other functional pieces of steel, big brushes and strong steel combs, riding-boots, tins of dubbin, and whole harnesses on staring dummy horse-heads. But what caught my eye in all this were the horse-whips and the plaited leather riding-crops, slender and pliant. I cannot think that there was anything remotely psychopathic about my interest, which was aroused by the fact that my brother and I played top-and-whip, as most children did, and I conceived the idea that a very long whip would give me an insuperable advantage in our endless games. So one day I went into the shop on my own, with some pennies in my hand, and said that I wanted to buy a whip. Very reasonably, Mr Crozier asked me what I wanted a whip for, and I replied, with a completely fabricated untruth which I still find breath-taking, that I did not want it for myself but for Gertie, who, I boldly claimed, owned a horse. I was rightly sent packing, and the story got back to Holyoake. The family were highly amused; but I am still bothered by this incident and its deeper implications. Just where did I learn to lie with such cool and easy coherence? Ridiculous as it may be, I remain deeply ashamed of myself.

I was still very young when I first began to suffer from eczema. Even on the postcard view of Leyland Cross, a bandage covers the ointment that had to be applied to the back of my knee. But it is not so much the ailment that I can remember as the remedies: special bland food preparations, a patent blue soap called Neko, and above all calamine lotion, pink and thick in corked medicine bottles, and calamine ointment (or 'salve' as we always called it), pink and sticky in cardboard tubs. In search of effective relief, in those pre-N.H.S. days, we did the rounds of the local doctors with their stuffy waiting-rooms and tiny dispensaries – Willmott, Fotheringham, Carroll, Cank. It was Harold T. Cank who was adjudged the most effective: a fat, friendly man with heavy horn-rimmed spectacles and a fruity, matter-of-fact, manner. He became our family doctor for years afterwards. As for the eczema, I fancy I just grew out of it in time; or it may have trans-muted itself into the mild, seasonal hay fever which is the only permanent health problem I have had throughout my life.

It was in these very early years that another world, an altogether different construct, began to gather and impose itself. It was not my own, though I was expected to make it my own and live in it. Its immediate source was not in any strange out-of-body experi-ence, but in the bricks-and-mortar presence of Leyland St Mary's, our Catholic church a hundred yards down Worden Lane, just beyond the Cross. Not that I realized it then, of course, but this religious world – the world of Catholicism – whose source was in a Palestine and a Rome of the remote past, was destined to replace my ordinary world before I was out of my teens.

I do not remember when I first began to attend this potent source of a new and completely different 'take' on reality. I would certainly have been walked there by Gertie and my father when I was still very young. I could tell it was meant to impress. I have already mentioned the bright sanctuary in its arched alcove. Its walls shone white and dried-blood red in expensive marble. The polished panels were cut and patterned so as to resemble – but not deliberately, I fancy – the bloody, cleavered-open carcases of slaughtered, perhaps sacrificed, animals. I was reminded of what I saw hanging in Mr Shorrock's cold-store. In cool contrast, the altar was pure white marble, backed by smaller alcoves in glitter-ing gold mosaic, and surmounted by a brilliant golden-doored tabernacle, the obvious focus of everybody's devout attention. We were meant to be impressed, and we were. Gold was not a material encountered in my ordinary world, except in Mr Shorrock's heavy watch. The sanctuary had an exotic, even mysti-cal air about it. Heavily carved wooden rails enclosed a lavish floor of even more marble, and held the world of the profane at a distance. There could be no doubting that here was the local centre of a world apart.

The rest of the church, where the Leyland Catholics stood and knelt and sat, only confirmed this impression by its starkness. The body of the church was a broad and high, without pillars but with hard, unpadded pine benches and kneelers divided by two aisles. No home comforts here. But as a child, I could pass the time at church by sitting on the kneeler and playing with a Dinky toy in the hymn-book shelf which was part of the bench in front. This helped to allay the boredom induced by the routine rituals of Mass and Benediction, performed, for the most part, in unknown Latin. Unintelligible sermons and a familiar repertoire of soupy hymns did nothing but add to the impression that in going to church we were entering an alien world, and certainly not one meant for children. True, there was Children's Benediction early on Sunday afternoons, but this proved to be nothing more than a cut-down version of the grown-up service in the evening, with catechism instruction in place of the sermon. The good monks themselves confirmed the general other-worldly impression. Devoted to their pastoral work as they were, they had never belonged to the ordinary world of Leyland, nor did most of them stay at St Mary's for long. After a few years they were likely to be recycled either to another Benedictine parish or back to Ampleforth. In any case, their roots were in the other world, not in ours. Their strangeness was underlined by their non-Lancashire accents and by the voluminous choir dress they wore round their fine old presbytery. They were part of my second world.

But besides the surface differences there was also a deeper quality in the world of Leyland St Mary's which set it radically apart from the ordinary world: a quality which allowed it to float free of the ordinary workaday world next-door in which people had to live, the world of actual time and physical space. The quality was, I suppose, what I would now be tempted to call 'metaphysical', additional to the ordinary physical world, and possessed of a kind of transcendence. The quality characterized another world which had to do with what was changeless and eternal, a world which contrasted with, if it did not openly contradict, our own. Just as it was independent of time, this second world was also independent of the confines and limitations of space, since it could exist just as it was without change anywhere on earth. It was also a world ineffably superior to our ordinary world, promising infinitely better things than ours could ever offer, as well as claiming authoritative control over us. Even a child could not help being impressed and attracted by its special quality, however impossible it might have been to define it. And the impressiveness of this second world, the way it imposed itself on the lives of Catholics, was far from unwelcome in our small, dull, provincial manufacturing town. It brought more than a dash of the exotic and the exciting and the non-trivial to local life – much more, certainly, than was available from the still unusual wireless broadcasts or in the town's two cinemas which, apart from the other local churches, provided the only other popular access to a different world. And as for the authoritative control it claimed over ordinary life – was it not important to know just where you stood in this ordinary world and just how you were supposed to be living in it? The local centre of this potent world lay just beyond Leyland Cross.

I was taken there regularly and I began to assimilate, in my childish way, its importance. We were never what you would call a religious family, in the sense that some Catholic families were. We knew families whose homes were bedecked with religious images and coloured lamps; where the day began with morning prayers and grace was said at every meal from breakfast onwards; and where the evening Rosary was recited before bedtime prayers. As far as my brother and I were concerned, brief bedtime prayers, sometimes forgotten, represented the peak of daily religious performance. Harry, of course, would have been learning his catechism at school by this time; but I was still picking up impressions from my experiences at church. Despite the lack of appeal for children, there was always a certain social feel about church. You got used to seeing the same families every week, and you noticed when they were absent. I liked putting my big penny in the inevitable collection.

It all had to do with someone very important called 'God'. You did not expect to see God at church, chiefly because, apart from being invisible, He was so busy that He had to be everywhere at once, and in any case He had more important people and matters to attend to than us. So God remained unseen, a figure who was ageless and friendly and kind, but who could get angry with you if you upset Him. Not that He was in any way like a bad giant or an ogre. You only had yourself to blame if He got angry with you; and in any case He got angry with you only for your own good. The sooner you said you were sorry, the better. He was doing his best to run the world well, and you should not do anything to make it harder for Him. You would see Him one day, but He waited until you died before He welcomed you – perhaps after some corrective detention in Purgatory – into Heaven, where you would be happy for ever, provided you had really tried your best to be good. If you had not tried your best, you left God with no choice but to punish you – though not necessarily for ever in Hell, which is the place you finished up in only if you tried really hard to offend Him and did not get round to saying you were sorry before you died. In any case, there were lots of good, holy people whose job it was to help us to get along with God – Our Lady, of course, and St Joseph, as well as other saints. There were angels as well, and one of them had been given the job of being your own Guardian Angel. There was not a lot of talk about Jesus, but as 'Our Lord' he was entirely special both because of the cruel way he had died, and because of his coming to life again after-wards. This made him more than a little remote, but the whole business of going to church somehow centred around him and his dying on the Cross. All round the walls of St Mary's there were large and lurid paintings of Our Lord carrying his Cross and falling down under the weight of it, and they were called 'the Stations of the Cross'. This confused me for quite some time. We passed Leyland Cross on our way to church, and there was no station, let alone a railway with stations, there. There was only one station in Leyland and it was at the far end of the town, not far from where my father worked at the Co-op Drapery in Chapel Brow, but that was not where the Cross was. In time the matter must have sorted itself out.

So there I was, about five years into the life which I was growing round me – a life which was already beginning to be lived in two quite different worlds, the ordinary world of Leyland Towngate and the Catholic world of Leyland St Mary's: two 'limited wholes', two quite different 'takes' on reality, and the one much more limited than the other. Not that the difference between the two worlds was going to cause me anything of a problem for a long time to come. Most people, if they are fortunate, manage to live in different worlds of their own making: the world of work, for instance, and the world of home and family, the world of cultural pursuits, of hobbies and sports, of leisure activities, and so forth. Less fortunate people have to live in worlds that are not of their own making, but which are made by others and imposed on them. But when all is said and done, what are worlds if not, in the end, somebody's imagined and willed constructs? – the 'limited wholes' in which we choose, or are constrained, to make the lives in which we live out our human existences? Of course it has taken me a long time to find that this is probably the best way to see the human situation – and also the best way to see religions. What, from the human point of view, are religions, if not systematized constructs based on their founders' inspired insights into what confronted them in their particular experiences of life? Different religions stem from the different culturally and personally determined interpretations of reality imagined, willed and imposed by the genius of their founders on their historical times and situations. However grandiose a religion's claims may in time have become, at root it remains one kind of 'limited whole' in which people can choose to conduct their lives.

As I see it now, we all live in limited wholes, worlds, constructs, where the problem is, not that they differ, as they obviously do; nor why they differ, to which there are obvious answers; nor even in what sense they are real and objective, which seems to me an unintelligent question as it stands – unintelligent because it is unanswerable, given that by definition our limited worlds have their origins in someone's imaginative, and therefore inevitably subjective, interpretations. In any case how can you step outside a world you live in to measure it against objective reality? Or what measure would you use which you had not first imaginatively invented? And so on. The practical problem with living in, say, two different worlds arises when you come to the realization that they are both laying claim to the same *kind* of truth – as, for instance, when the ordinary world and the religious world are both claiming to be descriptively and literally true. Then competition eventually turns into contradiction, and the kinds of truth they are laying claim to have to be urgently redefined. They cannot both occupy the same ground in the same way in some 'equiliteral' kind of way.

All such clumsy attempts at sophistication lay decades ahead. The two worlds I was faced with from childhood were both presented to me as being real in the same descriptive sense. There was the simple, regular, mundane world of Towngate – a pleasant home, its own close confines, its kind and familiar inhabitants, every day a day for playing games or for making the occasional trip to see other kind and familiar people. It was a world which bespoke nothing much beyond itself. Then there was the transcendent, religious world centred on St Mary's, real in just the same sense, and claiming to encompass all possible space and all possible time, past, present and future, from the creation to the end of the universe. As any child of normal, uncritical understanding does, I was led to suppose that both worlds offered true descriptions of the same kind of reality, and for a long time to come I had no problem with this simple notion.

I now realize, however, that what was being sown in my mind was not all 'good seed' (Matthew 13.24) of the same kind. As straight descriptions of reality which were true in the same sense, the two worlds were as terminally incompatible as the wheat and weeds of the parable. But for the moment nothing could be done except to 'let both grow together' undisturbed until such time as I might be mature enough to be able to try sorting them out, one from another, for myself. I fancy that with many people the seeds of the problem simply do not germinate; or they are kept suppressed by a heavy mulch of other concerns, until eventually they perish. But where, for one reason or another, they do germinate, and take root, they will emerge sooner or later as a full-blown problem. In my case, the seeds of the problem germinated when I was about forty years old, took root when I was about fifty, and finally emerged in full vigour when I was already getting on for sixty. A late developer, I was to take my time – in fact, most of my adult lifetime – in coping with the problem of relating my religious world to that of ordinary life. I say 'coping with' and not 'solving' it, since talk of a 'solution' suggests that I am claiming to have discovered some kind of intellectual nostrum for dealing with it. 'Solving' seems inappropriate in a matter which cannot be other than deeply personal. I do not think I have solved the problem – but I do think that, with help, I have managed to make my own personal peace with the two worlds I inherited and lived in for so long, and with the relationship of the religious world to the ordinary world of human living. So I shall try to describe how the problem slowly grew in the course of my strange career, and at the end how I came to 'cope with' it. There is nothing particularly dramatic about this long process, if only because, in my view, in the end it accords with what Ludwig Wittgenstein said of philosophy – it simply 'leaves everything as it is' (*Philosophical Investigations*, 124).

Chapter 2

A Wider World

Of my two so-called equiliteral worlds, ordinary and religious, it was the former which expanded and began to fill rapidly over the twelve years of my formal schooling. But the worlds continued to exist side by side. The religious world continued to be thought important, because it existed to tell you how to behave in the ordinary one, and to serve eventually as a reward for behaving well. But the ordinary world was the one in which you could expect to have to live, so you had to work hard and do well at school. You could certainly not afford to neglect either.

Since I always seemed to be one of the youngest members of every class I belonged to, I suppose I must have started to attend St Mary's R.C. Elementary School in Leyland in September 1936, when I was not yet six years old. My memory of going to school for the first time is still vivid. I was taken there by Gertie, who happened to work close by. We would have gone along Towngate to the point where it turns a right-angle bend into Hough Lane, but then we would have gone straight on down what seemed the long steep hill of School Lane to the very bottom, where there was a brook and a large school playing-field. Beyond that, looking out over the field and with its back to Golden Hill Lane, was the fine school building still labelled with a heavy dark stone inscription as Balshaw's Grammar School. Leyland had had a Tudor grammar school in 1524, and its quaint building (1580–1620, now the local museum) still stands in the corner of St Andrew's churchyard. It functioned until the 1870s, when it was subsumed into the recently founded Balshaw's. In the early 1930s, when Balshaw's moved to its present superior site near Bent Bridge in Church Road, Fr Parker astutely bought its ample old site to accommodate the small Catholic school which was housed in an inadequate building in Towngate. At the bottom of School Lane was a little iron gate through which the children passed into the school grounds. But what I can recall most clearly is Gertie in tears, looking through the gate as I trotted off for the first time into school.

The main school building had junior classrooms round three sides of the large central hall where the Headmaster, Mr James Coffey, sat and worked in the open at his elevated desk from which he could monitor any movement outside the lower classrooms. Classes ranged from 'Infants' up to Standard 6 or 7, at which point the fourteen-year-old pupils left and started work, usually in local factories or offices. The senior classes were housed in 'temporary' wooden sheds – 'the Huts' – off to the side of the school. Behind the main building were separate boys' and girls' playgrounds with their respective lavatories. The school catered exclusively for Catholic children. Once in the system, the only way out of it before reaching the leaving age of fourteen was to become one of the tiny annual group who 'passed the scholarship' at ten or eleven years old and then went off to one of three Catholic Grammar Schools in Preston, two run by nuns for girls and one for boys run by the Jesuits.

St Mary's was a very good school, well-run and with kindly and efficient teachers who had to cope with children of very mixed abilities and backgrounds. I enjoyed being there very much. I recall the successive order of the junior classes round the central hall. Behind glass and wood partitions on one side were the two classes of 'Infants', with very low tables and little chairs, on which we sat in formal rows, writing and drawing on sand-trays with our fingers until we graduated to writing on very heavy wood-framed slates with hard squeaky pencils. Of the processes of being taught and learning I can recall very little, possibly because there was nothing that was individual or personal about it. It all seemed to be a matter of being just another member of the class. Daily, like a community of small and scruffy monks, we chanted our multiplication tables, sometimes antiphonally from side to side of the class, sometimes in unison. We all learned to read by perusing tattered copies of the same forgotten books. Mental arithmetic and spelling were more competitive exercises, and I was keen and good at them. But they involved everybody. In just the same competitive way we learned the answers to all the questions in the junior version of the Penny Catechism of Catholic Doctrine. Oddly, if there was anyone who could not read or who had other particular 'learning difficulties', I cannot remember them – which at least means, I suppose, that they were not singled out or stigmatized in any way. Of course, we all got things wrong from time to time, but this only drove others who thought they knew the right answer to more frenzied attempts to be asked to come out with it. Some children liked shooting up their hands and answering questions more than others, but I do not think it ever occurred to me that some children were brighter or better than others. I was certainly never given to think that I was particularly clever, and in fact there always seemed to be one or two girls in the class who could beat me at most things.

All the children went home for dinner at twelve o'clock or thereabouts, and there were two brief 'playtimes' morning and afternoon. There were no school meals. At morning playtime we were given a cold one-third pint bottle of milk with a cardboard top inside the rim. You stuck a straw through a central hole and sucked the milk through it, remembering to keep the top and wash it carefully for use in raffia work in class. By wrapping each top in coloured raffia, round and round from the edge to the central hole, you eventually produced a coloured disc which you could then sew on to other coloured discs until you had made a table-mat. Everybody in the class did this, and I much enjoyed doing it. These days raffia work is an occupation associated with those who are said to be intellectually challenged, but it was the first creative work I can recall doing. In the boys' playground it became clear that some boys were tougher and noisier than others; but in class these differences did not count. There were no discipline problems and no bullying, and we worked hard from start to finish of the day. There were no fashionable teaching methods or other distractions to waste our valuable time. The school hummed with concentrated learning activities directed by devoted and greatly respected teachers. There was no homework, and school holidays were short. But we did enjoy our Catholic privilege of a full day off on Holydays of Obligation – but, of course, you had to go to Mass at St Mary's. Once a week we played games if it was fine outside, chiefly soccer and rounders. I quite liked them, and I was just about good enough not to be a duffer at them. I was never concerned to become competitive in sports, though in my time I have played a good number of team sports – soccer, rugger, cricket, volley-ball, and even rowing – with considerable pleasure, but always at a comfortably mediocre social level. My whole memory of my early schooling, as of home, remains a very happy, if an oddly vague, one. I cannot recall much that happened outside our own tight little cohort.

Occasionally there was an assembly of the whole school in the big hall. Mr Coffey, or sometimes even Fr Parker, made announcements, often about events at church; though the school assembly had no overtly religious purpose. At the only assembly I can actually remember, we all sat on the worn, dusty parquet floor and listened, on a newly acquired radiogram, to the launching of the Cunard liner *Queen Elizabeth*. Mr Coffey made a joke which even then I recognized as weak, about the amount of Lifebuoy soap it must have taken to grease the slipway. Religious activity took place in church. The atmosphere of the school, however, was unmistakeably Catholic, but its Catholicism consisted in learning the catechism questions and answers by heart; saying a brief prayer at the beginning and end of each day in front of the statue of Our Lady which each class kept decorated with flowers in the summer; and, on Monday mornings, answering up honestly when the teacher opened up the Mass Register and checked each pupil's attendance at church on Sunday. Thus: 'Tommy Jones?' – 'Mass, Communion and Benediction, Miss' (rather proudly). Or sometimes: 'Missed Mass, Miss' (shamefacedly). I hardly think this degree of intrusion into how a child performed his or her religious duties would be tolerated these days. But we made nothing of it in those days; and, in any case, I think we were quite able to understand, even as children, that it was unlikely to be a child's fault if they missed Mass.

As far as I can remember, we all seemed to manage with far less individual and distinct personalities than modern children are constantly being encouraged to develop. We seemed much more herd-oriented in everything we did. We were sedulously prepared, in due course, for the important sacraments of Holy Communion, Confession and Confirmation in large, unindividuated batches. Neither personal success nor personal failure struck children with the excitement or traumatic intensity that is fostered by the aggressive individualism which children learn from modern television and their over-ambitious parents; and both success and failure must have been far easier to handle in those days than children now seem to find. If you add to that the remarkable freedom that children enjoyed in traipsing safely far round the surrounding countryside on their own, inventing their own adventures, travelling widely, again on their own, on cheap public transport, or playing their own games outside their homes and in neighbouring streets, you might judge these to have been good times in which to be a child. I happen to think they were, but they belong to an irrecoverable past to which I have remained rather attached. Towards the end of a lifetime spent dealing academically with students far younger than myself, I decided I was wrong to try to get close to them or even understand them. I found I liked them, but felt rather sorry for them. I got on well with them on the whole, and I enjoyed their company, and I was happy working hard on their behalf. But I also found I got on best with them if I thought of them as visitants from another planet. I felt that, strictly speaking, they belonged to a world which was not one of mine. Besides having to grow up and face an unbeliev-ably more complex and difficult world than we ever had to cope with, the young seem to me to be expected to bear the dreadful burden of a largely factitious individuality – an individuality which seems in many cases to be aimed at achieving, without effort, celebrity status. This was an aspiration which we were happily spared in our far simpler provincial world, both in school and at home. With us, if there was any sin that was near to being unforgivable it was any kind of 'showing off'. It will be obvious by now that – and perhaps why – I have never been a parent. I have no regrets on this score, and I doubt that I would ever have made a good family man.

What I really enjoyed about school from the start, and what I felt my family most wanted from me, was learning – just knowing and understanding things. And yet I have never become a high flyer. I have never had that quick, sure-fire cleverness which I have from time to time admired in many bright people. Faced with the opportunity of learning something, I would take my time, confident enough that I would probably get there in the end. In this respect (but perhaps not in others) I am easy-going, and I prefer to take my time: a rather lazy, late-ish developer. I have sometimes regretted my lack of ambition, my reluctance to spot the main chance and make the most of the excellent educa-tional opportunities I have undoubtedly had. But right from the start, at St Mary's, I liked above all belonging to the group, our class. Of course, I also liked being recognized as a significant member of the group. I liked being among the leading lights: towards the top of the group, but not necessarily at the top itself. So I would try to do well at whatever the group was supposed to be doing: and in the case of school – and for much of the rest of my life – this had to do with learning. I imagine that this means that my liking for learning comes, not from any dispassionate or unworldly devotion to learning as such, nor from directly personal ambition in the field of learning (where I think I have probably failed to fulfil my potential); but from the fact that having the necessary and sufficient learning was my way of getting myself recognized and accepted as an individual by what-

ever group I happened to be in. Learning was my way of belonging to the class or group or elite to which I wanted to belong. This
attitude to learning has its dangers and its potential dark side. It
can lead to the pursuit of learning as a means of exercising power
or control over others, of asserting authority. It may have had
something to do with my eventual choice of vocation.

I climbed the ladder of classes at St Mary's without difficulty. I
considered school to be an excellent way of passing the time, and far
better than playing out. Everyone was friendly and helpful, I was
never bored, and our varied pursuits, including the raffia work,
seemed always congenial. From Miss Smith's Infants' class I moved
into Miss Prescott's, and then into Standard 1 under Miss Anderton,
a small, sharp, red-haired lady whose classroom was at the east end
of the hall, opposite Mr Coffey's central control desk. I can remember one single piece of learning from Standard 1. With Miss
Anderton we made an igloo by cutting an old terrestrial globe in
half, painting it glossy white, putting it on a white surface, and
adding an entrance tunnel from half a cardboard tube. I thought this
a thing of wonder, and no doubt we learned a lot of other things
about Eskimos. The year after, I moved back across the hall behind
Mr Coffey's desk. Standard 2 belonged to Miss Dobson, a tubby,
mannish figure in a skirt and jacket, a red face and Eton-cropped
blonde hair. She was given added interest by her possession of a
small car – no common thing for a single woman in Leyland in the
1930s. Much later on I learned that Miss Dobson had once been a
nun, but I would not have known what a nun was when I was in her
class, since I had never seen or met one. Miss Dobson taught us long
division, which I thought was magical. She stood no nonsense, and
she worked us hard.

For Miss Reddy's Standard 3 we moved out of the main building and into 'the Huts'. She was later to become a long-serving
Headmistress of the school. I stayed in her class for a very short
time – a matter of hours, as I recall. With a few others I was made
to skip Standard 3 – no reason was given and my parents were
not consulted – and I was moved rapidly into Mr Walbank's
Standard 4. I suppose that by this time we were being, so to
speak, fattened up or groomed for 'the scholarship'. The date
must have been September 1940, and I was still not ten years old.
It was about this time that we experienced a few daring daylight
air-raids on Leyland Motors, part of which was very close to the
school. We had air-raid shelters dedicated to our English saints –
St Thomas More, St John Fisher – and once, as we rushed out of
class towards them with the warning sirens wailing all around

us, a lone Heinkel screamed very low right overhead, showering us with bullet cases, much prized and swapped afterwards. We stopped in our tracks to take the whole scene in. We could see the crew – real Germans! – inside quite distinctly. They dropped one large land-mine very close to the factory power plant. It did not explode, however, but wrecked the workers' bicycle shed. The plane got away over the Irish Sea and was shot down off Blackpool by our Spitfires. The crew survived, and the story goes that the German pilot was found to have been an apprentice engineer at Leyland Motors in the 1930s, and he was completely familiar with the precise lay out of the whole factory. All this served to make school even more interesting.

ॐ.

But whilst the school dimension of my experience of the ordinary world had begun expanding, more interesting and potentially far more important developments had been taking place in its home dimension. In 1937 my father re-married. Our cosy Towngate household was dispersed. Grandma Butterworth, her job as housekeeper and nursemaid well done, went to live with one of her daughters in Preston, and it was at this time that Gertie set up house on her own in Farington. A new family regime was inaugurated under entirely new management at a new address, 42 Balcarres Road, Leyland, about half a mile from Holyoake in Towngate. We all still kept in close touch, and I cannot recall that life in my ordinary world was disrupted, for all that it was going to become very different. As far as the religious world of St Mary's was concerned, too, life went on in the usual fashion.

Neither Harry nor I ever referred to my father's new wife as our step-mother. We always called her Mother, just as we referred to the two new family members who eventually joined us as our sister and our brother. I imagine that this was due to some typically wise plan on the part of our father. A successful plan it was, too – over half a century later I have to stop and remind myself that we were a family of two halves. I remember going to my father's second wedding at St Oswald's Catholic Church in Coppull near Chorley, where the Dugdales lived. The formal wedding photograph shows my father looking handsome and very serious, and my new mother equally handsome and smiling, perhaps a touch triumphantly, in her long blue velvet wedding dress. I instantly acquired a new set of ready-made relatives; and though they were never to feel as close as the Butterworths and the Tomlinsons, the Dugdales were interesting and welcoming people, and we saw them frequently. They had rather more dash and flair than the older sides of the family, though they shared the same lack of demonstrativeness, and could seem rather cold. My mother was ranked in the middle of five Dugdale children, three daughters symmetrically flanked by two sons.

It was from the two sons, my new uncles, that I quickly got my lasting taste for cricket. Jack, the elder, was a star of Chorley Cricket Club, and he had once been a county prospect for Lancashire. He was a man of wonderfully imperturbable temperament who moved through his long life in the same low gear, unfailingly pleasant. He was a left-handed batsman, elegantly unhurried on the off-side, and very difficult for bowlers to get out. He was married to a remarkable woman, the same Amy Morris who witnessed how my father had seen to opening up the Co-op Drapery on that Christmas Eve morning of 1930 when he had just lost his first wife and had acquired me as his second son. It was Amy who engineered the first serious encounter between my father and her husband Jack's sister Hilda who was to be his new wife and our new mother. Tom, the younger Dugdale brother, was also a fine cricketer, but of a wholly different stamp from Jack. Tom was a swashbuckling all-rounder of real talent who worked for several years as a full-time professional in Lancashire League cricket before emigrating to Canada. Dorrie, my new mother's older sister, was married to Bill Holland, a colliery winder from Wigan, and a self-made original who wrote creditable dialect poetry. Her younger sister, Florence, married a farmer, Gerry Clitheroe, and they ran a large farm close to the centre of Chorley – Gillibrand Hall Farm, one-time estate of the old Catholic Gillibrands. Gerry was said to be of the same family as St Margaret Clitheroe, the York martyr for the Catholic faith. They were a pleasant pair with three daughters, and during the war I was regularly sent to visit them at the farm, chiefly to pick up contraband eggs. During harvesting I learned to drive, not without mishap, a horse (called Camel) and cart. My ordinary world was certainly taking on some surprising new dimensions.

42 Balcarres Road was a solid semi-detached family house in a pleasant tree-lined road with grass verges. The double front gates bore the legend 'Greycot', a silly name we had the sense never to use. A steep short drive led to large back gates which gave access to the garage beyond and the back garden. The house cost, I recall, £360, bought outright by my new mother with a small Dugdale legacy. It became the basis of such future prosperity as the family has enjoyed. Behind the back gates and on the back

lawn Harry and I played endless cricket, sometimes coached by one or other of our new uncles. From this new base I began to move round Leyland more freely, and I got my first bicycle. It was somewhat further to school now, but otherwise I noticed few differences in life. School just went on, as did 'Mass, Communion and Benediction' at church. We were slightly closer to the farms and fields which surrounded Leyland on its south-east side in those days, and we took to going for long Sunday walks *en famille* in the country.

My new mother was a tougher proposition to deal with than Gertie or my Grandma, but I liked her well enough from the start. She was a very hard-working and efficient housekeeper, and we were well cared for. I think I very soon got the message and buckled down quite happily under the new regime. I was not stupid, and perhaps rather calculating; and in any case, as I have said, I liked conforming and belonging to whatever group I found myself in. I liked the way in which my mother involved me in household matters. I felt I was making a contribution. I could join in without fuss, feeling useful. I became good at household chores and even at elementary cooking – two skills which have proved quite invaluable since. I enjoyed this new home life, different as it was from the more indulgent days in Towngate. I continued to find school no trouble, to go to church with the family, and to live a larger life quite happily in this new dimension of my ordinary world. Occasional tensions – it cannot have been easy for a mother to cope with two rather spoilt and fast developing boys – were soon put aside. At any rate, it all bothered me very little.

Nor was I at all bothered by the birth, in December 1937, of my new sister, Barbara Mary. She was born – as far as I was concerned, without the slightest warning – in a small private nursing home nearby. She simply appeared, and after a few days she came home. No one bothered to spin any tales or offer any explanations. I am glad they didn't, since I had neither interest nor curiosity in the matter, and it never occurred to me to ask how she came to be there. She was chubby and cheerful, and a cot and a large blue pram appeared. I recall none of the traumas, jealousies or sibling rivalries that psychologists have prompted us to expect. I fancy I had to do a few more little jobs round the house and run a few more errands. But I had learned to know and like my place in the family. I also began to see more of the ordinary world outside the home than I had done in Towngate. I began to acquire solid and regular friends who lived in our new part of

Leyland. There were several Catholic families – Warrens, Holdens – in the area with children of my own age, and we stuck together as a flexible group for many years to come. We walked to school and played together. We still had no homework to do, and on summer evenings and on Saturdays (but never on Sundays) we would stay out, roaming the countryside, climbing trees, damming streams, trespassing in Squire ffarington's Worden Park, making a general nuisance of ourselves, and, above all, collecting railway engine numbers as we sat for hours on the embankment of the busy main line railway that passed through Leyland. This train-spotting triggered off a permanent interest in steam railways, and I can still recite a litany of the numbers and names of the great L.M.S. locomotives that pulled the long-distance trains up and down the country. We did all this in perfect safety. There were no child-molesters or abductors, and we met no one we did not know – nor, sometimes to our cost, anyone who did not know us. There was one well-known mentally handicapped man – Galoshe Dick, everyone called him, because of his peculiar footwear – whom we often met roaming the fields, but he would just greet us and proceed on his simple way. My mother sometimes tried to get me to employ my spare time more profitably. I remember she tried, not unreasonably, to improve my new joined-up handwriting by getting me to copy out a practice sentence which referred to 'Athena, the grey-eyed goddess of the Greeks'; but I was happier copying out family recipes into a new cookbook. I had to hold my fountain pen properly, a long way from the nib, because, my mother claimed, Winston Churchill did so.

ॐ

The dimensions of the Catholic world of St Mary's church were also expanding, but less dramatically than those of home. I was learning more and more of the Penny Catechism all the time, of course, but without finding anything of greater significance or interest in it than I did in learning multiplication tables or in spelling more and more tricky words. My new mother came from a strongly Catholic background, and we attended church as regularly as ever. Night prayers took on rather more prominence than before, not least prayers for deceased members of the family. I learned to enjoy reciting the psalm 'De Profundis' – 'Out of the depths I cry to thee, O Lord ...' – and it became the first religious text to evoke a felt response in me. But my experience of the Catholic world of St Mary's deepened considerably when I became an altar-boy. I can remember going by car one morning with Dom Anselm Parker out to Runshaw Hall to serve Mass for the very first time. Runshaw Hall was a residential home for mentally handicapped men run by the Brothers of Charity, and the Benedictine monks provided its daily Mass. I had been meticulously trained. I had all the Latin responses by heart, without understanding a word of them; and I had been carefully rehearsed in the complicated choreography required of altar-servers in the ritual of the Tridentine Latin Low Mass. I can evoke easily the stuffy, prim, little chapel, with the Brothers and the 'lads' in their charge shuffling in the background, the flowers and the candles, the stiff white altar linen, the shining glass cruets for the water and the sweet-smelling red wine, the low-muttered Latin, the embroidered vestments and the deep, deep gold inside the chalice. It was a sensory experience that I was enjoying close up for the first time, and it gave rise to feelings of some indefinable mystery that I can savour even now. I must have served Mass satisfactorily – not that Dom Anselm would have noticed much: he was as deaf as a post and of a detached, scholarly disposition (he had once been the eponymous Master of Parker's – now St Benet's – Hall in Oxford). From then on I became a regular member of the altar-serving team, graduating from torch-bearer to acolyte at High Masses, *Missae Cantatae*, Benedictions, processions, weddings, funerals, and whatever else needed doing. There was quite a horde of us, and that made the world of St Mary's fun. Harry was already a practised and prominent figure among us, and at rehearsals he often displayed his unlikely gift for clowning in the Buster Keaton mode. Well out of sight of the priest, he would assume his dead-pan face and an outrageous limp, whilst swinging the unlit thurible about wildly. We all admired his surprising skills enormously.

I made my First Confession and Communion with the rest of my class from school, and shortly afterwards we were all routinely confirmed together. I find it hard to distinguish these rather soulless events from one another. As boys we had to be sure to dress in our best suits and have our shoes polished; but the girls could transform themselves into angelic bridesmaids, so the occasions may have meant more to them. What I can recall is that at the Confirmation there was a short, fat, grumpy Archbishop from Liverpool called Richard Downey, whereas after our First Communions we had a party at which we were given brightly coloured certificates and green jelly. We all had to know, of course, the catechism questions and answers relevant to each Sacrament. I cannot say that the occasions were especially

religious, except in the sense that they marked the taking up of
new responsibilities to behave better and to pay more attention in
church services. Like the rest of the normal and regular performance of one's Catholic duties, they were not meant to lead to
anything that one might call a personal spiritual experience. Such
a thing would have been considered outlandishly cranky and
quite out of place. Being a Catholic simply did not involve that
sort of thing: it was primarily a matter of faithfully fulfilling your
duties in church. I am sure, of course, that being a Catholic did in
fact help people to cope with whatever life had in store for them;
but largely, if not entirely, by persuading them that whatever
happened, they would be all right if they stuck to the system and
performed their duties. Spiritual experiences did not really count.
A kind of devout stoicism was what really mattered.

As if to contradict that stark sentiment, I must report that it was
about this time, during those early years at Balcarres Road, that I
had what must be the nearest I ever came in my life to what I
might almost be prepared to call 'a spiritual experience'. I was
probably ten years old, or possibly slightly older, and I had been
serving early Mass at St Mary's on a bright sunny morning. I had
just started out on my way home on my bike, and I was crossing
the still deserted area round Leyland Cross, with Towngate
ahead of me, and the turn into Church Road on my right. I have
no recollection of there being any traffic or people around at the
time. But suddenly, quite without warning, I felt completely
happy – happy in the strong and clear conviction that everything
in my ordinary, day-to-day world was right, and that everything
was going to be all right, whatever might happen. The experience
came across as an immediate and very powerful validation of the
way things just were, of the right existence of everything just as it
was, and this included myself and everybody I knew, my whole
life and my whole ordinary world. There was nothing otherwise
extraordinary or supernatural or transcendent about this, nor
anything religious. Far from being transformed or even different,
the familiar and accessible ordinary world of Leyland remained
just as it was – just more like its old familiar self than ever. It
seemed that it had somehow been given to me to 'realize' that my
ordinary Leyland world, and everybody in it, existed just as they
should exist, in their own right and for what they really were. It
came over as an epiphany which validated my ordinary world
with great force and precision. I do not think the experience can
have lasted more than a few seconds. Unlike Paul on the road to
Damascus, I did not fall to the ground and hear a voice (Acts 9.4

etc.). I saw absolutely nothing. Observers would have seen nothing. I stayed firmly in the saddle and pedalled off up Church Road on my way home. As I write about it with the hindsight of 60 years or more, the experience does not become any more transparent – or any less gripping. It left a unique and indelible mark on me; and no later experience, even in some of the world's most awesome and religious places, has ever been able to compare with it or reduce its importance. I have, in some sense, lived on it ever since, though I have never managed to account for it any better than I have done here. I have hardly ever spoken about it, since I thought it would seem out of character, and I could never be sure whether what I might say would make any sense, or sound just vacuous, or – far worse – cause me embarrassment.

One fact about it remains quite clear: strictly speaking, there was nothing that was identifiably 'religious' about the experience at all: 'religious', that is, in any sense related to the ways in which our Catholicism was being presented to us in school and at church. True, I was learning my catechism and being gradually initiated into the Catholic Sacraments. True, I happened to have just been to church. True, I had just received Communion. But there was no content to the experience that seemed to link it with any of these things. Nor was any access to some transcendent realm of religious reality vouchsafed. There was only an instant, brief transfiguring 'epiphany' of the completely ordinary Leyland world. At the lower end of the scale of possible interpretations, it might be said that after the long fast that preceded Communion in those days I was simply light-headed and ready for my breakfast. But somehow neither that view nor the 'religious' view of the experience does any justice to it. It seemed far outside the scope of piety or hunger. I cannot even say that I have ever been able to draw any conclusions from it. It would never serve as the premise of an argument. The idea that it may have determined in some way the course of my later life strikes me as rather facile, trivial and extremely unlikely. It had no connection with the religious world apart from the superficial circumstances. It may just have been the kind of romantic Wordsworthian experience that children are said to have from time to time – some intimation of the inherent 'transcendence' of the ordinary natural world. I simply do not know – but I have never forgotten it and I never shall. Since then I have passed by Leyland Cross many times, and never without a strongly felt memory of that childhood experience.

Meanwhile our new and growing family went on enjoying a stable and comfortable life together. In our Northern fashion, we were not an outwardly demonstrative lot, and an outsider might have thought that we lacked warmth or were cool or off-hand in our relationships; but the show of feeling or affection – like touching or hugging, for instance, or words of endearment – simply did not belong to the ordinary range of acceptable self-expression within the family. Somehow neither warmth nor cold came within the register of normal Northern reactions. We would have found any warm expression of affection or love impossibly mawkish – 'soft', or even (with a short 'a') 'daft' – at the same time as finding any deliberate coldness, of course, quite intolerable. True, some families seemed to live more closely to one another than we did. We seemed to embody that habitual reserve of my father which was consonant with solid and, as later experience has confirmed, lasting relationships. All the same, I think that Northern reserve or reticence can serve to detach and distance people from their own and other people's feelings; and I fancy that to some extent this happened in my case. I learned over a long period, and especially in religious life, to discount feelings as unimportant, and that had the consequence that I did not bother to cultivate them in myself or acknowledge them in other people. I might have been learning quickly with my brain at school, but I had very poorly educated emotions and a fairly seriously underdeveloped sensibility. I became inclined to indulge in those occasional moody withdrawals which are said to signal the onset of adolescence. I thoroughly disliked myself for this, but I lacked both skill and practice in articulating my feelings and coping with them knowingly. Perhaps what I could have done with was the increased self-assurance which comes with knowing and feeling that I was loved, as I am quite sure I was. Without that kind of reassurance it becomes very difficult to love oneself or anyone else properly. So for many years I tended to fall back on my liking for just belonging to the group I found myself in, and for a long time this sufficed; but in the end its insufficiency caught up with me, and I have been very fortunate indeed to have had time to cultivate a richly personal relationship on soil that, in my case, had lain fallow far too long. I think I had been trying to learn to survive without the feelings of love, and this strikes me now as a perilous strategy. It prolongs emotional immaturity, and it can lead – as I think it might have done in my case – both to mistaken choices in life and to perseverance in erroneous decisions. This is not meant to sound ungenerous towards my family. No family is perfect, and I continue to count myself extremely fortunate in mine.

Family solidarity was reinforced by Neville Chamberlain's declaration of war on Adolf Hitler's Germany at eleven o'clock on Sunday, 3 September 1939. My father and mother, Harry and myself listened to his broadcast with all due attention. We did not know how life in remote Leyland might change in wartime. I suppose we expected our small accustomed freedoms to be somewhat further limited by various mild privations in food, clothing, entertainment and travel; and this expectation proved true. In no sense can it be said that we really suffered from the war, as so many millions tragically did. In fact the only real effect of the war for young boys like myself was that it made life a lot more interesting, even exciting. We were far too young to think that our country would ever need us. The Allies would deal with Hitler and the Germans long before it came to that. Leyland was a long way from occupied and war-ridden Europe, but it made, of course, its own very considerable contribution to 'the war effort' through its engineering and munitions industries. We all felt part of the war without having to take much of a part in it. For those of us still at school a normally humdrum life was transformed by all the novelties that the country's amazingly thorough commitment to the war brought our way. Overnight, or so it seemed, and right on our Leyland doorsteps, there occurred a total mobilization of everybody's efforts and resources. Local economies boomed.

The national propaganda drive to activate and focus people's energies and to direct their undistracted attention to the conduct of the war was outstandingly brilliant and effective. The Leyland factories went into instant overdrive and overtime. We came to live the war the whole time. Somehow even small boys like myself had their sense of life and purpose enlarged and swept up into a national crusade. We became conscious of the rest of the country, and then of the rest of Europe. It did wonders for our knowledge of geography and even of history. We watched the factory workers being bussed in and out of the town to work seamless shifts at Leyland Motors and the other factories. Mr Ainsworth from across the road was transformed into an armed member of the Home Guard, and Mr Threlfall, the newsagent, into an Air Raid Warden. Mr Littler, next door, became a key figure at Leyland Motors, the chief engineer responsible for the maintenance of essential power. Any plane that crossed the sky became an object to be identified and noted down. Uniforms appeared everywhere, and our aluminium pans disappeared, gladly given away to be turned into Spitfires. Iron railings, even the ones round old Holyoake, were hacked down to become guns and bombs and tanks. Daylight had to give way to pitch darkness in 'the blackout'. Everyone had to carry an identity card and, slung round them in a cardboard box, a gas-mask. The familiar Leyland factories – the Motor Works, the Rubber Works, the Paint Works, and the recently built Ammunition Works at Euxton on the way to Chorley – were elaborately camouflaged and became secret installations. We were severely cautioned never to mention what went on in and around Leyland: 'Be like Dad, keep Mum!', 'Walls have ears', and so on. Army trucks and then huge Churchill tanks, already with the Red Star on their turrets and with their markings in Cyrillic script, began to clank and rumble out of the Motor Works and take to our familiar streets on their way to the testing-grounds, before being shipped, via Hull and Murmansk, to attack Hitler from the East. To stop the street junctions in the town being shredded daily by turning tank-tracks, tough cobbles – not good for our bicycles – replaced the soft tarmac at every corner. We were told to be on the watch for German spies. Leyland had suddenly become an exciting place for a boy to be.

It was in the midst of all these excitements that certain other events occurred which expanded and altered the new family life that had been developing and solidifying at Balcarres Road. The first was the birth, on 17 July 1940, of another member of the family, John Alan. Once again, I had no notion of his impending arrival. I find it hard to believe that I can have been completely unaware of my mother's pregnancy, but I was. What happened was what had happened in my sister's case. My mother went off – no doubt Grandma Butterworth was once more recalled to the colours to look after us – and she returned, this time from St Joseph's Hospital in Mount Street, Preston, with Alan. I have a clear memory of being shown him for the first time. He looked tiny and crinkled and reddish-brown. He fitted in without fuss. The established routines went on largely unchanged, though I was expected to pull more of my weight round the house, and pushing prams and go-carts began to limit my outdoor pursuits a little.

A second event that stirred the waters at home was Harry's leaving school with a joyous heart at the age of fourteen in 1940, and his going to contribute to the war effort by joining Leyland Motors as an apprentice engineer. Rebel as he had been at school, he began work, quite literally, sweeping the factory floor, and I can recall his daily return from work, a slight, slim figure in filthy overalls. His first weekly wage-packet contained 14/-, or 70 pence. One day a week he spent at the Leyland Motors Day Continuation School, close to our house, and it was here that he finally began to find himself. He learnt mechanical drawing and the use of fascinating instruments like the micrometer and the slide-rule – beautiful, precise, complex objects which were a delight to handle. He had to produce large, fine machine drawings which looked very competent to me. He was fortunate in having a boss who spotted his potential and gave him much encouragement – Mr Donald (later Lord) Stokes, who lived just round the corner from us. Harry began to show that he was bright and extremely able. He was moved around from place to place within the Motor Works, getting a first-class education in engineering which proved to be the basis of his highly successful career. My regret is that our paths diverged so sharply, once the war had led to his moving from Balcarres Road to live temporarily with Gertie about a mile away. On her own, she was finding the blackout and the nightly air-raid sirens a considerable strain. I do not think Harry was all that reluctant to go. He had known our mother Minnie, as I had not, and perhaps he did not look to the family as much as I did for support and interest. I remain very proud of him and of what he made of himself without the opportunities, connections and background that others like myself came to enjoy. We were still in close contact with him, of course, and when Gertie was drafted to Mansfield, Harry came back to us. But a fault-line in the family had been opened up and it never really closed again.

The third event which had its effect on family life in Balcarres Road was my 'passing the scholarship' in 1941, and my subsequent move from St Mary's School to the Jesuit grammar school, Preston Catholic College. I recall the scholarship examination very exactly. I was just over ten years old. Candidates from all the local elementary schools went to Balshaw's Grammar School in Church Road to sit their first public examination in the usual clinical conditions. There were not many of us from St Mary's, but we had been very well prepared. Vigorous selection even before the examination was not frowned on in those days. The morning examination consisted of an intelligence test and an arithmetic test. I then came home for my dinner, which included, I remember well, a large bowl of rice pudding. Then in the afternoon there was an English test with, I think, comprehension and precis. But the only detail I can remember is that I ran very short of time for the essay which had to be attempted at the end. The set topic I was faced with was 'Air Travel', and I can remember my satisfaction in framing the concluding sentence to what had to be a short, one-paragraph essay: 'One of the benefits of air travel is that it makes the furthest countries our nearest neighbours.' I can only have read this dashing thought, or something like it, in a book. But I produced it as the purest and most pleasurable invention. I had, of course, no experience of air travel, and I knew no one who had. There was little air travel anyway before and during the war – which perhaps makes it odd that the topic was ever set. We had not been coached in that or in any other topic. So the thought must have emerged as if fresh-minted from my imagination, though it was surely prompted by the books that I was at last beginning to read.

By this time I was showing a marked liking for books of almost every sort – a liking which has only strengthened over the years. I was acquiring a growing number of Wonder Books, encyclopedias, large picture-books on ships and railways, and a number of bound volumes of the Wide World Magazine. These I leafed through endlessly, becoming very familiar with the adventures of Louis de Rougemont and with some Gothic tales by a strange person called Baron Corvo – it was much later that I came to realize that he was the bizarre F.W. Rolfe. In my early grammar school years I read through the whole of a multi-volume illustrated encyclopedia which I solemnly borrowed, volume by volume, from my Dugdale cousins in Farington. I became well known at Leyland Library, run by the redoubtable Mrs Farrelly, a pillar of St Mary's Church, whose son was a Franciscan missionary in darkest Borneo. I read a great deal of Percy F. Westerman and Anthony Hope. I also read any comics I could lay my hands on. Gertie bought me *The Beano* regularly from the first copy onwards – it had a roll of liquorice inside, an early marketing ploy. Later I graduated to the weekly *Hotspur* and *Rover*. I had very little interest in canonical children's literature, which struck me as coy, snobbish and insipid. Nor did I like the remote worlds of Kipling, Saki, John Buchan or Sapper. But I enjoyed Conan Doyle's Sherlock Holmes, and I thought I would like to be Dr Watson, when I grew up.

When Mr Coffey read out the scholarship results to the assembled school at St Mary's, I was named among the handful of successful candidates. I think I was the only boy, and I was certainly the youngest. I felt the glow of success all the way home from school. When I announced my success at home, it went down well enough, of course, but rather as if it had been expected all along. Once again, family reserve was in firm control. They had been taking it for granted that I would get my Lancashire County Scholarship. Later I found I had been rewarded with the gift of a fine model yacht with the not very apt name of 'Endeavour'.

The scholarship gave my growing ego a considerable boost, and my career a great thrust, in the direction my life was already beginning to take – towards finding acceptance and a sense of belonging among those who valued learning and who aimed to be 'in the know'. I was perhaps discovering, in my childish way, that in learning lay the possible means of escape from the confines of my very ordinary life; and through learning lay access to a status and a superiority which I might have been craving deep down. It was in such a still unconscious frame of mind, I feel sure, that I paid a brief, introductory visit to Preston Catholic College in Winckley Square sometime during the summer of 1941. This was to sit another examination, an entrance test on the results of which the College Governors awarded scholarships of their own. For me the results were already irrelevant, and in any case they did not have the prestige of the scholarship I had already won. I never even found out whether I passed or not. They were usually awarded to good Catholic families who needed some help even with the low College fees. The only thing I can recall from my first visit was the gloomy size of the place, empty on a Saturday except for few very confident-looking prefects with green ribbons round their caps. They looked dashing and not a little forbidding, as if they belonged to one of the public schools I had come across in the kind of books I had learned to dislike.

In September I began to attend the College. My bus fares to Preston were paid for by my scholarship. About five of us from Leyland turned up as new first-formers in our belted navy-blue gaberdine raincoats and our bright maroon caps, carrying shining satchels and, of course, our gas-masks. Underneath our coats we wore as much of the full school uniform as wartime clothing coupons would cover. I was not to know that this move to the Jesuit grammar school was going to bring the tension between my two worlds to a head, and that at the end of seven years there I was going to try to resolve the tension once and for all, and in a fateful way.

Preston, for which Leylanders like myself affected a deep contempt – we pretended it was a recent growth, and nothing like as venerable as Leyland and its Hundred – was an untidy manufacturing town, with the central part of which I was going to become very familiar. The natural links between Leyland and Preston were the train and the bus, and I used both at different times during the years I was at the College. Schoolchildren from Leyland had to be off the buses by five o'clock, the time the day-shift finished in the wartime Leyland factories. All the buses were then needed to ferry night-shift workers from Preston into Leyland and to take the day-shift home. Factory workers did not have their own cars in those days. This meant that as far as I was concerned almost all after-school activities at the College were ruled out, at least for the rest of the war. In any case, and especially in the longer winter part of the school year, it paid to get home before the blackout. These were, in their way, quite grim years, and I missed out on many normal grammar school activities. But restrictions were such a universal fact of life, so well organized, so rigorously imposed and so completely accepted, that they came to constitute a normality all their own, and life just went on – off to school, classes, back home, homework, off to bed. The comforting fiction of business as usual was maintained wherever possible. Even though I still had two or three years of education after the war was over, they were years that brought even more deprivation to the country than we had seen in wartime, so grammar school and war conditions belong together in my mind and imagination.

Preston had two grammar schools for boys: Preston Grammar School, with which we had no contact whatever, and the flamboyantly named Preston Catholic College, founded and run since the late 1800s by the Jesuits. It stood on a handy site in the town centre in a pleasant early Victorian development, Winckley Square. The green and bushy gardens in the centre of the square were defaced during my time at school by a large Emergency Water Supply tank made of steel and full of old prams, bedsteads and bicycles. It hardly befitted the gentility of the surrounding buildings. Next to the College were the convent and school of the Holy Child sisters, whose girls provided many a pleasing distraction for the older College boys. The nuns and the Jesuits had clearly planned their schools to be close to one another, though there was another convent school, Larkhill, run by the Faithful Companions of Jesus. It is now the site of the sixth-form Newman College which has superseded all three Catholic establishments.

Preston was not only a strongly Catholic town: it was also strongly held Jesuit territory. Jesuits were responsible for four of the town's central churches as well as for the sole Catholic grammar school for boys.

The College numbered about three hundred boys in 1941 – scholarship boys from the town and from the county, boys on bursaries and some fee-payers. Any idea that a grammar school like the College catered only for a brainy or a social elite would be seriously mistaken. Brains and social class were mixed and cross-mixed to produce a school which was genuinely comprehensive yet able to offer individual pupils very sound, though, by today's standards, limited opportunities. In 1941 the chief difference from the College of pre-war days lay with the staff. About five or six of the younger laymen on the staff had been called up into the armed forces, but their places had been filled by a surprisingly large number and variety of Jesuits. Clerics, both ordained and unordained (provided they were formally tonsured), were exempt from military service, though a good number of priests, of course, served as chaplains to the forces throughout the war. Preston, because of its Catholic coloration and its large Catholic population, was deemed a suitable place for young but exempt unordained Jesuit clerics to spend the couple or so years of school-teaching which regularly formed part of their long train-ing. Fewer eyebrows might be raised in Preston than elsewhere. The effect of this was to enrich the College both academically and on the sports field well beyond its normal pre-war level. The younger Jesuits – called 'scholastics' – tended to be lively, the older priests to be learned. What these attractive characters perhaps lacked in long-term commitment to school teaching they made up for in an energetic devotion to games and particularly to serious classical scholarship. Dull our lives were not; though in our studies we may have suffered from the lack of the consistent application of humdrum methods of teaching. We were rarely taught the same subject two years running by the same person or even in the same way. But more importantly, the Jesuits were almost all from elsewhere. Preston, it must be said, is a deeply provincial place. It may have been recently declared a city, but in the small-town context of those days most of the Jesuits figured as somewhat larger than life – big fish in a small pond. They were by no means all brilliant, or even efficient, in the classroom. But from the start of my time at the College, as they strolled across Winckley Square to the school in their winged gowns from St Wilfrid's Presbytery where they lived in community, they made an impression on the likes of me that was to have its effect later.

I was not aware, of course, that there was a measure of illusion in the impression they made. Not unlike the Benedictines in Leyland, they represented a great international and historical institution, irrespective of the actual extent to which they individually deserved to take the credit for its achievements. The English (now British) Province of the Jesuits, as I was to come to learn in time, was something of a backwater in the Society of Jesus at large, and was largely given over to running public schools, grammar schools and parishes. Commitment to the broader fields of scholarship, culture and even spirituality, for which the Order was, at least in the past, rightly famous, was limited. Among the Jesuits there are, and always have been, some few individuals who are directly responsible for the Order's high reputation, which is then enjoyed by the many who are of little or no distinction. As in most institutions, it is comfortable mediocrity which characterizes the majority. But such critical thoughts were not available to a young provincial lad like myself who had an urge to please and to belong and to do well. I got to know most of the Jesuits who taught me at Preston at later stages of my life. They turned out to be the good and worthy people I had known them to be when I was a schoolboy, though of course they made a less forceful impression when viewed at closer quarters in a wider setting.

More immediately impressive during my schooldays were the older lay masters and mistresses who had remained behind at the College on the outbreak of the war. The impression they made was different from that made by the Jesuits and, humanly speaking, more telling. Among them were teachers of already legendary commitment to the school – a quality not to be discerned in the more transient Jesuits. Unlike most of the Jesuits they were known by affectionate nicknames: Big Ben (Herbert) Bolton, Dicky Bragg (Mr W. Allen), Sergeant Jack Keogh, Little Len (James Lawson), Flush (W.C.) Park, Nutty Almond – and the women, too: Beness (Big Ben's sister, Miss Bolton), and the Art Mistress, Maggie Meagher. These were all part of the College's fixtures and fittings. Only gradually did one learn about their personal lives. A number of the men – so I later learned – had earlier left religious congregations, after 'trying their vocations', and they had taken to teaching as a way of remaining faithful to their aspirations to help others. None, of course, had any chance of promotion in a school owned and run by a religious order. Their pay was said to be poor. But they did have the status of teacher, which was still, in those days, something socially prized; and they showed a dogged devotion to their life's work which made many of the Jesuits seem, even in our schoolboy eyes, ephemeral, recyclable creatures of perhaps only a single school-year. The lay staff belonged to the same ordinary world we all belonged to, whereas the Jesuits belonged to another, alien, religious world located behind the polished brass plate which marked St Wilfrid's Presbytery.

It was rather different, though, with the Jesuit who was Headmaster for most of my time at the College, Fr B.A. (Barney) Malone. Of somewhat simian appearance, with half-moon spectacles, he limped round the school, swatting miscreants (painfully) with his large bunch of keys, imposing order and unerringly naming every single boy he addressed in his familiar sing-song voice. Barney was, I think, no fool. For one thing, he had been, prior to his promotion on the death of the previous unpleasant 'Boss', Fr Grafton, an excellent teacher. Barney was of Irish descent and had a good sense of humour. He was the best bee-keeper I ever met, and no school year was over until we had all listened to his annual illustrated lecture entitled 'Among the Hymenoptera'. If this was supposed to serve as an introduction to 'the facts of life', at a time when sex education had not been invented, it failed badly, but it certainly entertained us. Later on the Jesuits foolishly promoted him to a post in which he was unfairly exposed to the critical wit of some frustrated young Jesuits, and his reputation suffered. I frankly liked him, and he was kind and encouraging to me as long as I knew him. I rather think that, unlike a number of the Jesuits who served at Preston, he did not secretly despise Lancashire folk. There was a homely touch about him that was missing in many others.

Like most grammar schools of the period, the College modelled itself, even if only distantly, on the English public school, but with a strong Catholic coloration. There were Sixth Forms, even a Fifth Remove, an A and B stream, a School Library, a Hall with quite a good stage, an annual Shakespeare play, an annual Cabaret, a school orchestra, a Glee Club, and twelve Prefects. In the newer part of the school, built not long before the war, there was a swimming-pool, a gymnasium, science laboratories, and a dining-hall with kitchens. Outside the narrow back gate into Mount Street there was a school Tuck Shop, a gold-mine for the people who ran it, at least in term-time. The school was even divided into 'Houses', though obviously these had no residential implications. They were named after English martyrs – Fisher,

More, Campion and Mayne. Their purpose was to provide a framework for inter-house sporting and academic competitions. House points were awarded, and these were added up annually to produce a winner and three losers. The prize was a large silver cup and a tea-party. It all left me rather cold. But pretensions had their limits. It was as if bits of public school veneer had been stuck on to the College but only in the more obvious places. Although the Scouts were active, there was fortunately no OTC. I do not suppose we were thought to be officer material anyway.

One experience in my first year at the College was new to me – the experience of not being able to understand something, a genuine *aporia*. The topic was minus-numbers in arithmetic. Nobody seemed willing or able to explain them to me, or perhaps I had a blind spot about them. The difficulty was, as it seemed to me, miraculously cleared up when Barney Malone came to visit the classroom. I do not know how he came to be teaching us. Possibly the Jesuit who was our maths teacher (later a successful Province Bursar) had been found wanting, and the Headmaster had taken the matter in hand himself. All that Barney found it necessary to do was to tell us a perfectly lucid and homely tale: 'If I've got only £2 in the bank, but give you a cheque for £5, I'm worth minus-£3.' I got a great deal of pleasure and relief from the evident correctness of his explanation. What on earth had been so difficult about that?

But apart from wanting to master things I did not understand, I have no memory of ever feeling ambitious about learning or of ever actively exploring knowledge. Although I read avidly at home, at school I preferred to be a passive learner, happy to be learning the infrastructures of learning: methods in maths, the useful rhymes at the back of Kennedy's *Shortbread-Eating Primer* (as 'Shorter Latin Primer' invariably appeared on our defaced copies), grammatical paradigms, vocabulary, syntactical rules – the more esoteric the better. It is perhaps not surprising that I have never developed great powers of concentration. I still work effectively, as I have done all my life, only in brief dilettante bursts, a matter of, say, half-an-hour at a time. I like to think, of course, that somehow 'much more' must be going on in my head, and I am capable of reflecting – even brooding – on things for long periods. But then I find that things get done pretty smartly, once I know how to proceed. So visible and tangible 'work' is quick and brief, and then nothing seems to take place for quite some time. But I imagine and rehearse things a great deal before doing anything; and I dislike having to do anything that I have not thoroughly imagined myself doing beforehand. I am notably unspontaneous. I was once thought a good lecturer and a passable preacher; but my success was due to my having imaginatively rehearsed almost every word I ever spoke. I have always liked trying words on for size. But the real workings of my mind are well beyond me, though I have acquired a usefully rough idea of their pattern or rhythm, and I know what I can – and cannot – expect from it. Little, if anything, has changed since I was a first-former in Preston.

During the seven years I spent at the College (1941–48) I was taught by a staff of very mixed abilities, from the plainly incompetent to the one or two with a real touch of teaching genius. One factor which obviously makes a lot of difference in a teacher is enthusiasm for the subject. Hence good teachers would have been good teachers of any subject they happened to be enthusiastic about. Enthusiasm is not only infectious: properly informed, it also breeds clarity and understanding – and with clear understanding comes, I find, the pleasure and satisfaction which accompanies all intelligent learning. Compared with the few teachers who can bring that pleasure and satisfaction about, the rest are little more than competent, even if sometimes learned, ushers. At a deeper level, though, in the course of a monstrously long formal education from elementary school to doctorate (twenty-six years of full-time education, not counting another five years of training) I have been led to believe that in the last analysis the quality of a good teacher lies not only in enthusiasm, but also in the way they themselves have habitually learnt their subject. The best teachers are the best learners, and not necessarily the most learned; and bad teaching rests on faulty or at least inappropriate learning in the first place. It has probably much to do with a second important factor, with imagination. Good teachers seem to have the imagination to acquire their learning 'teachably' – in a way which renders anything they might learn teachable. In other words, they are good teachers because they have first learnt by teaching themselves. Good teaching is a performing art, and the good teacher has an imaginative, even histrionic, quality akin to that of a good actor. 'The boards' and the blackboard are not all that far apart.

In contrast with what I had been used to at St Mary's in Leyland, from the start at Preston I had more poor teachers than good ones; but the proportion of poor to good was roughly what I was going to find at every subsequent level of my education. I was in the A-stream for my first five years at the College, before passing into the Lower and then the Upper Sixth. Life was much more competitive than it had been back in Leyland. I was now among boys of whom many had been selected for their intelligence from the town and county. Some of them were very highly intelligent indeed. Form IA were, as I remember them, a thoroughly pleasant group of around thirty boys who stayed more or less together until Form VA. Occasionally someone was judged to have better chances in the B-stream, and sometimes a B-stream boy was promoted to our group. Demotion and promotion depended on twice-yearly examinations in all subjects. Three times a year reports were sent to our parents, and a position in class was assigned. It was not possible to doubt just where you stood. I burned all my reports many years ago – with good reason – but I can recall that in my first examination I came sixth, and in my second I came nineteenth. There was instant concern in school and at home about my performance, and also about the reports, which were mediocre, to say the least. Everyone seemed convinced that I could do better, and I never again sank any lower in class. I slowly climbed up the ratings over the years; and I think I finished up with a hat-trick of first places in the Sixth Form. Perhaps the competition was not as strong as it had been lower down the school. I won a handsome book prize for this. But for the most part I had been happy in my habitual position, trailing along not too far behind the leaders, well-placed enough to satisfy my vanity and sense of security. I would not have cared for the responsibilities or the expectations that might have attached themselves to coming out top all the time.

As far as the various subjects were concerned, I do not think I was obviously better at one than at another. I was not too good at physical training – until, that is, I grew bigger and stronger in the Sixth Form, and then I began to enjoy it. Not that I was ever physically a weakling. In fact, I used to surprise some of the more belligerent members of the class by my ability to force them down and hold them there in our mock scraps. I was never bullied, and never heard of any bullying at the College. I took to English grammar and syntax easily, and this interest was strongly reinforced when I began to learn Latin in the Second Form. I liked sentence analysis, spelling, reading, and learning a lot of poetry by heart. Every boy had to have a copy of Palgrave's *Golden Treasury* which he kept throughout his time at school. Inside the cover there was stuck a programme of poems, listed by number year by year, and these had to be known by heart. I suppose we learnt between fifteen and twenty thumping old favourites per year, apart from gentler lyrics and some speeches from whichever Shakespeare play we happened to be engaged on. The very first poem we learnt by heart was Thomas Gray's 'On a Favourite Cat, Drowned in a Tub of Gold Fishes'. It must have sounded hilarious to hear a piping Lancashire accent come out with:

> 'Twas on a lofty vase's side,
> Where China's gayest art had dyed
> The azure flowers that blow ...

I daresay we understood only some of the words. But what other wonderful words and ideas there were to encounter in that single poem: 'demurest, her conscious tail, their scaly armour's Tyrian hue, Presumptuous Maid!, Malignant Fate, she mew'd to ev'ry wat'ry god, no Dolphin came, no Nereid stirr'd' ... and so on. These cadenced words and phrases have stayed with me for life. We did not come away from the poems we learnt with any general idea of what poetry was or how it worked; but we did begin to hear and feel words. Otherwise English was taught as much as possible like some other dead language. But even so, much of the poetry and even more of Shakespeare managed to escape alive.

It was somewhat the same with art. We received a most useful grounding in lettering, penmanship, the history of English archi-tecture, elementary drawing – all culminating in the endless painting of posters. We never had to draw or paint a landscape, a still life or a human face or figure. Posters – that, it seemed, was what art was all about. We had to design and draw them, and then colour them in, chiefly in lurid poster paint. The subjects of our posters were dictated by the war: Battle of Britain Week, The Spitfire Fund, Eat More Fruit, Eat Potatoes, Buy Savings Certificates. In the School Certificate we all took a written paper on the history of architecture – one of the most useful subjects I ever studied. The College produced at least two well-known Northern architects, just as in classics it produced a dispropor-tionately large number of excellent classical scholars. But they would all have done posters in their time, and have recited Gray's poem on a drowned cat.

French was taught as yet another dead language, and since we had no conceivable use for it until after the war, what should have been a life-enhancing subject became the biggest bore in the timetable. But it has meant that I can read academic French easily, and that has proved very handy. The only place to learn a foreign language is abroad, as I discovered when, later on, I was sent to Germany for a year's study, and I picked up German in no time. Of course, I was much helped by having the clear and firm grasp of grammar and syntax derived from Latin and Greek. What passed for history and geography I liked and was good at history, which, even when it was reduced to learning facts about Egypt, Babylon, Greece and Rome, can do wonders for the imagination. Later on, a couple of us were encouraged to undertake a little research into local history, going to the splendid Lancashire County Records Office in Preston, and even round non-Catholic parishes in search of baptism and marriage registers – that sort of thing. From that I developed quite a taste for researching the past and its sources, and it has remained strong in me ever since. Geography proved very interesting too. We studied physical geography. We pored over maps and made terrains out of putty, and sliced them up to indicate the contour divisions. We learnt to read the shape of the world, the lie of the land, the effects of climate. I have, ever since then, loved maps and enjoyed land-scapes in many parts of the world. In my ideal school syllabus, history and geography, like art and English, would be compul-sory subjects, but French I would try to manage without.

What then of the other subjects we studied? Science we did, but not seriously. Neither physics nor chemistry were well taught. I feel about school science what I feel about French: physics and chemistry are better studied where they are to be used – rather as my brother Harry learnt the engineering science he needed through his apprenticeship at Leyland Motors. With mathematics it is quite different. Here is a subject well worth learning, and I could have become quite good at it. But mathematics was also poorly taught, except for geometry, and this appealed strongly to my logical sense and my imagination. The sad upshot of the poor teaching of science and maths at Preston was that the bright boys were left with no real alternative to taking classics, and this was not necessarily the best subject for all of them.

In those days no Catholic grammar school could fail to teach religious doctrine as a prominent element in its curriculum. At the College it was neither well nor interestingly taught. All that we were offered, for much of the time there, was intensified by-heart learning of the Penny Catechism, the junior version of which was already familiar from our days in elementary school. Where nowadays serious attempts – sometimes highly successful – are made to offer children at least something of the bread of the

Catholic tradition, all we got were bigger and heavier catechetical and theological stones. Still, in defence of the barrenness of the religious syllabus of those days, it has to be acknowledged that it did accurately reflect the official view which was taken of the Catholic faith in those days. Here you had Catholicism rendered down to a system of pre-cast questions, each with its unchallengeable answer, about what the institutional Church had decided that Catholics had to learn and practise. All that schoolboys needed – and all they would ever need, even when they grew up – was to be indoctrinated, while they were still in captivity, into a reach-me-down system of second-hand ecclesiastical certainties. There was to be no talk about the religion or spirituality of Catholicism and no notion of its meaning or value. These catechetical and theological stones *were* our Catholicism. Any need for spiritual experience or religious feeling (instantly suspect as these would have been) had to be satisfied with bracing doses either of stern preaching against sin or triumphalistic *ferverinos* wildly overselling the 'Faith of our Fathers'. Solid certainties to last a lifetime and into the world beyond – that is what Catholicism had to offer: certainties formulated, guaranteed and imposed by a Church infallibly headed by Christ's Vicar in person. What more could you possibly want? You would always know exactly where you stood as regards your eternal salvation, since once you had learnt the system any divergence from it would instantly and inexcusably put you in bad faith and a plain state of guilt, if not sin, from which only the same system could then release you. I would not blame the College for taking this approach to the teaching of the religion that inspired it, since this was the only approach on offer at the time. No one, and certainly not the Jesuits to whom the teaching of religion was usually assigned, knew any better. They were there to plug the party line, if not always very efficiently. But there was one Jesuit scholastic, 'Wogga' Smith, who seemed interested in opening our minds to the deeper implications of our Catholic faith. When I was in the Second Form, and aged eleven, he started up a library from which we could borrow suitable religious and spiritual books. I read quite a number of them, and with profit. But Wogga was exceptional in many ways: an enthusiastic soccer fan and an older entrant into religious life, he displayed human qualities not found among the other Jesuits. Uncompromising as he was in class, he somehow contrived to mix toughness with a measure of discreet personal warmth. Much later, after a successful parish ministry, he left the Jesuits and the priesthood and got married.

The rest of the Jesuits remained coolly and professionally distant from us.

Of course there were the predictable signs of Catholic life round the school: statues of Our Lady in the classrooms and corridors, edifying pictures of saints, and so forth. Each week there was Benediction for the whole school across the road in St Wilfrid's Church, and we had High Masses there on big feast-days. These were impressive occasions, and they were religiously much more valuable, in the sense that they provided access to a far richer Catholicism than anything we met with in school. It very occasionally happened that one of the Jesuit priests would preach a sermon that was mildly interesting, but far more important was the music involved in the services. Music was a firm fixture in the College curriculum, and we spent many of the music classes preparing carefully for our performances in church. We learnt the hymns, both Latin and English, in *The Preston Catholic College Hymn Book*, and also the plainsong Latin Masses of the simpler kind from *Plainsong for Schools, Part I*. This was not only fun to do, but a little elementary music – I only wish it had been much more – stood me in good stead in later life. Not that all our singing was religious. Along with Palgrave's *Golden Treasury*, each boy had to have *The Oxford Song Book*, from which we learnt a hearty selection of old favourites: 'Forty Years On' (little did I then realize the significance of that!), 'Camptown Races', 'Early One Morning', and the like. As our voices broke, we growled our way through most of the book. Surprisingly few boys did not enjoy singing lessons. Popular music was nothing like as widely available as it is now, and singing was a release from the dry, impersonal labours of the classroom. I would certainly want to have music and singing in my ideal academy.

Looking back now, I realize that I enjoyed most of the subjects taught at the College despite the often lackadaisical way in which they were taught. After elementary school the idea of each subject's being taught by a different teacher was novel, of course, and potentially exciting. The curriculum resembled one of my encyclopedias in the way it unfolded, subject after subject, without any conscious linkage, and this I liked. Underlying all the subjects, it seems to me, whether they were languages or not, was a single, rather boring rationale: learning was a matter of learning the infrastructures and principles of the subject, cost what it might in terms of effort and concentration – and boredom – on the part of the teachers and the pupils. This is what school – and perhaps especially grammar school – was about: getting the inner parts and workings of the subject at the basic level into the heads, and especially into the memories, of those who had come to learn. It was about getting them to know their own way about a subject, so that they also learnt about learning, and could then go on and learn what they wanted or needed for themselves. In no subjects could this unfashionable approach have been more rigorously applied than in the learning of Latin and Greek. These dead languages served, usually without acknowledgement, as the practical paradigms for learning all the other subjects. They embody in themselves the model to which the grammar school was invented to conform. Rightly, to my mind.

Latin, as I said, we began in Form IIA. Our first teacher was the remarkable Wogga, whose own knowledge of Latin was pretty elementary. For the first few weeks he even taught us the ecclesiastical pronunciation, before being told to change to the pronunciation commonly accepted in English schools. But what mattered were his tough methods. He knocked Kennedy's primer into our thick heads – he literally hit us if we did not know by heart the paradigms, the parts of verbs, even the gender rhymes. The upshot was that I permanently acquired a total recall of the whole of Kennedy – 'a possession for ever', I might say; and certainly one of the most useful pieces of learning I ever came by. Years later, during a Latin prose examination at Oxford, I found myself reduced to mouthing the rhyme

> A, ab, absque, coram, de,
> palam, cum and ex, and e,
> sine, tenus, pro, and prae.
> Add super, subter, sub and in,
> when state, not motion, 'tis they mean.

And all in order to confirm that 'coram' took the ablative case. I learnt that in 1942, and it has survived more or less intact in the memory for nearly 60 years so far. I later had a few Latin teachers who were better informed than Wogga, but none to whom I am more grateful. His Latin teaching was just what was needed at that stage. I came to love Latin, with its right-or-wrong precision; and I still maintain that it provides, along with mathematics, by far the best initiation into accurate learning. Long experience of teaching has convinced me that at some point, at some time, all students need to come up against a subject which they cannot just pretend to know: a subject that depends on getting things right, and where there is no room for error, and where you either know it or you do not; where questions cannot simply be 'discussed', and where you cannot fake the answers. Latin, to my mind, is just such a subject. Good Latin will not let you get away with anything.

Greek I began a year after Latin, and I never received quite the same grounding in it. This meant that for a long time I did not have the same confidence in reading and writing Greek – which is strange, since Greek is the easier language. We were taught chiefly by Jesuits who, even when they were competent, lacked the interest and commitment to make us learn the basics properly. For a time our prospects looked up when a layman, James Lawson – Little Len – a fine classical scholar with a severe physical handicap, took us over, and we responded well to him. But sadly he was replaced by yet another indifferent Jesuit. Little Len was moved to teaching English, which he did for years afterwards with distinction. The wartime shortage of lay staff meant that sometimes we had to make do with second-best.

So my grammar school education went on from year to year. I suppose I was making progress. School reports were a mixture of frustrated, angry, encouraging and lukewarm comments. Most of all I disliked the bald comment: 'Fair'. I was beginning to get noticeably more fractious and non-conformist in my behaviour and attitudes. On my weekly report card, which had to be signed at home over the weekend and returned on Mondays, I achieved notoriety in class for getting an 'Excellent' for Application and a 'Bad' for Conduct – both in the same week. I must have been difficult to deal with, but I was also able to do well when it suited me. In time I sat the School Certificate, in which without any effort I can recall I achieved a 'Credit' in all nine subjects. This was rightly read as indicating some ability, as well as some potential to spare. A much smaller group of us – about six or seven – then moved into the two years of the Lower and the Upper Sixth to take the Higher Certificate in Latin, Greek and Ancient History. Once again, the teaching was done by Jesuits who, though they were respectable enough scholars, did not have their hearts in teaching. To be fair, I cannot say that our own hearts were always set on learning, either. Classics in the Sixth Form should provide the essential foundations for a possible career in the subject; but for our group it turned out to be a disappointing experience. The class a year ahead of us, however, produced a good crop of academic classicists in the established tradition of the College, so it cannot have been entirely the fault of our teachers. My last two years were rather wasted, and I have regretted it ever since. One possible reason was that classics did not suit most of the boys in

our group, and it would not have been their subject of first choice
– had choice been available. But there again we were up against
wartime restrictions.

◌

Not that schooling and the attendant homework filled up all the
time I had. There were the long school holidays. I suppose that in
normal circumstances I could have begun to travel around a little,
in England if not yet abroad. But travel was actively discouraged
by the authorities so as to leave the transport services free for
more serious traffic. Bus and railway stations were plastered with
the forbidding question: 'Is Your Journey Really Necessary?' So I
occupied myself for a great deal of the holidays by working for
the Co-op in Leyland. Holiday jobs there were easy to come by,
thanks to my father's position, and I often worked at his drapery
branch in the hardware department. In the loading-bay at the
back I would unpack kitchenware and crude pottery from huge
straw-filled crates. Sometimes I would help in the shop at the
sales. I met all kinds of people, and not least the girl shop assistants. I was paid a little money for my labours. A Saturday's
unpacking would bring in about 15/-, or 75 pence. A week's
work would bring in £2 or £3. I also moved round the other
branches of the Co-op, too. I did stints in several grocery stores –
Canberra Road, Golden Hill, Leyland Road, even back in
Towngate – working in the back or in the cellar, packing bags of
sugar or weighing out potatoes. I even worked in the central
warehouse. I was a sort of peripatetic drudge, well treated by the
shop staff and quite happy to be passing the time in a useful way.
Best of all, though, I worked with a cheerful van-man, Bert Lee,
on the Co-op Travelling Shop. The two of us (though I cannot
remember what there was for me to do apart from keep him
company and open and close farm gates) motored round the
outlying country districts, calling at houses and farms and selling
Co-op groceries. Bert was an affable man, and I listened to – and
joined in – many conversations with his customers, who, I
suppose, were glad to have someone to chat to in their isolation. I
developed a taste for listening and talking to people, especially
old people. I enjoyed all those holiday jobs. They kept me occupied, and I had no time to spend the money I earned. I put it into
National Savings Certificates. Following the advice of another of
my lurid school posters, I Saved for Victory.

We also had a family holiday every year, though never a very
exciting one. It was only for a week, but we solemnly went off to
Fleetwood or St Anne's on the train with a trunk to a boarding-

house. We walked along the promenade, and I spent a great deal
of time sailing my model yacht. We played on the sands, and
there were donkey rides and ice-cream. Everything was geared
down to the pace of Barbara and Alan and the small pram that
went everywhere with us. The food was good, chiefly because we
took quite an amount of it with us in the trunk – a common practice in order to supplement wartime rations. Only rarely was this
pattern broken. In the summer of 1943, when I was twelve, I
joined the College Scout camp (though I was never a Scout
myself) at Chaigley outside Chipping for a fortnight under
canvas with about thirty or forty boys and a few laymasters. On
arrival I was instantly overwhelmed with the most dreadful
homesickness. I was comprehensively miserable, in a way I have
never been, before or since. I wrote a quick card home, begging to
be rescued immediately. It must have been wisely intercepted,
since it never reached home. Within the fortnight I then grew to
love the place and the life. My father even cycled all the way out
from home to visit me. In the end I was quite prepared to stay
there for life, and I hated coming home. Later, in 1947, still soon
after the war, I went with a group from St Mary's Leyland to
Switzerland for a fortnight. For this I did dig into my savings to
the tune of £25. We travelled by boat and train via Paris (where
we paid for restaurant food with very acceptable tins of ground
coffee) to Seelisberg on Lake Lucerne, to stay in a hotel and to eat
food such as we had not seen for years. On the way I saw London
for the first time, as well as Paris, Basle and Lucerne. I had, of
course, never before experienced the hot, dry mountain air of
Switzerland. There was no mass tourism as yet, and facilities
were limited, local and cheap. We had great fun. It took nineteen
hours to get back from Basle to Calais, because many miles of
railway track were still out of commission as a result of the war. I
was sixteen years old and seeing some wider dimensions of the
ordinary world for the very first time.

Weekends and shorter holidays as well were times I spent with
friends. The days of moving round the surrounding countryside
in a 'gang' were over, and friends became more personal and
more close. I saw a great deal of a couple of them, one in Leyland
and one in Preston, and both became lifelong friends. These
friendships rested on shared interests: in Leyland, on bird-watch-
ing, cricket, country walks, and even a little train-spotting; in
Preston, on cycles rides and long hikes into the Lancashire hills
and moors – Pendle, Parlick, Fairsnape, Anglezarke, White
Coppice. We talked incessantly, but not about much that was

important. We smoked secret pipes, drank illegal beer at the back doors of pubs, and biked round old churches. They were long, happy, innocent days.

℺

Thus at home and at the College a further seven years elapsed. It was not an especially exciting time, but a happy one. I liked school work, and I liked belonging to my group of peers, while at the same time I was developing a taste for objecting to the system. I had a good home, and I liked living there with my family. My ordinary world had steadily grown into a much wider world, and I was beginning to feel comfortable in it, and even to know my way about it, if only in a very limited way. I was beginning to get out and about: not socially but, in a mild way, culturally. I went to the cinema on Saturdays, and I enjoyed dramatic adventures and romances. I thought *Mrs Miniver* was wonderful. I took to going fairly regularly to the concerts by the Hallé and the Liverpool Philharmonic Orchestras in Preston, and I much enjoyed them – John Barbirolli and Constant Lambert were my heroes, and Tchaikovsky my favourite composer. Lower down the cultural scale I went to most Preston North End football matches every other Saturday afternoon in the winter, and I got to see most of the great names of post-war football: Matthews, Lawton, Mortensen, Shankly, Swift, Mercer, Mannion, Carter, and, of course, Preston's own incomparable Tom Finney. I also went occasionally to Old Trafford, either for a Test Match (I have a vivid memory of the second day of the Indian Test Match of 1946) or for the Roses Matches against Yorkshire. I can still recite football and cricket teams of that period with the same ease as I can L.M.S. engine names and numbers. Not all my memory bank was stuffed with Latin and Greek paradigms and the parts of irregular verbs and gender rhymes. Saturday afternoons in the summer were reserved for the family outing – my mother, myself, Barbara and Alan, to be joined later in the afternoon by my father – either to the Leyland Motors or to the Leyland Cricket Club, to watch a Ribblesdale League game in which one or other of my Dugdale uncles might be performing. Both grounds were close enough to allow us to nip home for tea at the interval. It was a good life.

But it was a life that was going to have to move on. Inevitably questions were arising about my future. I was by now close to the end of the Sixth Form, but I had no fixed idea about what I wanted to do after school was over. Having clearly shown, when I was lower down the school, that I was inclined to have a mind of my own, I am not at all sure why I was appointed a School Prefect in my last year. It turned out that I was a good prefect, efficient in my duties of supervision and in my ability to deal with disciplinary situations. At the end of the school year we had to sing our 'Prefects' Song' before the assembled school:

> Our duty is to aid the weak,
> To check the erring lad,
> Shepherd and fold the wayward clique,
> Suppress the bold and bad.

As far as the school authorities were concerned I was known to be non-conformist and inclined to be recalcitrant. Perhaps efforts were being made to get me to join the school establishment. I was the first prefect in the history of the College who was not, and never became, a member of the pious group known as the Sodality of Our Lady. I was also the first prefect ever to be beaten (with the ferula) for insubordination – I had flatly refused to attend the nominal weekly class in science for classicists, and some token punishment had to be meted out. I had publicly denounced such classes as a total waste of time – which they were. The new Headmaster, Fr John Duggan, changed the timetable. I had somehow learnt to be outspoken when I felt strongly about an issue, and extremely stubborn and quite fear-less in declaring my views. I have no idea how I had gradually come to be like this. It was not as if I was unhappy or discon-tented, or that I felt particularly aggrieved or aggressive against anybody or anything. My guess is that as I rose to the top of a group to which I liked belonging, I began to feel in some way responsible for the way it ran itself, for the system; and when I thought that it was being run badly, I felt it right to criticize it in ways that took other people by surprise. At any rate, from then on John Duggan, a French scholar, took to describing me, in an elegant understatement, as 'un peu difficile' – an epithet which pursued me, quite justifiably, for many years. Meanwhile I was doing well as a prefect, and even better at my studies. But I must have looked, to anyone concerned, a very uncertain prospect.

What my prospects in the ordinary world might be was still unclear. There can be no doubt, I think, that I was ready to start making my way in it, and that I was capable of going quite far, once I got going. But at what? Lower down the school I had toyed with the idea of joining the Lancashire Constabulary, but Barney Malone had laughed me out of it. It would be ridiculous to suggest that Barney was secretly working at some plan to get me to join the Jesuits themselves. The idea was in itself inconceivably far-fetched; and the Jesuits, to my knowledge, never encouraged their pupils – and certainly never myself – to join the Order. In any case I would have thought that I had demonstrated my own radical unsuitability on more than one occasion. The next ambition I had was to go into librarianship, with a view to being an archivist. This I think I would have enjoyed. But that idea was overtaken by a more definite plan to become a doctor. By now I was in the Upper Sixth, and I would have taken up the place I was offered at the Liverpool University Medical School with the help of the Lancashire County Bursary, awarded to me on the results of my Higher School Certificate. I now seemed bound for some university. If not medicine at Liverpool, then the most obvious alternative was to read classics at Manchester, where I had already represented the College at an excellent school classics conference run by Professor T.B.L. Webster. I do not know what my family made of all this. It was all, I suppose, a bit beyond them. They never failed to give me maximum encouragement in whatever direction I happened to be moving, but they were hardly in a position to give me any positive advice. There was, of course, no such post as 'Careers Adviser' at the College in those days. People just seemed to be standing back, waiting to see what might happen.

Whatever it was that happened, happened in the bath at home at Balcarres Road. I suddenly, and very much to my own surprise, decided to become a Jesuit. I had, to the best of my knowledge, never before given it a single thought. I hardly ever said a prayer. I indulged in no pious exercises, and although I remained true to the practice of my Catholicism, my performances were pretty perfunctory. I later came downstairs and informed my father and mother. They did not seem overly bothered or impressed. They kept their thoughts to themselves. I next told John Duggan at the College. I must also have told some of my friends. Rather eerily, no one showed any surprise. Were they trying to be kind? Or were they too embarrassed, perhaps too shocked, to react? For some reason unclear to me, can they possibly have been expecting it? I suppose I must have been seen as a rather palely serious, studious and unworldly young man, inclined to be 'un peu difficile' on occasions perhaps, but not in any apparent difficulty with his religion. None of this amounts to what is commonly thought of as having 'a vocation' to the religious life and the priesthood. I certainly never felt even remotely 'called', not even in pious hind-sight. I just seemed to make my mind up to it. The causation of the sudden decision in the bath completely escapes me. The immediate effect was that I dropped all the other alternatives.

My decision was taken only very late on in my final year at school. I could not have thought about the matter, and still less have mentioned it to anyone, before the Lent of 1948. The school reacted by inviting me to join 'the Leavers' Retreat', which was to take place in the Easter holidays at Loyola Hall, Rainhill, Liverpool. I would not otherwise have thought of putting myself forward for anything so overtly devotional. It was the first personal spiritual exercise I had ever undertaken, and I found that I thoroughly enjoyed myself. The preacher of the retreat was Fr Bernard Basset, a highly intelligent, academic, witty and imag-inative Jesuit who long enjoyed a well-deserved reputation as a writer and spiritual guide. I was impressed by the routine of the retreat house – the silence, the talks and so forth; but especially by one sermon by Fr Basset which he preached before the Blessed Sacrament with great sincerity and conviction. What he actually said I now have no idea; but he struck me as a man who knew whatever Catholicism was about from the inside. It all clearly meant everything to him personally. I never spoke to him, but I had never before even imagined that anyone could be as coher-ently sincere, convinced and committed about Catholicism as he was. This impression was confirmed years later when I twice stood in for him when he was absent from the tiny parish he was then running on St Mary's in the Isles of Scilly – I suppose he must have been, in his way, a holy man. It was not that I was overwhelmed by an urge to imitate Bernard Basset, whom I did not know and never really got to know. But in his presentation of his Catholicism there was, I fancy, a strongly romantic strain. He had distinguished himself as a historian at Oxford, where he was a fellow-prizeman with Harold Wilson. Perhaps behind my gruff Northern façade there lurked an unfulfilled romantic. At any rate, I returned to school for my last term and my final examina-tions knowing, at last, what I thought I really wanted to do.

That first attraction to the Jesuits is now too far away, as well as too deeply overlaid with other anachronistic developments in my religious views, to be worth too much consideration. I would be prepared to say that I 'got religion', but only in the sense that I broke through to the fact that there had to be more to Catholicism than had thus far met my eye. It may have been a result of my long familiarity with Benedictines and Jesuits, devoted as they were to a life apart, that I saw in Catholicism a world separate from my ordinary world, and as a world which made sense in itself; a world that I might enter and in which I might learn to live my life; a world which contrived to be a viable and contradictory alternative to the ordinary world of my experience. But it is true that there was little or nothing traditionally 'religious' about my attraction to it: nothing explicit, that is, to do with grandiose determinations to serve God or Christ or the Church. There was little feeling, piety or warmth about it, either. It seems to have been the way the Jesuits lived that attracted me, more than any of their professed religious purposes. In fact, I precisely liked the way in which they apparently did not feel they had to flaunt their religion. Their way of life – officially meant to be 'ordinary' – I had glimpsed when, in the Sixth Form, it was usual for one of us to go over each day to their dingy, club-like presbytery at St Wilfrid's to read from some diverting book to the whole Jesuit community as they ate their dinner. Here we saw them all in full view and in their natural habitat. The reader was also given a splendid dinner afterwards – with cider – in a tiny parlour. They lived, it seemed to me, practical lives: good men, in their way, with worthwhile jobs to do, whether in the school or in the parish. They had certainly shown me notable tolerance. They also represented a wider view of Catholicism than anything I had picked up in Leyland – a much wider religious world. They came from all over the United Kingdom, and belonged to an Order of well-deserved international renown. Above all – and increasingly I think this was one aspect of the Jesuit life and world that particularly attracted me – many of those I had seen or known in my time at the College appeared to be learned and academic in their interests. Learning, as I have stressed, had always attracted me. They were also priests – or priests-to-be. But their priesthood seemed to me – but not, of course, necessarily to them – to be little more than a set of functions that they were well prepared to perform efficiently as occasion required them to do, rather than a central element in their lives. In any case, for anyone joining the Jesuits, the priesthood was a very distant prospect indeed – an average, in those days, of fifteen or so years into the future, almost another lifetime. I would say that behind my attraction to the Jesuits lay my old attraction to learning.

Of the religious inspiration and purpose of the Jesuits I had no more than a schoolboy's knowledge. In school we had celebrated Jesuit feasts and saints from time to time, and there were school holidays connected with certain leading Jesuits like Francis

Xavier. What Ignatius Loyola stood for, apart from the supposedly military discipline of the Order he had founded, I did not know. We had interesting evening lectures at school on Xavier and on Teresa of Avila from no less an expert than Professor Allison Peers of Liverpool. But of religious life and its meaning, or indeed of Jesuit origins, I was simply ignorant. The English Jesuit martyrs we had heard of, but they ranked somewhat lower than John Fisher and Thomas More, our twin Catholic bastions against the usurping Church of England. Whatever else the Jesuits in Preston had done or had not done, they had certainly not indoctrinated us about their Order. Still less, as I have said, had they encouraged anyone to join. The attitude they displayed was – well, go and try it, if you must, and see what happens.

Before I could do that, I had to be formally accepted for entry in September 1948. Candidates were normally vetted during the course of the year previous to entry, and I was officially 'examined' during the summer term. This meant a visit to four Jesuits over at St Wilfrid's, including the then Jesuit Provincial, the inspirational Martin D'Arcy, who was on his annual visit to the community. The four interviews I found all very pleasant and undemanding. Each priest had to fill in a questionnaire in Latin. The only mildly probing question that I can recall came from Fr D'Arcy: why did I want to join? I have to confess that, unlikely as it might seem, I was rather stumped at the time by this elementary question. The only quick – and perfectly honest – answer I managed to produce was that I could not think of a better way in which to spend my life. This off-the-cuff answer went down well. I seemed to have said the right thing. The other interviewers ran through their list of questions in a pretty perfunctory way. They knew most of the answers already, since I had been in the school for seven years. Nothing personal or sexual was mentioned. One of my interviewers was Fr Johnnie Turner, old and very deaf, who conversed with the aid of an ear-trumpet. I was told that Bernard Basset's mother, confronted in the confessional with the bell-end of this instrument protruding under the grille, put sixpence in it for the Foreign Missions. Fr Turner impressed me by knowing the Latin for step-mother (*noverca*). The others were very familiar figures: Barney Malone, by then the Rector of St Wilfrid's, and John Duggan, who (I imagine) no doubt noted in Latin that I had a tendency to be '*aliquantulo difficilis*'. I must have passed my mild ordeal, since I was later informed that the Jesuits were prepared to take me into their novitiate in September. I immediately wrote to Liverpool University to tell them that I would not be taking up my place in their Medical School.

In view of what happened much later, was I wrong to do so? The more I reflect on the question, the stranger it seems to be. It is one thing – and a normal thing – to gain, as life goes on, more insight into one's past, one's motivations, one's character, the meaning and purpose of one's human existence. It is altogether another to try to re-interpret one's past, or, still worse, to try and re-write it. I do not think that I was at all wrong to join the Jesuits. It was not at all untruthful of me to tell Fr D'Arcy that I could not think of a better way in which to spend my life. I simply could not have thought of a better way at that time. What is more, my motives, however ill-informed, however immature, were entirely sincere. According to my lights I knew what I was doing, and what I was taking on. I was not deceiving myself, nor was anyone else deceiving me. I was determined to do my best by my Catholicism as I then saw it – as another equiliteral world strictly alternative to the ordinary world in which I had been busily developing the life that was going to be mine. I was prepared to give that ordinary life up entirely, and go and try to live another life in another world. I thought it was the best thing to do, and I have no regrets that it took me all of forty eventful years in what slowly became a wilderness to discover, and then still reluctantly, how and why I had come to be in what had turned out to be the wrong place. All kinds of factors would have prevented me from the mistake I was making: greater insight into myself, more professional guidance from others, a less triumphalistic notion of Catholicism, a critical awareness of the limits of knowledge in general and especially of the functions of language in the creation of forms of life and worlds of meaning, a more solid appreciation of the reality of the ordinary world as opposed to the world of religion – these are the spiritual and intellectual refinements that might have helped me to avoid joining the Jesuits, and that finally contrived to convince me that I had to leave them. But they were neither immediately nor generally available in 1948, let alone in a provincial youth aged just seventeen. I was going to reach the age of sixty before I acquired them. As for the Jesuits, they were certainly not wrong to accept me. After all, admission to the novitiate was no more than admission to a two-year trial run before the real obstacle course had to be faced.

Chapter 3

Out of this World

On 7 September 1948 my classmate Barney McCann and myself were seen off by members of our families from Platform Six of Preston Railway Station as we departed for the Jesuit novitiate in Roehampton, London S.W.15. Barney had become a friend over the last four or five years at the College, and was to remain a friend for the rest of his life. Unlike myself, he had long fostered an ambition of joining the Jesuits, but he left the Order, still as a scholastic, after twelve years or so, and then took up a successful career in teaching, first back at our old school in Preston, and then in a large Catholic comprehensive school in Washington, Tyne and Wear. At the start of 1999 he died a bachelor after a very long and uncomplaining struggle with cancer. Just over fifty years previously we had boarded the fateful train together, dressed in deep sub-fusc, with black hats and stiff white collars. Perhaps in those days this already semi-religious garb did not make us stand out among our fellow-travellers quite so much as it would nowadays, when we would be taken, I fancy, for a couple of Mormon missionaries. Our families had to kit us out completely for the new life into which we were entering. Only recently I was told that my mother had been saving up for a fur coat, but the money had to be spent on my new clothes. The tale sounds apocryphal to me. First, I am surprised I had never heard it. Second, she was certainly not a fur coat type of person. Third, I cannot imagine on what occasion she could possibly have worn it round Leyland without looking rather silly.

Our goodbyes were typically unemotional, and we were off on an adventure that was meant to last the rest of our lives. I wonder, though, what we were all thinking. As far as I am concerned, the answer is simple: nothing very much beyond getting to a new and exciting destination. No Jesuit saw us off from Preston. Entry into the Jesuits was a low-key affair, of little concern to those already in the Society, and understandably so. It was the novitiate itself – the first part of the Jesuit system – that was supposed to sort out those who would leave from those who would stay. The official attitude was impersonal, cautious, and severely empirical: 'you say you have a vocation to the Jesuits, so go and test yourself out on our system. If you can come through the rigorous initiation to which we will subject you in the difficult two-year novitiate, we will then provisionally agree with you that, as long as we find nothing to object to in your attitudes, you may possibly have a fixed future in the Society. You will be carefully trained and instructed within the system in everything you will need to know to enable you to proceed to the next stage of your training for whatever kind of work it is decided you are suited for. You might eventually – but only in perhaps fifteen or twenty years, time, and after you have been ordained priest – be given permanent Jesuit status'. The whole systematic structure of Jesuit training and vows reflected this attitude exactly. So for the moment there was no need for the Jesuits to take any interest in a couple of ex-schoolboys departing for the novitiate. Time – lots of time – and strict conformity with the system would be what counted. I should add in fairness that I describe things as they were half a century ago. What kind of system exists nowadays in these deregulated days I no longer know.

I have often wondered what my parents would have been thinking. Typically, they never said. Whatever their expectations of me had been – and they had always seemed to expect that I would do my best at school and that I would finish up in a world that was different from their own, but one that would cast some kind of solid and well-deserved credit on themselves – such expectations had been rudely overtaken by my sudden attraction to the Jesuits. As sound and unspectacular Catholics they would not have considered it proper to question whether I might be doing the right thing. A vocation to the priesthood or to the religious life was an eventuality that Catholic families were told by the Church to hope and pray for. It would have been wrong to question or obstruct it in any way, however many other legitimate family hopes and expectations and needs might thereby remain unfulfilled. The family attitude was meant to be one of deep gratitude to God that in His inscrutable wisdom He had seen fit to vouchsafe the blessing of a vocation to the priesthood and religious life. So my father and mother remained silently grateful, not daring to raise queries, if they had any. They were good, uncritical people and remarkably generous in facing what could well seem, in worldly terms, a writing-off of their considerable investment in my already lengthy education – not to mention the loss of the apocryphal fur coat. Perhaps they felt compensated in some way by the social *éclat* they would enjoy as the parents of a priest and a Jesuit. Priests are figures of power in the Catholic community. Not only do they wield considerable influence over the faithful; they are also in close daily contact with the unseen and unpredictable ways of the Almighty.

This was not quite how I saw things. If their interest was in me as a future priest, my interest was definitely in becoming a future Jesuit. As far as I can recall, I never had a very strong attraction to the status and functions of the Catholic priesthood. Whatever I was joining the Jesuits for, this was not exactly it. Priesthood would play an accidental role in whatever work I expected I would be doing as a Jesuit. I am not at all saying that I did not like the idea of being a priest. I could, and did, fairly easily imagine myself celebrating Mass, preaching and performing all the other priestly functions. But the priesthood as such exercised no specific appeal. It happened to be part of what it was to be a Jesuit. If this seems like culpable ignorance on my part, I can only say in my defence that I was very ill-informed, and explain that by the time I was seventeen years old, I had never actually met an ordinary diocesan pastoral priest – one who worked under a local Bishop in an ordinary Catholic parish. I knew only the Leyland Benedictines and the Preston Jesuits. True, the former exercised their pastoral responsibilities admirably in St Mary's Leyland, but they clearly belonged elsewhere, in Ampleforth; and most of the Jesuits I had known had no pastoral responsibilities at all. So it would have been odd if I had given the pastoral priesthood priority in my intended membership of the Jesuits. The Jesuits I had come to know seemed to wear their priesthood lightly. I am sure this does not mean that they did not take it seriously; but they certainly seemed more centred on their teaching and learning. I was also not without my own personal spiritual aspirations to what I liked to think of as holiness: vague, romantic, adolescent, but intensely real and sincere. I suppose I thought that these aspirations would be refined and fulfilled in the Jesuits, given some substance, made more personal.

These were not my thoughts as the train ran on down south. Having arrived at Euston, we took a No. 30 bus on its mazy trip through central London and off into the leafy south-west suburbs to its terminus in the little, still unspoilt village of Roehampton. There the anonymous gates and right-angled drive of Manresa House took us in as part of another annual batch of would-be-

Jesuit hopefuls. Before the Jesuits had adapted it and renamed it to suit their purposes, the house, then called Parkstead, had been an elegant villa, built for William, Second Earl of Bessborough in the 1760s by William Chambers, the original architect of Somerset House. The white stone façade, which looked out over Richmond Park, was in the strictly Palladian style. In 1823 it led the diarist Thomas Creevey to remark: 'I had a really charming day at Roehampton yesterday. It is quite a superb villa, a house with 500 acres of beautiful grounds about it, and all Richmond Park appearing to belong to it.' The Jesuits bought it in the early 1860s and aroused both local and royal disapproval. Queen Victoria is said to have ordered a screen of trees to be planted round her property at White Lodge in Richmond Park so that she would not have to gaze on the new Jesuit settlement. Once their novitiate had been transferred to Roehampton from Beaumont in Old Windsor, the Jesuits, not noted for being conservationists, set about vandalizing the building and the estate, adding a chapel and dormitory wings and other domestic offices, and carving up the carefully landscaped grounds at will. Obtaining local planning permission was a procedure that still lay well into the future. The original villa was all but overwhelmed by the unappealing bulk of the tastelessly bolted-on functional accretions which now faced us as we approached Manresa with our suitcases for the first time. Had I been prescient I might have seen the ill-sorted combination as prophetic of the religious life into which we were about to be initiated.

So we stepped into another world, where strong tea was available in a low room on the ground floor. Old words lost their meanings, and new words began to take over reality. We were in the hands of fussy 'Angel Guardians', half-a-dozen trusties who had just completed the first half of their two-year stretch in the novitiate, and who were thought responsible enough to guide our ignorant steps for the statutory period of the 'postulancy', the quarantine period of about ten days before we were deemed fit to join the rest of the novices. The Angel Guardians seemed decent enough, and they laughed a lot, probably out of nervousness. Only one or two seemed rather full of themselves. The chief one was an ex-Major from the army, obviously chosen to be a high-flyer in the Society. I had never realized, of course, that my fellow-novices would be an extremely mixed bag as regards age and background, with a high proportion of ex-servicemen who had done some remedial study of Latin and undergone some basic rehabilitation, not to civilian life but to life in a seminary or novitiate, at the Jesuit-run Campion House for 'late vocations' at Osterley. My own group, the class of '48, turned out to be a very mixed bag indeed. To start with we were about thirty-five in number, but I imagine that between fifteen and twenty of these had some experience either in the armed forces or in some other field of the grown-up world; whilst the rest of us were straight from school, and mainly from Jesuit schools at that. Some of these had been at boarding school, so for them the novitiate must have felt like a continuation course, with a reorientation towards the full-time religious life.

To pass on anything like an adequate impression of life as lived in the world – the 'limited whole'– of the Jesuit novitiate is hardly possible, if only because the novitiate consisted in a deliberate attempt to realize a form of life not shared by any human group outside very similar religious novitiates. But more than this: it was deliberately set up in contradiction of so much that passed for normal in most developed cultures and societies. It was unique in its way; hence it becomes impossible to draw comparisons or give descriptions which do not require continual and tedious qualification to make them even half understood or appreciated. It would take a considerable artist to give even a fair impression of it all. Evelyn Waugh at his wicked best is the only writer known to me who, given sufficient experience, might have been up to the job of providing a helpful, not to say hilarious, description. The truth is that the novitiate was a completely factitious world apart in itself, consciously constructed as such, and conscientiously preserved, as far as possible, from contamination of any sort from other worlds outside. But then there are many other forms of life that have their own strange ways of going on, and which stoutly resist outside influences. It is true, for instance, of most professions, or of the armed services, or of any club that thinks its own identity and procedures matter. But in all such cases there is usually some life beyond and outside the group. Members do, at least occasionally, go home and become relatively normal, meet non-members or not as they wish, travel around, go out to dinner, produce babies, care for their families, do the shopping, go on holidays, and so forth. Not so the Jesuit novices. Life in the novitiate was an all-inclusive totality. It covered every detail, waking and sleeping, twenty-four hours a day for two whole years. Every aspect of it was simply compulsory. Everything must be done according to the order of the day or other commands dictated by the authorities – the Master of

Novices or those delegated by him to run the daily life of the novitiate – getting up, washing, shaving, dressing, praying, meditating, thinking, looking, eating, washing up, slopping out, laying tables, speaking (in Latin normally, with English allowed at times), cleaning, sweeping up, gardening, walking, reading, relaxing, playing football, conversing, studying, taking a bath, doing penance, receiving the sacraments, undressing, going to bed, falling asleep. There were no alternatives on offer, unless a novice was plainly too ill to follow the common regime for a while. There were no normal freedoms, individual or communal. You spoke when it was time to speak, and you spoke to those you were allowed to speak to, and you spoke in whichever language was permitted at the time. You did not gravitate towards those you once might have considered your friends, or avoid those you happened to find uncongenial. You were allowed out only with the companions assigned to you. You obeyed instantly and in every detail the sound of the bell or the command of the one in charge. If the bell rang when you were writing, you did not try to finish the word, let alone the sentence, you had begun. You worked without interruption at whatever task you had been given until it was time to stop. You did exactly as you were told, simply because your life was no longer meant to be your own. You had voluntarily and permanently abdicated your selfhood and your individuality in favour of those responsible for running this Jesuit boot camp. The only possible analogy would be some super-strict and severely punitive prison regime of the kind that no longer exists in the civilized human world. I am unaware that there is any exaggeration in this summary account of the novitiate I entered over half a century ago.

Life in the novitiate was unreal because it was meant to be unreal. It was based on a pure concoction of ideas which had no real basis in the past, present or future of any known world, and not even, as it turned out, in the original religious vision of the Jesuits themselves. It was meant to embody, not a living religious spirit, but the dead structures of a religious tradition which had been mercilessly rendered down into a simplistic and all-embracing system. It is systematization, reduction to a system or a code of conduct, that kills off religious traditions and their spiritual values, however inspired and admirable they might have been in their origins. Take the Jesuits, for instance – though much the same could be said, *mutatis mutandis*, of Catholicism at large. They had been founded by a religious genius, Ignatius Loyola, whose insights into his traditional Catholicism looked well beyond so much that had been systematized and codified in the late medieval church of his day and in most of the other religious orders of his time. His *Spiritual Exercises* alone must rank as one of the outstandingly imaginative re-interpretations of the key doctrines and of the central thrust and mission of Catholicism. His letters reveal all the sensitive strength and flexibility of a first-rate spiritual leader and spiritual guru.

But towards the end of his life, he wrote detailed *Constitutions* both in response to the needs of the remarkable Order which he had founded almost in spite of himself, as well as to satisfy the requirements of ecclesiastical authority. This was understandable enough, since the tradition, the handing on, of the essential vision or insight must lie at the heart of any religious movement; and written tradition seems, at first sight, the obvious way of preserving that insight. Hence, for instance, the early collection of the New Testament writings. But the attempt to commit an inspired insight to paper runs the certain risk of distorting the insight and of failing to transmit the inspiration. It also sets a precedent for others, not personally party to the originating insight, to try their hand at writing it all down. With the Jesuits, the precedent set by Ignatius was followed first, and laudably enough, by the generation of his followers who knew him and survived him; but secondly, after the restoration of the suppressed Society in the early nineteenth century, by later leading Jesuits who, almost disastrously, reduced the Ignatian vision, which they had neither shared nor properly understood, to a conveniently universal system for training entrants and maintaining general discipline and sufficient numbers in the restored Order. A renegade Jesuit of the early twentieth century (and something of a hero of mine, as will appear), Fr George Tyrrell called this systematization 'Jesuitism', and he carefully distinguished it from the real Ignatian thing. (Tyrrell, incidentally, had other pet dislikes that he called '-isms'. Favourite targets of his were 'theologism' – the dead scholastic theology of his (and my own) day – and 'Medievalism', as we shall see.) Little though we realized it at the time, Jesuitism was the system into which we were being initiated at the Roehampton novitiate.

Yet even so I have to report – perhaps perversely – that, both in my ignorance then and even in the light of the far greater awareness I now enjoy, the two years I spent as a novice at Manresa House were happy ones. The chief reason is that it was not beyond the scope of the imagination to read the novitiate as a richly comic experience: not perhaps in the sense that it was calculated to produce many laughs (though in fact we did laugh a lot, as I remember), but in the deeper sense that it was subversive of everybody's accepted values. Whilst it was obvious that there were gaping differences between the novices – marked variations of class, wealth, social background, education, experience, intelligence, age, temperament, and so on – absolutely none of these things was allowed to matter or count in the slightest. Everybody was instantly reduced to a mad equality as total and as surreal as could be imagined. Ex-schoolboys suddenly found themselves in charge of a work-squad which contained ex-army commandos, retired officers, highly qualified scholars, fellow schoolboys, R.A.F. ground staff, merchant seamen – all of them assigned to pulling deliberately fostered thistles bare-handed out of a potato field, either in complete silence, or, at a signal, forced to converse laboriously in sub-medieval dog-Latin. Totally uncongenial trios of badly dressed novices of ill-assorted ages – people who would hardly have known, or even have looked at, one another in the ordinary world – were sent on recreational walks in the pouring rain over Wimbledon Common without a penny piece between them. People who had lived elegant, much-travelled lives in foreign parts were given sixpence each to get themselves to Westminster Cathedral and back in the depth of winter, and told to visit as many Christmas cribs in as many Catholic churches as possible in the process. Without exception, everyone took daily turns at cleaning and mopping out lavatories (perhaps consoled by the fact that Gerard Manley Hopkins had once been entranced by the frozen spray on the very same slate urinals when he was cleaning them); at sweeping and polishing long linoleum-covered corridors; at peeling potatoes and preparing other vegetables whilst listening to the tedious animadversions of Fr Alphonsus Rodriguez on *The Practice and Perfection of Christian Virtues*; at gathering up fallen flying leaves in windy autumn; at serving at table, at washing up and drying crockery and cutlery; at weeding and digging and hoeing; at teaching catechism on Sundays to difficult and distracted children in the surrounding parishes; and, with complete disregard for any skills a novice might have, at bookbinding, gown-patching, language-learning, making instruments of penance (spiky wire leg-chains and small whips), and at flower-arranging in the sacristy. We lived in a house which was an artificial bee-hive of crazy make-believe industry and of deliberately contrived labour-intense non-production. Meanwhile, of course, the real work – cooking, housekeeping, the running of essential services, healthcare – was being done by the Jesuit lay-brothers, that devoted but largely unrecognized section of the Society of Jesus who represented as much normality as it was possible to foster amid the encircling madness. The only safe way to look back on it all is to see it as very comic indeed.

So we moved through the day, dropping one pointless task at the sound of the bell to take up another, or to move from one more or less religious duty to another: to 'spiritual reading', for instance, of books which were carefully vetted for their suitability, to study, and, occasionally, to enjoy brief 'ad lib. time', when you might perhaps write a letter, though not more than one a week. Letters were posted unsealed via the Master of Novices, who was free to read them, just as he opened all incoming mail. There were no newspapers and no radio, though 'gramophone concerts' of strictly classical music were held sometimes on special feasts. Periods of 'recreation' were compulsory after dinner and after supper, and always sitting or walking in whatever trio happened to be formed as one went through the door. Visits to the chapel were frequent throughout the day – first thing in the morning, for daily Mass and Communion, after each meal and most duties, for evening Benediction or for Litanies, and finally before going to bed. All this was quite apart from any private devotional life you might dream of developing. For such individual spiritual luxuries there was very little time left over, and personal pieties were quite severely discouraged. Space, as well as time, was scarce. We did not have individual rooms, but lived and slept in long dormitories where we had a desk and chair and a prie-dieu outside the curtained cubicles where we slept. But most of the time we spent round the house and in public places. Privacy was impossible to come by. To all of this there has to be added the Master of Novice's daily lecture, in which he dealt with the Jesuit *Constitutions* and spirituality. Then there were weekly elocution, reading, singing and voice production classes, and occasional liturgical engagements outside the house. Then at certain times of the year the devotional pace would be stepped up with more talks and sermons in the twice-yearly triduums and the annual retreat. Our idea of a holiday was a fortnight's 'Hay Season', when we took to the grounds and had daily picnics – and more practice sermons, preached out-of-doors. So our lives were arranged for us over two full years. You had to put in the full time, otherwise the novitiate could be ruled canonically invalid; though I do not think you had to start all over again.

It is pointless to resist the obvious comparison with prison. I fancy that prison, even in those relatively bad old days, offered a far less rigorous regime, but one that consisted of a somewhat similar round of compulsory communal activities designed not to have any positive or satisfying outcome for the inmates, but to pass the time to which the prisoner had been sentenced. Still, at least the mail-bags sewn by prisoners, or the oakum they picked, had some purpose in the ordinary world. Of course, there are differences between novitiate and prison. One is technically free to leave the novitiate, and since one's fellow-novices are unlikely to be criminals but on the whole very decent folk (though, come to think of it, the novitiate would serve as an excellent refuge from the law for any villain tough enough to face it), the general atmosphere among novices is probably more pleasant. As I have said, I found those years quite often hilarious. A sense of humour, was, I believe, essential to survival, both then and afterwards. In any case, the novitiate could hardly have been a depressing place: had it been such, it would have collapsed under the weight of its own nonsense. Perhaps the most lasting and gratifying effect on myself has been that when I have seen films about Colditz or other places or forms of detention, or popular sit-coms like *Porridge*, or even visited people I know in prison, I get intense pleasure out of instantly recognizing a form of life which is already very familiar. I am led to wonder at how much more comfortable the inmates are than we were as Jesuit novices. But to the schoolboy that I was, the change from home and school was so complete, and the new life so completely novel and absorbing, and so many of my fellow-novices so surprisingly different from people I had ever met before, that it remains true that I found the experience enjoyable. It was just as well that I had neither time nor skill in those days to look more deeply, either into myself or into the religious system I was slowly being led to assimilate.

I am now, I think, in a position to discern the deeper principles that were embodied in the way the religious world of the novitiate was run. Just what the whole theory behind the novitiate was would require a long enquiry into its history and into the minds of those responsible for its development, in particular during the nineteenth century. I have no intention of inaugurating such a project; but it could be helpful to say what leading ideas seemed to govern the minds of those who dictated the way in which we were expected to behave as novices. I think they may be handily reduced to three.

In the first place, the aspect of novitiate life which I have referred to as richly comic and subversive of accepted values stems, I believe, from a principle that dominated the spirituality of the nineteenth century 'restored' Society of Jesus: in Latin, *agere contra* – that is, acting in direct contradiction of whatever natural thoughts, inclinations, feelings or desires happen to suggest themselves. The idea rests on the alleged paradox that it is only by contradicting yourself at every level that you achieve real – that is, reliably genuine – self-fulfilment. What had to go, if any spiritual progress was going to be made, was any ambition to achieve your own independent personhood. For instance, if you feel you have a tendency to think yourself clever, play the fool, and hope to convince others that you are not clever. If learned, act as if you were ignorant. If you find you rather like good clothes, then go around in the dirtiest old hand-me-down Jesuit gown that comes your way. If good food is your fancy, then eat the oldest crusts around. If there is a particular person you find boring or repellent, do not avoid his company but seek it out. Of course, in all this there is a built-in brake which puts a stop to any excess – if you find you are inclined to be something of an exhibitionist in your self-contradicting asceticism, contradict that tendency, too, by keeping your self-denial to yourself. 'But when you fast, put oil on your head and wash your face, so that your fasting may be seen not by others but by your Father who is in secret ...' (Matthew 6.17f. NRSV). Still, in the novitiate, it was the spirit of self-contradiction that was meant to be most exercised; and the cultivation of such personal spiritual lives as we had came down to the imposition of this essentially negative spirit. We were in no position to inquire into the validity (or the authenticity) of the underlying paradox. It was obviously basic to the take-it-or-leave-it religious system we had come to the novitiate to accept.

Now it seems obvious to me that a dose of self-denial or even self-contradiction is probably no bad thing at least from time to time in most people's lives – a measure of vigilant self-control, and a fairly vigorous attitude towards countering one's wayward habits and inclinations and one's self-indulgences. It is not hard to imagine that the general quality of human life might be considerably improved if more people learned to curb and deny their sinful propensities. But in the case of the *agere contra* presented to religious novices, it was not just habits and inclinations that might be deemed sinful that were in question. It was, of course, taken for granted that these would be exorcised through the habitual use of penance and self-denial and the frequentation of the Sacraments. *Agere contra* was meant to be a programme for an entire way of life. It was the whole of one's natural interior life, both present and future, that needed, and would always need, contradicting. The life of the novitiate was built round this principle. Once inculcated by two years of unquestioning acceptance in the novitiate, the principle was meant to serve as the only really valid basis for the rest of one's Jesuit life, whatever it might bring. Thus the overriding need for self-contradiction could always be invoked when, say, one found oneself opposed to a Jesuit Superior who might wish to wring compliance out of one of his subjects, however unconvincing the command. You had been programmed to do, not what you might think appropriate, but what you had been told.

The root difficulty with this cult of self-denial is not that self-denial is necessarily a bad thing – as I have said, there is likely to be room for it in anybody's ordinary life – but that it was presented in such a negative and comprehensive way: without, that is, having any regard for the potentially positive benefits of personal freedom and growth. It was un-Christian insofar as it promoted death – indeed, crucifixion – to self without any countervailing resurrection. Carried to its theoretical limits, *agere contra* left no scope for whatever talents or gifts a novice might have brought into the Society in the first place. But the Jesuits were not so stupid as to throw these away, and they were allowed to surface in time after the novitiate, and in practice they were – at least in some cases – well cultivated and used to fairly good effect. But not in all cases: the negative emphasis of the principle did, I think, prevent some Jesuits from making the most of themselves or from being more use to the Order; and, what was worse, it did give unintelligent or unscrupulous Superiors the whip-hand for use in exploiting their more compliant subjects – though in fairness I should add that in my forty years in the Jesuits I cannot honestly say that I ever personally suffered from such a Superior, though some I had were obviously better than others. Either I was very lucky, or perhaps, being 'un peu difficile', I was never compliant enough to be exploited. But others, I know, were not so lucky, or were, I would say, too prone to submission. Having absorbed the negative theory of self-denial all too faithfully, they did not choose to develop either the character or the gifts they had. For them the theory meant that whatever their self-assessment – or their self-respect – amounted to, it was never to be trusted: it must be contradicted, and certainly never

asserted against the will of their Superiors, which, by prior definition, was identical with the will of God. Like God, the Superior
would know the person's potential and usefulness best. The
novice had to become habituated to being, in the dramatic
imagery of Ignatius' *Letter on Obedience*, as passive as a corpse or
as a staff in an old man's hand. As a prime principle of the spiritual life, or as part of any theory of human living – however
useful it may be in forming some part of a person's self-discipline
– *agere contra* is, I believe, a 'vicious' principle – vicious, that is,
not necessarily in a moral sense, but in a logical sense, as in
'vicious circle' – and certainly in any theological sense derivable
from a Catholicism whose God, far from wantonly contradicting
the humanity He had created, is believed to have identified
Himself fully with it in the mystery of the Incarnation, and to
have graced and enhanced it in order to save it.

A second principle at work in the life of the novitiate was
consistently deployed to add both weight and colour to the basic
doctrine of *agere contra*. This was the principle of 'the imitation of
Christ'. The self-contradiction I have mentioned turned out to be
an ideal reliably grounded in the whole practice and purpose of
the life and death of Christ himself. To read *agere contra* as no
more than some abstract idea, therefore, would be wrong. It was
meant to be put into constant practice; and that practice
amounted to seeking always to imitate the Jesus whose Society
we novices were bent on joining. Now the imitation of Christ is
an emotively very powerful ideal. It dramatically simplifies into a
single, uncritical, raw demand the only proper relationship
between Christ and anyone who may wish to follow him. It pre-
empts and excludes alternative modes that might be assumed by
other forms of sound religious devotion to Christ and his teachings. If you are not willing to imitate Christ, it says to the novice,
and to do it as closely and continually as possible, then you can
only be in the wrong place. But the principle, as with the *agere
contra* principle it was used to license, suffers from the same kind
of crude spiritual overkill. No Catholic would care to deny that
the life and death of the Founder possesses an exemplary quality
which will naturally impose itself on anyone who wishes to
follow Jesus – just as, presumably, the life and death of Socrates
had its effect on a devout Platonist. Disciples, followers, are
drawn to imitate those whom they take as their masters. In so
doing, they need to sink or merge their own personalities to some
extent in the personality of the Master. So some measure of what
might be termed 'imitation' will obviously have its place in the

life of any follower. It is simply part of the whole-hearted devotion looked for in a follower. But devotion (in the serious and wholly commendable sense of the word) is one thing: the kind of imitation of Christ proposed in the novitiate was another.

The chief way in which the imitation of Christ was proposed to us as novices was through the *Spiritual Exercises* of Ignatius Loyola. The *Exercises* are essentially a carefully worked out and graded series of earnest considerations, meditations and imaginative 'contemplations' designed to lead the exercitant to decide to spend his or her life working for God and Christ. I have already said that I consider that the *Exercises* present a brilliant summary of essential Catholic theology. This alone would make Ignatius an outstanding figure in his own age and in any other. It is one of the key reasons why the *Exercises* have been so effective for so long. They offer doctrinally- and spiritually-starved Catholics a thoroughly bracing remedial crash-course in their own traditional religion. But they are more than a brief theology text-book: they employ a sales technique whose pressure is renowned. Of course, the exercitant can always opt out of the process if and when he wishes. But not even the carefully and humanely crafted guidelines for making a decision – 'closing the deal' – about your future life can leave you in much doubt that, in opting out, you might just be choosing the easy way out from what is a divine call to service – and, more specifically, that you would be in some way playing Judas, betraying Christ, in choosing not to follow Christ to his glory through imitating him in his suffering and his death. This threat puts enormous psychological pressure on the exercitant, and it is applied in a steady *crescendo* from the start to the finish of the *Exercises*. From the 'Principle and Foundation' onwards it is to be understood that human existence has only one possible purpose, the glorification of God; and, as the exercitant proceeds from that point, it is made clear that this purpose is achieved through as close an imitation and following of Christ as is imaginable or feasible. It is from inside this powerful context alone that it is possible to appreciate the appalling horror of sin and of any falling short of the ideal of imitating the sinless Christ. This ideal is presented in scene after dramatic scene, drawn either from the gospels or from pious tradition, in which Christ, his cosmic role, his ministry, his preaching, his suffering and his death, and eventually his resurrection, are pictured for the exercitant in forceful detail. The sheer pedagogy of the *Exercises* is quite stunning. It leaves no room for respectable doubt that one's life is best spent in as close an imitation and following of Christ as a person can possibly manage.

I had been in the novitiate for some four or five weeks before all of us new entrants, now proudly wearing old and patched (and sometimes still dirty) Jesuit gowns over our worldly clothes, began the 'Long Retreat' – the full, thirty days course of the *Spiritual Exercises* – under the direction of the Master of Novices, Fr George Walkerley. There was a certain inevitable artificiality about this whole experience, in that we had, of course, already decided in our own ways to join the Society; though it was also expected that the Long Retreat would lead some of the novices to reconsider their decisions and leave without more ado. But clearly, since we were already in the novitiate, the situation was loaded in favour of our staying put. The Long Retreat was intended, I think, more to reinforce our decisions than to alter them. But it would be wrong to give the impression that the rein-forcement was effected by any kind of overdriven or fanatical presentation of the *Exercises*. Nothing could have been further from George Walkerley's style. He had the look of a gentle, schol-arly man. He had been destined for further studies in theology when the war broke out, and he became an R.A.F. chaplain. It was difficult to envisage him in this role. He carried about him an air of ethereal mysticality, which was probably misleading, though it impressed the novices. He remained a distant, even rather shadowy figure, for all that we listened to his talks almost every day throughout the novitiate years. Few, if any, ever got to know him, I fancy; and I certainly cannot recall a single substantive conversation with him, although we all went in to see him for 'spiritual direction' fairly frequently. He seemed to watch each novice carefully, whilst avoiding much personal involvement. With sixty or seventy very assorted novices in his care during this post-war vocations boom, I imagine there was little else he could hope to do. Given the bloated number of entrants he had to deal with, his role must have been limited to monitoring the effects of the system on each of us. Positive, personal guidance of so many would have been impossible. He was thoughtful, intelligent, occasionally humorous, but remote. His chief concern, a wise one, was that a novice should never 'strain'. He took us through the *Exercises* with no sound or fury, letting them, and especially their uncompromising emphasis on the imitation of Christ, do their work.

But the imitation of Christ is, in itself, a problematical concept. As a preaching motto or device, or as a supplier of spiritual motivation, it no doubt has its place as a serviceable short-cut to what must appear to be an obvious form of sanctity. But who is this Christ? And what are the realistic limits of possible imitation? The Christ proposed for imitation is in fact an icon uncritically simplified in the interests of piety. In this context hard-nosed exegetical questions about the Jesus of history are not raised. How reliably can we possibly know the real human being behind the different theological constructs of the Gospels? The Gospel Christ – or, better, Christs, since each Gospel presents a different Christ by putting a different spin on its protagonist – is already a preacher's abstraction drawn from a lengthening tradition of devout, partial, and sometimes contradictory memories. Notoriously, later preachers and teachers have always been inclined to manipulate the Gospel portrayals of Christ in favour of their own prejudices. Christ comes in so many different guises. Which Christ are we supposed to imitate? The gentle Jesus, meek and mild – or perhaps the severe critic of his own religious estab-lishment? And just what does – or can – imitation mean? What can it amount to in our quite different world? Such are only some of the more obvious problems that are airily by-passed in the giving of the *Exercises*, and they did not arise in our Long Retreat.

But what did quickly become clear to us was that the particular Christ who was being proposed for our imitation neatly exempli-fied the key principle of *agere contra*. The prime quality of Christ held out to us for our imitation was his constant self-denial, the quality that made him a self-sacrificing and obedient victim to the divine will. To imitate Christ was to subordinate one's will, at whatever cost to one's mind and reason, to the authority of one's Jesuit Superiors. As Christ had willingly accepted that his Father's will be done, and had revealed his utter obedience in his bloody suffering and death, so we, in imitation of him, should willingly accept that doing the will of our Superiors at all costs was the Jesuit ideal to which we were called, because the will of our Superiors, even the least sign of it, was unquestionably the sure revelation of what God himself willed for us. Obedience to Superiors at all costs: this is what the Society of Jesus and the imitation were all about. This would involve willingness to deny or contradict one's own will and inclinations at every step if need be, and this in turn involved the acceptance of the *agere contra* principle which we had already begun to experience at work in the life of the novitiate. The Jesuit case for permanent conformity to the will of Jesuit superiors, for total obedience, was thus coher-ently stitched up.

A third principle served to anticipate and disarm any unease with the novitiate practice or theory, and so to head off possible objections. This was the principle of 'Trust The System'. A system there certainly was, as will be evident from what I have already said about the novitiate. But it spread much further into Jesuit life than the first two years. There was a clearly defined and almost wooden structure to the whole of Jesuit training – or to what would be called in later jargon, 'formation'. With some slight flexibility and a few exceptions, the would-be Jesuit was expected to pass through the required stages of basic training – novitiate, juniorate, three years of philosophy, some years of 'regency' (the period spent teaching in a Jesuit school, but often including a degree course at university), four years of theology, and then the 'tertianship' or third year of novitiate before final vows. The whole formation generally took fifteen or sixteen years. For one reason or another – age, aptitude, health, specialization – the formation could be shortened or lengthened by a few years. But there was no hurry. The system was long and expensive and certainly ponderous enough to leave its mark on the Jesuit trainee. The authorities felt enough confidence in it to sit back and let it do its work. Above all else, they had time to watch and monitor the progress of their future generations. Such a system, with its many and varied stages, could surely be relied on to reveal the suitability, or otherwise, of the trainee for final acceptance into the Society. And just as the authorities felt they had a right to entrust their charges to the system, without having to take much of a personal interest in them, so they also felt that the trainees had a duty to trust such a well-wrought system as they went through all its phases. In effect, suitability for final acceptance into the Jesuits was routinely dependent on a very long endurance test based on the principle of the obstacle race. Personal gifts and aspirations were not exactly ignored, and it would be unfair to suggest that over the years no thought was given to how they might best be fostered and encouraged, at least in more obviously able individuals. After all, a few square pegs did contrive to finish up in square holes, and filled them with distinction. Then again, running the system itself was labour-intensive: a fair number of individuals had to be singled out from the system to provide the specialized and qualified manpower needed to keep the system itself going. But personal qualities were always secondary to one's willing acceptance of whatever the system might throw at you as it unfolded. *Agere contra*, backed by a convenient interpretation of what was meant by the imitation of Christ, in order to get you to trust the Jesuit system for life – this, on reflection, is pretty well what the novitiate had to offer.

I feel now that those who might have gone to the novitiate in search of the bread of personal spirituality, a way of faith and love that might lead them into the mystery of God, were really offered little more than a questionable system of loaded and hand-me-down piety carved in stone. In fact, come to think of it now, the two years of the novitiate were, at least in my own case, almost wholly bereft of anything that might be reasonably called personal or spiritual experience. It was as if the whole two years were devoted to ensuring that any personal spiritual experience (and *a fortiori*, any other kind of experience) would never really be allowed to count against the declared will of one's Superiors. Personal spiritual experience was no more than one of those obviously dangerous tendencies in oneself which, if it ever raised it head, would have to be severely countered. It might even be true to say that, with the intense stress on Jesuitism as a system, there was something almost 'counter-religious' about the novitiate. Personal religion might, after all, disrupt and endanger the smooth workings of the system. I can understand this attitude on the part of the authorities; but I hardly think that it can possibly have been the attitude of Ignatius Loyola. One important feature of the early Jesuit novitiates, for instance, were 'the experiments' – periods spent well away from the novitiate when the novices were set a variety of religious tasks to see how they performed in action. These might be involve such religious adventures as going away for a time on pilgrimage, or having to teach or preach, or to work in a hospital or a school, and the like. On their return, account would be taken of how the novices actually found the experience as an exercise of their own religious commitment and devotion. For some reason we had no such experiments at Roehampton, no such tests of our religious faith in engagement with the ordinary world. The best we could manage was to spend a month pretending to be a lay-brother novice in the same house. All that this involved, as I recall, was an increased amount of washing-up and a pleasant change of company. I heard it remarked later that the novitiate prepared us, not to be Jesuits, but to be Cistercian monks. If this was a deliberate policy on the part of the authorities – and I am quite sure it was not – it would at least have served a practical purpose, in that the bulk of our subsequent training at Heythrop in North Oxfordshire had to be spent isolated in Cistercian-like surroundings. But our novitiate would have given us as poor a start at being a real Cistercian as it did, I am afraid, at being a real Jesuit of the type originally envisaged by Ignatius. I remember a couple of well-known Latin hexameters from somewhere:

> *Bernardus valles, montes Benedictus amabat,*
> *oppida Franciscus, magnas Ignatius urbes.*

> Bernard was attracted to valleys, Benedict to mountains,
> Francis to towns, Ignatius to large cities.

The suggestion is that Jesuit life is ideally as full of bustle and change and flexibility as life in a modern city centre. The novitiate was certainly no preparation for that.

Of course, I had no such thoughts as I emerged from the Long Retreat in mid-November 1948. There was little that I find memorable in the experience. I quite enjoyed the daily retreat talks and I did not mind the regime of long silences and strict seclusion. The whole event had lasted four weeks or so, but we had had a day off at the end of each period of about a week. There were letters waiting from home and from Gertie. Harry, as I knew, had been married whilst I was shut away in retreat at Manresa. I would have liked to have been at the wedding, but my attendance was just one of those things that I had to deny myself. It would be another five years before I was allowed to go and visit my family up in Leyland, but they all gallantly came down to Roehampton to see me in my second year, and we walked round the grounds and had tea together in a gloomy parlour. I wrote to them regularly, and my mother wrote to me every single week for the next fourteen or fifteen years, whether I was in England or abroad. Just what this degree of denial of one's family was meant to effect, at least in my own case, I am now entirely unsure. It was not as if they were well-to-do or in a position to alleviate or undermine the austerities of the novitiate. No account whatever, of course, was taken of the effect of my removal on them. It could all, of course, be justified by Christ's grim declaration that a worthy disciple had to love him more than father, mother, son or daughter (Matthew 10.37) or even hate them and his brothers and sisters as well, and his own life too (Luke 14.26). But then the dubious exegesis of scriptural bits and pieces is a time-honoured way of asserting religious claims – in this case the Jesuits' claim to the whole of one's life, and a way of ensuring a more complete dependence on the Jesuit authorities. Not that I bothered much about it at the time: I was, I have to admit, very much taken up with my new life.

The lessons of the Long Retreat, not to mention the general tone of the novitiate spirituality, were negative in the ways I have tried to express. But it has taken me a long time to come to a realization of this. It would be wrong of me to give the impression that, at the time, the negative aspects of the life which we were assimilating were all that burdensome. I was deeply intrigued and attracted by a form of life so different from what I had had before. I was, after all, still no more than a provincial schoolboy. I did not have much of a self to deny or a life to give up. The life I had had in Leyland was a restricted life, and it needed some kind of enhancement. Here, at Manresa, was a community of diverse people with experiences of belonging to social classes and occupations far beyond what I could be expected to share. True, there was the negative side of being deracinated, and of giving up one's self and one's past. But as I saw it then, there was a considerable compensatory enrichment of life. I mixed with better educated people than before, and with some social betters; and together we aspired to belong to a Society whose international importance could not be doubted. Did it much matter if we were being pressurized in ways that emphatically demanded the surrender of ourselves as the sole guarantee of our sharing in the evident grandeur of the enterprise? Or if we were being asked to sacrifice everything for the sake of that obedient *esprit de corps* which was supposed to be the glory of the Jesuits? Or if so few real insights into the religious and spiritual mystery of Catholicism were being vouchsafed? Or if key theological and religious issues were hardly mentioned? Was I not, after all, beginning to acquire the kind of learning that I found so fulfilling – that variegated, esoteric learning that set me apart, gave me privileges, and ensured membership of an elite?

It was in this uncritical and triumphalistic spirit that I spent the rest of my two-year novitiate. I enjoyed the feasts and the outings, the nugatory jobs we were all given to do, the ups-and-downs of the sheer routine of daily novitiate life. I cannot recall feeling either depressed or particularly elated. I must have been taking to it all with suspicious ease. The second-year novices moved on, and a new batch came in. I was appointed one of the Angel Guardians for the incoming group – a seal, as I took it, of official approval and a sign that I was coming up to the required standard; that I was really beginning to belong; that my face fitted, that I was in the right place. The whole body of novices was, in

those days, large enough to ensure a regular turn-over of congenial enough company, whether one was working indoors or
outdoors, or going for walks, or just talking in the daily periods
of recreation. There was no need to get bored with the same old
people. The older novices, mainly ex-servicemen, contributed
experiences and backgrounds and humour which were well
outside the range of the schoolboy set. Inevitably, as in any
human community, 'characters' developed among us and added
greatly to the general entertainment. Fits of uncontrollable
giggling were not all that rare, and they bubbled up from just
below the surface – a sign, I imagine, that we were perhaps under
more strain than we realized. The food was good, too. Personal
asceticism was very carefully controlled, and too overt a piety
was instantly frowned on. One might say that if there was one
sign which reliably informed the authorities that a novice was not
meant for the Society, it was the personal display of exaggerated
devotion. I am sure there is much to commend in this cautious
attitude. But I am surprised, on looking back, that despite my best
efforts I learnt so little about prayer and meditation, apart from
some ill-understood techniques which always turned out to be
boringly uncongenial and unproductive. But then was it not
against the perverse spiritual logic of the novitiate to expect
results? Prayer and meditation were meant to be hard. It was
what you were meant to expect. Perseverance at them in the face
of any evidence was exactly the right attitude. You could expect
no verification of the positive spiritual value of these exercises in
the present. To expect help and consolation from prayer and
meditation now was to fail in imitating Christ in his agony in the
garden. The least self-deluding thing, the only thing you could
put your whole-hearted trust in, was to practise continual self-
mortification, try to imitate Christ, and trust in the system.
Eventually, but not necessarily in this life, you would learn the
wisdom of this.

  Once I had taken on this mind-set – and not to take it on would
have meant having to leave – I found that the rest of the novitiate
passed uneventfully. About three or four weeks before the end,
when we were deep into our preparations for taking our first
Jesuit vows, the entire novitiate was moved at a stroke from
Roehampton to Harlaxton Manor, near Grantham. This was an
elaborate Victorian pile bought cheap by the Jesuits as an investment, and also with an eye to some future need to move establishments like Manresa in Roehampton out of the path of
post-war urban developments. The new Labour government had

targetted Roehampton as a desirable backwater to be ruined by a
new housing scheme in which London's war-battered Eastenders
might be rewarded by being relocated in tower-blocks. This
development, it was thought, would disturb the quiet and remote
calm needed for a Jesuit novitiate. It could well, of course, have
been the making of it. So we folded our tents and moved away,
lock, stock and barrel, in the course of a single day. Apart from
the coach ride, life went on unaltered, and on 8 September 1950
the class of '48 took their first vows at Harlaxton. The ceremony
was purely private and domestic. There were no visitors or
guests. The translated vow formula runs as follows:

> Almighty and eternal God, I ...., though altogether unworthy in
> your divine sight, yet relying on your infinite goodness and mercy
> and moved with a desire of serving you, in the presence of the most
> holy Virgin Mary and your whole heavenly court, vow to your
> Divine Majesty perpetual poverty, chastity, and obedience in the
> Society of Jesus: and I promise that I shall enter that same Society
> in order to lead my entire life in it, understanding all things accord-
> ing to its Constitutions. Therefore I suppliantly beg your immense
> goodness and clemency, through the blood of Jesus Christ, to deign
> to receive this holocaust in an odour of sweetness; and just as you
> gave me the grace to desire and offer this, so you will also bestow
> abundant grace to fulfil it.

The formula made our position clear in a way that perhaps not all
realized at the time. We, on our side, were fully bound by the
three traditional religious vows, and fully committed to eventually joining the Society. But the Society, on its side, had not yet
committed itself to us. We were not yet being allowed to enter.
Entry into the Society, and at what grade or level, was reserved
for the authorities to decide in time according to how one was
judged to have successfully assimilated the system. All the same,
we were, I am sure, a proud lot on that day, dressed in our new
black suits and new Jesuit gowns, grinning over our gleaming
clerical collars, and self-consciously flourishing our birettas.

I have in front of me a group photograph of those who took
their vows on that day at Harlaxton. There are twenty-one of us.
On our initial entry, two years previously, we had been, I think,
about thirty-five. A one-third drop-out rate during the novitiate
would have been considered normal in those days. Of the surviving twenty-one, seven were so-called 'late vocations', and fourteen were ex-schoolboys. Fifty or so years on, I note that seven of
the twenty-one (another one-third) left the Society later, and six

of these got married. To my knowledge, six of the whole group in the photograph are dead. I think there are ten of the class of '48 still in the Society. I have not researched the matter, but this represents, I think, quite a respectable showing on the part of a group who were certainly good to be with. Most have achieved predictable success, both in or out of the Jesuits, as teachers, academics, scholars, administrators, good priests. The group produced an Oxford Professor of Poetry, a notable papal biographer and commentator, a remarkable army and prison chaplain, a Jesuit lay-brother, and several missionaries who did important work in Zimbabwe, Guyana, and Japan. None of them proved a failure in what he undertook. This may seem to say something in favour of the rigours of the Jesuit novitiate; but I am inclined to think it says more about the basic toughness of the human organism, about the human ability to outwit and outlast the system, and about the quality of those who were attracted to the Jesuits in the first place.

Two or three days after taking our first vows we were sent straight back to Roehampton to start the next stage of our systematic formation – the juniorate. For a year or so we would be attending to the revival of the studies which had been suspended in the long lay-off from academic life demanded by the novitiate regime. In our fine new clothes we all boarded a hired coach and set out for London. We stopped at Peterborough to view the splendid Cathedral. We had little luggage, but we were full of ourselves and our new Jesuit identities. We had been given to suppose that the novitiate had raised us to a spiritual plane on which we were to try our best to maintain ourselves for the rest of our lives – that we had reached a spiritual height from which, if we did not take great care, we could only decline. We felt we finally had arrived safely in our world apart.

❧

In this truthful account of the Jesuit novitiate as it was half a century ago, I have re-appraised the experience by using, in hindsight, a distinction between the Jesuits, as they were originally founded to be, and Jesuitism, as the system to which history had reduced their remarkable spirituality. The distinction rests on no mere fancy of mine, or even on George Tyrrell's penetrating critique of a century ago. The Second Vatican Council implied just such a distinction in calling on religious orders and congregations in general to renew religious life in the Church. It pointed out that since the fundamental norm of the religious life is a following [not 'imitation'!] of Christ as proposed by the gospel, such is to be regarded by all communities as their supreme law.

Further,

it serves the best interests of the Church for communities to have their own special character and purpose. Therefore loyal recognition and safekeeping should be accorded to the spirit of founders, as also to all the particular goals and wholesome traditions which constitute the heritage of each community.
(*Perfectae Caritatis*, 28 October 1965, 2, a) & b))

The clear implication was that religious communities had tended to fall away from their original purposes and lose their individual characters, and they now needed to be recalled to 'the spirit of founders' and their own 'wholesome traditions'. In hindsight I can see that this critique could have been usefully applied to the Jesuit novitiate as I experienced it. Further experience of the Jesuits would only confirm that the Society had strayed from the spirit of its founder towards the wooden systematization of his vision. But then, of course, it should not be forgotten that this critical analysis is more generally applicable to any institution established on the basis of a founder's vision, not excluding the Church itself. Just how true had the Church itself remained to the spirit of its Founder and to its own wholesome traditions? Religious orders and congregations may only be manifesting in microcosm a failing that is to be found more blatantly in the macrocosm of the Church itself. Might the bishops at Vatican II have been missing the log in their own eye whilst pointing out the speck of sawdust in the eye of those in charge of religious orders? So as my time in the Jesuits went on, I – and by no means I alone – slowly discovered that there were solid grounds for criticizing the systems, both ecclesiastical and Jesuit, to which we had devoted our lives, and through which we now had to proceed. It would, of course, be some years before the criticism began to surface.

Chapter 4

Worlds Apart

So straight back to Roehampton and the juniorate went the class of '48. Problems with re-entry into a regime of ordinary academic studies, allied with the new problem of studying for strictly religious motives, would now have to be tackled. But it turned out that I did not have to face these problems. It was obvious enough that the older members of our year would by-pass this early stage in the Jesuit system. They were deemed to have sufficient academic or other experience, or at any rate little enough prospect of doing further secular studies anyway, that they were to be sent straight on to the next stage of training. But for reasons that still remain obscure to me, a couple of the very youngest members of the year were also made to skip the juniorate and were sent straight on to philosophy, and I was one of them. It felt like skipping Miss Reddy's Standard 3 back at St Mary's Leyland. After two or three days at Manresa, we were summoned by the Rector and simply told to pack (I had scarcely unpacked the few belongings I had) and take the 4.45 from Paddington to Charlbury in Oxfordshire, where we would be met and transported to Heythrop College, near Chipping Norton, the large ex-stately home where the Jesuits did their philosophical and theological studies. I was still only nineteen years old.

My shiny new vow of obedience prevented me, of course, from questioning this first decision of my God-inspired Superiors. But not long afterwards, and increasingly ever since, I came to consider that my Superiors had been wrong to send me through so quickly. Not that the juniorate was without its problems. Some subjects were not particularly well taught. But classical studies, still my field, were the exception. In the very short time I had been back at Manresa, I had already fixed up what promised to be a bracingly rigorous course in Greek and Latin with Fr Edmund Conyers D'Arcy, Martin D'Arcy's more academically gifted older brother. He was, by all accounts, an uncompromising teacher, an outstanding Oxford man in his day. He was exactly the teacher I needed at that juncture. I badly needed to make up for the more glaring deficiencies in my lackadaisical initiation into classics at Preston. But just as I was about to start my courses with him, I was pulled out along with the few roots I had managed to put down among my novice-contemporaries and transplanted into a new and older community. In any case, it was impossible to see what the hurry was. Naive as I was, I took it all simply as a mark of personal approval, a further sign that I must somehow be in the right place.

What was happening around me was that the Jesuits were involved in a rapid adjustment to their system of studies. In those days the English Jesuits ran and partly staffed some nine schools, public and grammar, in England and Scotland, as well as others on the 'missions' of South Africa, Rhodesia and British Guiana; but fear of what might be required of Jesuit teachers under a Labour Government had led them to try and ensure that all younger Jesuits would have at least the basic Teacher's Certificate, so that their employment in the public education system could not be brought into question. This was another reason why the novices had been moved from Manresa. The house was to become a Jesuit teacher training college, affiliated to the University of London's Institute of Education, and empowered to grant Teacher's Certificates to its students. Teacher training would be given to all likely young Jesuits, usually after the third year of philosophy, and so just before many of them would be sent out into the Jesuit schools for their first spell of teaching as scholastics. So Manresa would now become oriented towards 'pedagogy', and it would continue to house the juniorate, plus the third-year philosophers, transferred from a somewhat over-populated Heythrop, who would then spend a fourth year of 'pedagogy' getting their certificates. In being made to miss the juniorate, I was effectively being 'fast-tracked' away from teaching in Jesuit schools, though it was not at all clear why. In fact, I did teach for two years at the Jesuit grammar school in Liverpool, when the Government was no longer insisting that all teachers had to have a certificate, and I enjoyed the experience, as I shall relate below. With a teaching qualification I might, of course, have taught somewhat better. All I can suppose is that we two younger ones were moved on quickly because were seen as likely Oxford types, well prepared or not, who would do well in Classical Mods. and Greats, where success was still very highly prized among the Jesuits. Well, to that I can only say that the plan did not work in my case – although my colleague, Peter Levi, did eventually go on to become a don at Oxford, biographer of poets, and Professor of Poetry. Both of us later left the Jesuits and married. How much this now says for the God-inspired judgement of our Superiors back in 1950 it would be interesting to know. But I would learn in time not to expect too much of them.

Heythrop College stands about sixteen long miles north of Oxford, outside the village of Enstone. Until shortly before 1930, Jesuit scholastics had studied their three years of philosophy at St Mary's Hall, Stonyhurst, in Lancashire, and their four years of theology at St Beuno's College, St Asaph, in North Wales. It was then decided to amalgamate both student bodies and their 'professors' into a single 'Collegium Maximum'. The derelict stately home of Heythrop Hall was bought. It had belonged to the Duke of Shrewsbury and then to the Brassey family. To the central 'mansion', as we still called it, were added two wide-spreading two-storey wings, one of which surrounded the old stables and housed the philosophers; while the other, enclosing the Real Tennis court (crudely transformed into the College's main chapel), housed the theologians. There was a large self-contained estate all round the College: football pitch, cricket ground, swimming-pool, nine-hole golf course, tennis courts, bowling greens, deep woodlands, rockeries, waterfalls, two large lakes, a long Victorian 'nature walk', even a well-filled cemetery. All this lay at the end of a forbidding two-mile drive, which only led, in any case, to the A34, hurrying through the bleak sub-Cotswold countryside, an unattractive and little visited region. We had no neighbours. In the College we lived in a world of our own, looking inwards. There were individual rooms for about two hundred and fifty souls, lecture halls, chapels, libraries, laboratories, recreation rooms, offices, kitchens, a large refectory, and parlours to permit and repel intrusions from the ordinary world. We generated our own electricity and pumped our own water. There were four distinct communities in the place: the priests on the teaching and administrative staff, the stalwart lay-brothers, the 'philosophers' and the 'theologians'. As had been the case at Manresa, these separate communities did not communicate with one another, except in the course of teaching or business, or for a brief, formal period (called a 'fusion') on greater feast-days. Between the philosophers and the theologians there might be an age gap of up to ten years or so; and when, on my arrival, I looked across the refectory (once a huge palm-filled conservatory), I could see several theologians, either ordained priests or

about to be, who had taught me at Preston. Not that I could speak
to them, of course. I did not know that I was going to spend
rather more than a decade of my life in this esoteric world.

The changes in my life occasioned by the sudden move to
Heythrop were abrupt and far-reaching. From living in large
novitiate 'quarters' in curtained cubicles and little other privacy,
I now moved into a room of my own. It was strange to have a
door and even a view from a window. The furniture was standard, old and unpleasing, and only its arrangement was left to
my own taste. I was responsible for keeping the room clean and
the floor highly polished. The privacy was especially welcome.
The community I was to study and work and pray in was now
larger and even more varied than in the novitiate. By skipping the
juniorate I had caught up with a first-year set of philosophers
whom I had first known as second-year novices. A year above us
were the second-year set; but there was no third-year set, since
these had been despatched to Manresa, as I have explained. So we
were two large years of students, most of whom I already knew,
at least by sight. But there were also young Jesuits who had been
sent from abroad to study their philosophy in England – from
Spain, Malta and Germany, mainly. The whole Jesuit system of
studies was centrally and rigorously controlled in all its details
the world over, so it did not matter where the required studies
were done. And since the basic language used throughout these
studies was Latin, language barriers counted for little, too.
Exactly the same topics were taught and the same text-books
were used in Heythrop as in Munich, Rome, Barcelona, the
Philippines, Australia, California, and elsewhere. So communities of Jesuit students were nearly always mildly multi-national;
and this, as I was going to learn, induced a freedom of movement
within the Society, and some compensating breadth of outlook,
that added to the quality and interest of what would otherwise
have been a very constricted life.

So in our remote Heythrop world – a mixture of home, leisure
centre, monastery, and Alma Mater – the variegated community
of philosophy students settled down to make a life of it. The
general regime could afford to be fairly free and easy since our
desert location took care of many potential disciplinary problems
of the kind that would have arisen had we been living among
normal human habitations. There were still some domestic chores
to be done, but these were now chiefly confined to serving at
meals in the refectory. We had daily Mass, of course, and our
specified periods of prayer – one hour of private meditation in

the morning and two fifteen-minute examinations of conscience at lunchtime and bedtime. The main task in hand was study; but most people also cultivated what was the most obvious pastime, some form of country pursuit. Thursday (recalling life in Leyland) was our weekly day off – Out for the Day, O.F.T.D. Almost everyone went out somewhere, the majority to one of the 'huts' in the capacious woods. It was round the 'huts' that small, non-exclusive clubs of a dozen or more of us formed and settled and sometimes worked at cutting wood, keeping bees (which is what I did), laying pathways, clearing undergrowth or streams, or whatever. The authorities provided the raw food (bacon, sausages, eggs, bread, butter, jam), and Thursdays became days of huge fry-up dinners and long-drawn-out teas prepared on old wood-stoves, round which we would chat on until it was curfew-time and we had to get back to the College. There was nothing enforced about this way of spending Thursdays, and there were a few who treated the knockabout life of the 'huts' with a certain disdain. I think they might have been wrong. The 'huts' not only promoted innocent pleasures and friendships and some healthy exercise: they also represented an opportunity, gratefully taken by most, for common humanity to begin to assert and re-establish itself. They served as small oases in the desert of the Jesuit system; and I do not think that their contribution to the survival of most of us can be overestimated. Whether the authorities realized this, I do not know; but they were wise to subsidize them. I spent many of my happiest hours during my protracted Jesuit studies at Heythrop messing about in 'huts'.

On Thursdays, too, we could go out of the grounds for walks, or, as we became better informed and more astute, into Oxford. We were given just the right amount of money for whatever specific purpose we might have in Oxford and the change from that had to be handed back. Hence the cheapest possible form of travel became very popular – hitch-hiking. In all weathers we would depart in our pairs – going out alone was definitely not approved – over a farm road to Broadstone Hill, our closest access to the A34, which ran south to Oxford, north to Stratford. Flagging down lorries or cars was very easy. We were all wearing our clerical collars and suits, for a start; and in those now far-off innocent days, motorists and lorry-drivers would assume that the clergy were people of integrity and reliability. I fancy that many might read the signs differently these days and accelerate past. Conversations with drivers were often highly diverting, and heroic distances were covered – Bristol, Wolverhampton,

Cambridge, London, and back, before returning to the College by 5 or 6 p.m. The authorities knew, of course, that hitch-hiking went on, just as they knew that Oxford (and especially the Scala Cinema in Walton Street) was the most-visited venue. But they wisely turned a blind eye to it, even when they themselves, on their way by College car into Oxford, passed a pair of Heythrop hitch-hikers misguidedly trying to thumb a lift from their own Superior. To have tried to keep a steam-tight lid on Heythrop would have turned it into a pressure-cooker filled with an explosive mix of talented and fairly highly-tuned individuals who were already under the emotional strain of pursuing the religious life in what were, ordinarily speaking, deprived circumstances. So the general tone of the regime was kept reasonably tolerant.

Heythrop was not only a world of our own: it also had to be a world of our own making. The place worked according to the Roman pattern of two semesters a year, but with vacations at Christmas, at Easter and during the summer. The Christmas vacation in particular was very much an in-house domestic celebration, with large meals, community 'fusions', afternoon teas, 'oyster suppers' (a throwback to the age of cheap oysters, now oysterless), games and plays. Both the philosophers and the theologians put on plays, expending great efforts in preparing for the single performance in front of the whole College. Estate workers, servants and the lay-brothers were allowed to attend the dress rehearsal. It was with my first Christmas play that I began to realize that I had some usable histrionic talent. I successfully – perhaps even proleptically – played the Demon King in the pantomime 'Aladdin', hugely enjoying the hammy script ('Do what you can to catch that lad for me/ and I will pay you well – Ha, Ha, Hee, Hee!'), and all the usual comic business. Since then I have always favoured comedy, and especially farce and spoof, as the highest forms of drama, and in later years I got to play some plum Christmas roles in several comedies, including a Whitehall farce. I generally refused to take part in anything approaching serious theatre, and even at Oxford I specialized in Aristophanes and neglected virtually the whole of Greek tragedy. I have tried to make good this indefensible omission since. But during my time in the Jesuits – make of it what you will – I found serious drama, even in our very amateur dramatics, deeply unattractive. I think I perhaps sensed that the religious life itself ran the risk of lending itself to bogus melodrama anyway, and that an antidote to it would be more readily found in comedy, and particularly in farce. At any rate, spotting the comic potential of institutional life – an art that some of us consciously practised in later years – may well have provided the true beginnings of future well-based criticism.

The Easter vacation was more of a respite from the Holy Week ceremonies, which were done, complete with Tenebrae, with the same ferocious intensity that was expended at Christmas on the plays. Perhaps only Jesuits, who have no public liturgical commitments to speak of, could have done them in this way – with a precision that matched the Trooping of the Colour, but not with much evident prayer or devotion. In the summer vacation each large community went on holiday to an old, semi-derelict property on the outskirts of Barmouth in North Wales. This holiday was called 'Villa', and it lasted a fortnight. We had surprisingly enjoyable times there, roughing it in the house, swimming in the sea, walking in the mountains. We were given spending money (a 'hog') for the fortnight – £1.7s.6d., or £1.38 in today's currency. There were some who failed to spend even that amount and handed back their 'hog's tail'. Then back to Heythrop to prepare for another year of study.

One was, of course, never bereft of company, but close friendships could be a problem for some people. They were officially frowned on, and the religious principles inculcated in the novitiate inhibited their formation. It seems to me probable that their discouragement was in many cases unfortunate. Most close friendships I observed were non-exclusive and harmless, and, I daresay, helpful and rewarding to those involved. In any case, they could rarely last very long in the Jesuit system, because different postings inevitably meant the parting of friends. But I was still amazingly naive, not least in sexual matters; and in some cases there may have been sexual undertones to which I was simply not attuned. I still suppose that very few friendships came to anything even approaching forbidden expression. My impression remains that even in the tightly enclosed, all-male world of Heythrop, sex, whether as a topic or an activity, figured only rarely. Everyone was, of course, under the religious vow of chastity which they were sincerely trying to keep. But I would have thought that the ability to make strong and lasting relationships was a gift to be prized; and that the experience of such relationships schooled the emotions in ways not otherwise available; and that where the ability to form friendships was plainly lacking, there might be good reason to suspect that a person was unsuitable for the religious life anyway. I got on well with a good range of fellow-scholastics, both British and foreign; and one friendship, with Franz-Josef Mohr, a young German with one arm (the result of his having been forced as a fourteen-year-old to serve in Hitler's anti-aircraft defences towards the end of the war) is still a happy memory, though I have not seen or heard of him for almost forty years. At Heythrop there was a feeling that we were all stuck in the same boat, and there developed, not so much an *esprit de corps*, as the sort of general, rough *cameraderie* which, I imagine, grips young conscripts into the armed services, though they, of course can enjoy emotional outlets that were not available to us.

So we passed from one year to another of our study of philosophy. I began, of course, from scratch. I had no idea what philosophy might be, so I could have been taught anything in its name and been none the wiser. I suppose this, in a sense, is what all too literally happened. At least I had no expectations that could be disappointed. I threw myself with vigour into the courses that had to be completed. If this was philosophy, it was very like playing a new game you had been given for Christmas. After first familiarizing yourself with the rules, however arbitrary they might be, you stumbled round the board a few times before realizing that somehow you had finally won. It all came down to learning the method and the mind-set which the game required. Later I discovered that this was true not only of our philosophy but even more so of our theology as well – but not before I had turned myself into a competent adept at both. It is important to make clear that, as with a Christmas game, the scope and limits of our philosophy were very carefully dictated and defined by its overriding purpose. Our major courses, in philosophy as well as in theology, were precisely targetted on the eventual production of a certain type of Jesuit priest – no less, of course, than were the *Spiritual Exercises* in the novitiate. I am not saying that there is anything wrong with the practice of organizing courses so that they produce a pre-arranged result. Any institution with a system does it in the training of its operatives. I mention the limitations of our philosophical studies at this point to avoid the possibility of any misunderstanding that we were engaged in the open and critical study of academic philosophy; or that there were available to us alternative approaches to problems, different to the ones we were being sedulously trained to adopt. In starting philosophy at Heythrop, we were mounting the bottom step of what was, in its way, an efficient escalator, a mental production-line, which would deliver us in the end intellectually trussed and

packaged, ready to be distributed to the firm's outlets as fault-
free products stamped with the Jesuit Good Churchkeeping Seal
of Approval. This, in both senses of the phrase, was 'what we
were in for': not to become real philosophers or even competent
theologians.

Philosophy, in the sense we meant it, was a matter of working
your way through the six major treatises that constituted the
course, plus a number of minor courses. All this was dictated by
the central Roman authorities, right down to the details of the
course syllabuses. These appeared in the form of a series of
'theses' which had to be explained and defended through formal,
syllogistic arguments. Serious disagreement with what was
proposed was not an option which a student could realistically
entertain, if he wished to persevere in his 'vocation'. Hence philosophical thought was reduced roughly to the equivalent of painting by numbers. The principle that There is No Alternative
prevailed with religious force, and highly intelligent men with
clever, distinguished minds lent themselves unquestioningly to
the pursuit of this drab exercise. After all, in some distant sense,
it could be a way of imitating Christ in his self-denial. Giving
yourself over to the all-embracing system was to be religiously
obedient. I do not recall a single instance of departure on grounds
of dissent. Of course, it has also to be borne in mind that the
system had to cope with students of very mixed types and abilities; and philosophy is not everyone's delight. Most would not
have thought of criticizing the standard of the studies, since they
had no personal inclination towards philosophy anyway. Others
would have been incapable of criticism. There remains, however,
the troublesome thought that there must have been a few, even if
only among the teaching staff, who realized the nature of the
game we were all playing. But they too, just like the rest of us,
stuck to the rules dictated by the system.

The treatises or subjects dealt with in our philosophy courses
were: psychology, metaphysics, cosmology, epistemology,
natural theology and ethics. Three of these resounding titles were
taken in the first year, three in the second, with more advanced
courses in all of them in the third. In addition, there were supple-
mentary courses, often of rather more interest than the main ones:
the history of philosophy, experimental psychology, the philosophy of science and mathematics. These minor courses were, paradoxically, taught by Jesuits who were usually far more
distinguished than the 'ordinary professors' who taught the main
subjects. Perhaps our exposure to them was deliberately kept

fairly fleeting because too much interest in their minor contributions was considered potentially dangerous. After all, who knows where a serious interest in the history of philosophy or in modern psychology might end up? Certainly the appointment of the 'ordinary professors' was governed by a cautious policy, as I came to realize when I myself was appointed to such a post in theology. 'Ordinary professors' had to be, above all else, 'safe' men – doctrinally and religiously sanitized and unlikely to infect the young with ideas that might lead them into critical attitudes unsuited to their future Jesuit work. Some of them were certainly very able men; but it was not even up to them to arrange their own syllabuses. Whatever their interests or the personal views they had developed, these had to be rigorously subordinated to the overriding purpose of the whole course. We could have got much more out of them, I am sure, if they had not been hamstrung by the system. It would be easy to criticize them for being too cautious and too uninspiring; but they had their job to do, and they were fulfilling their 'vocation' through what may have been, in some cases, a form of constant self-denial. Later on, when I joined their community as a 'professor' myself and some of them were still around, I came to admire and like them. There was far more to them than had ever been allowed to meet our young eyes when we started.

What they contrived to teach us I now admire less. In all six main philosophical treatises the background thinking derived from the medieval 'synthesis' between the philosophy of Aristotle and the doctrinal system of the Roman Church. The creation of this synthesis, in which the developed beliefs and doctrines of Catholicism were boldly and brilliantly interpreted in terms of Greek thought, must rank as one of the greatest human feats of intellectual and imaginative construction ever achieved. The master mind behind the best of it was, of course, that of Thomas Aquinas, a philosophical giant who continues to fascinate even those who cannot possibly agree with him. As Wittgenstein put it in a famous remark, whatever you might make of Aquinas' answers, the questions alone are magnificent. George Tyrrell, a committed and knowledgeable Thomist, regretted that Jesuits were not trained to read Aquinas as they might read Dante. But alas! little, if anything, of the intellectual excitement of the greatest of Catholic philosophers was allowed to shine through the courses we had to attend. His great synthesis was shredded and filtered down to us in a careful selection of second-hand and pre-digested thought-bites, which were then spoon-fed – and indeed, force-fed – to students who were denied any other philosophical pabulum, save perhaps a corrective dose or two from the later Jesuit interpreter of Aquinas, the dull sixteenth-century Spaniard, Francisco Suarez. So the three years of philosophy came to little but a lost opportunity for really discovering the imaginative world that lay behind one of the greatest and most comprehensive interpretations of Catholicism. But clearly that was not really what we were supposed to be doing. What we were about was acquiring hand-me-down answers distilled from certain late varieties of Thomism – yet another formal and systematized '-ism' created to provide answers to questions that arose, not from ourselves or from any living issues, but from the artificial requirements of a centrally controlled and systematically dictated syllabus. These answers had to be learned virtually by heart (and actually by heart, especially if your Latin was poor) for regurgitation in the annual oral examinations. Fail to regurgitate enough, and you failed the examination. And failure, of course, brought with it not merely an academic or intellectual bad mark: failure at any part of the system involved a potentially demoralizing measure of personal and spiritual failure as a Jesuit.

Neither at heart nor in mind were we students of philosophy at all. In all that we studied there was at work a not-very-well-hidden agenda. It might be said that we were really occupied in assimilating a certain set of ideas, a mind-set, perhaps little more than a handy vocabulary, that was covertly preparing us for our later theological studies. Thus, for instance, in cosmology we studied the ideas of time and space and place – duration and extension and location – but not as a seriously critical enquiry into the nature of the categories in which we have to interpret our modern worldly surroundings, but rather by way of picking up and handling certain concepts which would turn out to be useful and important for the way we would eventually be meant to understand the Catholic doctrine of the Eucharist, with its emphasis on the real presence of Christ. Similarly, we learnt about Aristotle's 'hylomorphic theory' – his brilliantly imaginative view of the constitution of things through matter and form, of the way things might be thought to change, either substantially through the loss or acquisition of form by matter, or accidentally through what happens to a substance's accidents whilst the substance persists unchanged – but not in order to appreciate or criticize Aristotle's theory or Aquinas' adoption of it, but in order to familiarize ourselves early on with the concepts and words which we would need in trying to expound the Catholic doctrine of transubstantiation. Under the guise of studying philosophy, we were being indoctrinated with the means of understanding aspects of the Catholic doctrinal system in rigidly orthodox ways. Now I do not think that this process is in itself unacceptable, given the vocation we had chosen to follow. In fact, I still continue to wonder, with due qualifications, at the sheer organization and strict purposefulness through which the process achieved its ends. And, of course, we picked up a certain ready astuteness in the framing of arguments and counter-arguments, proofs and objections. But the swords we brandished at one another in our weekly 'disputations' (or 'circles', as they were called) were sorry, wooden things. Some learnt to use their critical faculties pretty smartly; but it was a pity that so much effort was wasted on questions that had nothing to do with any world other than one particular religious world of theology.

Other philosophical subjects had other connections with Catholic theology. Psychology sought to establish the status and role of the naturally immortal human soul as related to, but distinct from, the material body. This provided the beginnings of an acceptably orthodox way of understanding the Catholic doctrine of eternal life, which appeared to require that the soul should survive our present bodies to be rewarded or punished in some other form in Heaven or Purgatory or, if the worst came to the worst, in Hell. Metaphysics, or ontology, dealt with the notions of being, of essence and existence, as an introduction to the idea of a God whose very essence it is to exist, so who necessarily exists, without any possibility of not existing – which gives God a unique status not shared by any of his creatures, angelic, human or otherwise. Their essence contains the possibility of not existing at all, if it had not been that God had willed them to do so by his act of creation. Hence, in turn, natural theology, sometimes called 'special metaphysics', clarified the idea of creation, of God's infinity and the attributes that belonged of necessity to such a God: his eternity, ubiquity, indestructability, and so forth – as well as dealing with the conundrums of how God, whilst being both wholly and of necessity good and omnipotent, might evade blame for the unavoidable evils in the ordinary world; or how human beings could remain truly free in the face of God's technically overwhelming omnipotence. Faced with questions of this magnitude, real philosophers, wisely, would tend to wonder whether they have even got the framing of the problems and the questions right, let alone the solutions and the answers. Not so we. Solutions and answers we had to have, whether we had understood the problems or questions adequately or not. We could hardly have approached the later study of Catholic theology in an intellectual state of doubt or uncertainty about fundamental issues regarding God and man. These had to be settled now, in good time; and our philosophy – our proto-theology, in fact – was meant to settle them. What was never questioned, because of the complete acceptance of the medieval synthesis I mentioned above, was whether Greek-inspired metaphysics, even when filtered through the wondrous mind of Aquinas, was really an appropriate interpretative framework, for making the specifically Christian idea of God more intelligible anyway. True, we have to come to some human terms with the Christian God in any attempt to understand him; but are these philosophical terms the best? I think now that it all depends on how you decide to understand these, and indeed any other, philosophical terms themselves.

The fact is that the profound question of how you are to understand the terms involved in understanding – from another angle, the question of the nature of human understanding – was not seriously raised with us: and this at a stage when it would, in any normal course of studies, have been exactly right to do so. In our epistemology course (its Latin title was *Critica*) we were fobbed off with what I would call a sort of simplistic rationalism. There was no attempt to see how the knowing human mind works with the judgement of the will and the creative constructions of the imagination. We were told a bit about Locke, Hume, Kant, and others; but only about how wrong they all were. We were left innocent of the extent to which our normal acts of understanding involve interpretation – of the way we have to create and construct and refine our ideas in order try and render our world intelligible and meaningful before we can say what kind of truth-claim it can possibly make on us. But in that direction there lay before us only the bottomless mire of subjectivism, doubt, uncertainty, loss of faith. We had to go in the opposite direction, away from subjectivity, away from allowing any room for human interpretation, and towards the objectivity and certainty of the truth-claims which, once we were priests, we would have to make for the defined propositions of the Catholic doctrinal tradition and the infallible deliverances of the Roman Pontiff. Literal truth arrived at by human reason, even if human reason had to be illumined by 'faith' (that is, authoritatively told what it had to think anyway) – such was the goal bravely defended by our embattled epistemology against all the attacks of philosophy. Literal truth could be enshrined in clear propositions which reason and, when reason was found wanting, faith could grasp with complete certainty. Certainty – that was the real prize that we were after: above all, the certainty that would be found in the certainties of the Catholic belief-system. Since there was to be no room allowed for interpretation, none was allowed for variety of understanding.

It was much the same with our course on ethics. Once again, certainty was readily available. Anyone who exercised 'right reason' could know the natural law, which is a direct derivative of God's eternal law, and which could make perfectly clear what all our individual and social rights and duties are. It came as no surprise that when we studied Catholic moral theology later, we found that we already had a ready-made framework of moral understanding firmly in place, and that all we needed to do was to fill in, helped by some evident casuistry, the details from the Church's moral, pastoral and legal traditions.

So we were being set up intellectually for the study of theology which would crown our course of training for the Jesuit priesthood. I now much regret the loss of an opportunity to study – even to take – philosophy seriously. Such study would surely involve exposure to some acknowledged masters of the subject through the reading of their works. How often has it been the case later in life that reading a few pages of Kant or even a short dialogue of Plato or a curt paragraph of Wittgenstein has cast far more light on a philosophical problem than a shelf of second-hand exposition even from distinguished pens. We had little or no contact with either the masters or the expositors. We had to get used to being told what they said, and in the Latin, not of sophisticated Cicero, nor of lucidly elegant Aquinas, but of some hack producer of seminary textbooks and hand-outs (called *codices*) whose grasp of both the thought he was labouring to explain and of the language he was being forced to use was often dangerously slight. Being taught in this way induced bad study habits in all of us, and in particular, perhaps, a reluctance to consult primary sources and to learn to judge them for ourselves. But that was not the name of the game we were busily learning. We were locked into a system of purposeful indoctrination in which proper philosophical questions simply had no place. This is not to say, of course, that all philosophical systems do not have their own inherent and normally unacknowledged limitations, as I was later to discover.

Not, of course, that any of us minded much, if at all, at the time. The first two years I spent at Heythrop were generally happy ones. I was, however, fairly lonely, though probably no more than many of the younger members of a large community (about forty or fifty in all) in a big and isolated institution. I had lost the companionship of the class of '48. I was one of the youngest Jesuits in the place. My experience of the ordinary world was still confined to home and school. I was intellectually and emotionally immature. But being lonely seemed incompatible with being in the Society of Jesus. So it could only be a personal failing on my part, and I dutifully mentioned it in Confession just before my first Heythrop Christmas in 1950. My old confessor was Fr Henry Davis, retired but still the *doyen* of the English-speaking Catholic moral theologians of that time. I was not much helped by what he said: 'Never expect support from anybody in the Society.' Just what this surprising utterance was meant to mean, he did not reveal. He died about a fortnight later, well into his eighties. What he said did not, in fact, turn out to be true until much later when I left the Society, and by then I had realized that the sort of support I had come to need was too much to expect from anybody in the Society and I no longer bothered looking for it. But, to be fair, I would say that I was given a great deal of support from all sorts of people during my forty Jesuit years, along with much encouragement. Everything in all this depends, obviously, on what kind of support one happens to need; and for most of my time I needed no more than the support and approval of the system. It was when it came to more personal and emotional needs that Fr Henry Davis's remark became finally prophetic, and I had to look elsewhere.

So, standing on my own two lonely feet, I still faced life and work in a buoyant mood. I had no problems with the studies and the examinations. My early schooling in Latin gave me an almost unfair advantage. Lonely I may have thought I was, but I was rarely alone. I played soccer and touch-rugby (tackling was evidently considered too exciting), though not at all well. I was a regular member of the Bee Hut. I was used to living more or less in the country, and I liked country walking. I lived in a stately home on a large estate. We may have had no money, but we enjoyed a good standard of living. We were denied very little. We had no dependents and had a wrap-around security that very few people ever have, along with a predictably stable future. We were due to take up fulfilling work in an internationally renowned institution. It would have been madness not to have been happy enough. At the end of my two years at Heythrop I was supposed to return to Roehampton for a third year of philosophy and a fourth year of 'pedagogy' to get the Teacher's Certificate. Then, presumably, to Oxford to read Classics. This was not quite how it worked out.

౷

The Jesuit authorities decided to allow me to go to Germany for my third year philosophy, instead of back to Roehampton. In a fit of enthusiasm for learning German I asked to be sent, but their decision was almost certainly based on administrative convenience. I could fill up a place in the German philosophate vacated by a returning English Jesuit, and thereby maintain a balance, both numerical and financial, between English and German Jesuits who were abroad for their studies. Or was it that they thought that by avoiding my third year at Roehampton and my fourth year of 'pedagogy', I would get to Oxford more quickly after just one year abroad? Were they bent on compounding their mistake of letting me off the juniorate by letting me miss out another year from my training? Why the rush? The decisions of the authorities were never explained, though I fancy that financial considerations and the fact that I had asked to go gave them sufficient grounds for sending me.

I had not been home to Leyland for four years, and I naturally wanted to see my family before I went abroad. I asked for permission to make a brief trip North and the request was flatly turned down. So with a great deal of inconvenience and expense, my father and mother, with Barbara and Alan, trekked from Preston to Banbury (never an easy journey), and then cross-country by taxi to Heythrop, for the Whitsuntide weekend of 1952. They stayed in one of the estate cottages often used for visitors. They had certain meals in the College and others in the cottage. We went for walks, and talked, and viewed our country acres. It was very pleasant to see them. On Whit Monday, a Bank Holiday, they had to go back North. There were few trains and Banbury was twelve miles away. It so happened that one of the big College cars was going to Banbury Station, taking a lone Jesuit, a member of staff, to join the same train as my family intended to take. Not unreasonably, I asked if my family could be given a lift in the car, in which there was plenty of room for them. My request was refused; so my family had to order a taxi and pay for another expensive journey to Banbury, so that the Jesuit father could ride in regal isolation to exactly the same place to catch the same train. I was furious then, and my blood boils as I describe the incident now. It was not, of course, an incident of great importance in itself. Indeed I mention it only because I believe it marks an early sowing of those tiny seeds of disaffection which grew and flowered into the grand-scale disillusionment with the Society which eventually led me to seek my salvation elsewhere.

This may sound plain silly, but in all my forty years with the Jesuits I never had occasion to resent any treatment meted out to me more than that wanton and stupid refusal of a lift for my family to Banbury Station. I am not a person who nurses resentment, if only because I have really never had much reason to do so. But that refusal marked the beginning of the development of a critical attitude to the Society, and to the arrogance and snobbery for which it was known to many. I am well aware that I might be thought to be over-reacting; but I honestly think that the iron entered my soul at that point, and it was probably from then on that I developed a tendency to react sharply to any manifestation or threat of what I considered Jesuit nonsense on the part of Superiors. I was not destined to be an easy subject – 'un peu difficile' would turn out to be not too inaccurate a characterization of me after all. I have to say, in my own defence, that I became adept at choosing the right time and the right issue to protest, and I have never regretted any of my very few effective outbursts. I would also say, to be fair to my Superiors, that my protests were always met with tolerance and at least some understanding. I have always felt I was blessed with good Superiors, and that we lived and worked together in mutual respect. But I am also convinced that some of them needed a little help from me. I also have to admit that when I became a minor Superior myself, I was useless at the job, chiefly because I found it very boring. I found it hard to take an interest in helping to run anybody else's life. I came in time to admire even more those who had had the patience to be my Superiors.

After the annual Villa at Barmouth, I began to pack my trunk and make the arrangements for transferring it and myself to Berchmanskolleg in the small town of Pullach, a few miles south of Munich in Bavaria. The College housed a very large community of Jesuit philosophy students from five German-speaking Provinces – West, East, and South Germany, plus Austria and Switzerland – in addition to a small number of foreigners chiefly from Ireland and England. Its rating in Germany was high –it was a Philosophische Hochschule – and it had some noted scholars in its staff. But the course of studies, as I have explained, was the same as anywhere else in the Society, and all subjects were taught in Latin. I was to enjoy the year I spent there.

Apart from the trip to Switzerland run by St Mary's Leyland, I had never been abroad before. I had unusable schoolboy French, and only such German as I had picked up on my own at Heythrop. I much preferred German, and I proceeded to learn it quite effectively in the sink-or-swim context of community life at Pullach. I travelled, of course, by surface transport – London, Dover, Ostend, Cologne, where I slept on the Cathedral steps after an untimely arrival at one o'clock in the morning. I then caught a tram out to the Jesuit headquarters in the Stolzestrasse where I was to stay briefly. I liked the early morning smell of cigars in the streets. But I had forgotten that it was no more than seven years since the end of the war, and I was surprised at the jagged signs of bomb-damage on every skyline. The Germans were unfailingly friendly, however, and I enjoyed the different kinds of bread and sausage-meat, not to mention the beer. From Cologne I went on south, visiting Heidelberg and Stuttgart. Munich was still seriously bomb-damaged. The College in Pullach was a huge barracks-like affair, the result of the 1930s Jesuit policy of training students in ever larger establishments. During the war it had been occupied by the Gestapo. The place was now crowded with Jesuits, with two or three students to a room, but as a final-year student I got a small attic room of my own. The post-war boom in religious vocations was greater in the German-speaking provinces than in England, and the community contained a wide mix of ages and interesting backgrounds. Very many were ex-servicemen: a U-boat captain, an S.S. Major, and so on downwards to those of my own age who had been required to join up in their early teens. Two more English Jesuits joined me – Anthony Levi, Peter's older brother, and later Professor of French at the University of St Andrew's, and Ken Spence, later the Jesuit Provincial in Zimbabwe. An Irish Jesuit, Paul Andrews, added to the mutual support available to the English-speakers within the German community.

These were excellent conditions in which to have to learn German, and I improved quickly. The Germans were remarkably indulgent towards the English. Many of them had vivid and terrible memories of the war, and there was a group whose health had been so badly affected that they were still treated as invalids with special dietary and study arrangements. On top of that, less than a year before my arrival, they had lost nearly twenty of their number, including an English Jesuit, in a tragic railway accident at a level-crossing down towards the Alps. They lived much more stressful lives than the philosophers at Heythrop. Their Superiors were edgy and tough towards them. But for us English-speakers the community retained what seemed like a certain admiration, and they and their Superiors treated us with unvarying tolerance. In fact, it was difficult not to take advantage of the favourable situation. It was as if the English-speakers were expected to be eccentric, and so needed more latitude. We were from the strange island of the Queen (not yet crowned) and Winston Churchill. Our national temperament and consistent moderation resulted, like our weather, from the beneficent influence of the Gulf Stream. I am afraid we rather made the most of it.

We got out and about a good deal, sometimes with German companions, sometimes with one another. Munich, obviously, was a frequent destination, especially its well-stocked zoo at Thalkirchen. On Thursdays – that universal Jesuit O.F.T.D. – we would steal loaves of the grey bread baked in the College (surely the only substandard bread in a great bread-baking nation), and take them in a cardboard suitcase to feed to the elephants. This stopped only when a baby elephant, wise beyond its years, ate our suitcase instead. On other occasions we enjoyed the facilities of Munich itself: the cinema, concerts (where I heard Alfred Cortot play, to great acclaim), beer-cellars, the Bavarian State Opera, the Oktoberfest. There were church occasions, too, when I officiated as sub-deacon at High Masses in various city churches, and could sit listening to excellent church music, Mozart above all. We had bicycles available, too, and we covered quite large areas of Bavaria, visiting famous rococo churches, and, on one unforgettably moving occasion, Dachau, the former concentration camp outside Munich. In the Christmas and Easter vacations we went to Innsbruck to stay in the Jesuit theologate where there was a particularly distinguished faculty: Karl Rahner and his brother Hugo, and the supreme liturgical scholar, Josef-Andreas Jungmann. It was after Christmas that I spent a week or so on my own at the Zenzenhof, the Jesuit villa house near the Brenner Pass, high in the Alpine snows. The only other visitor was Karl Rahner, and I served his Mass each morning. A humane person, he brought me large slices of cake from some hidden source to eat at breakfast every day. He was making his annual retreat, and he never appeared again until the next morning. Until I sat down to write this bald account of my year in Germany I had not realized how much more free and normal life was in Pullach than in Heythrop, at least for foreigners. Of course, money was not much of a problem. Whatever we cost, and it was very little, was charged back to the English Province. It was a kind of expense-account living, but in a very minor way. I am now rather sorry I did not make more of it.

The standard of living in the College was certainly not as high as that of Heythrop. Lard replaced butter, coffee was made of acorns and chicory. There was little meat apart from sausage-meat, and, as I have said, even the elephants at the zoo despised the bread. Soups were good, however, and the eccentric English were awarded boiled eggs at breakfast. My mother, still writing her usual weekly letter, got into the way of sticking sachets of Nescafe in *The Tablet* which she sent. She also despatched occasional food-parcels. They were much appreciated. I had a small 'Tauchsieder' – a cup-size water-boiler – with which to make coffee; so I could entertain German friends from time to time. All this was forbidden, of course, but it was about as innocent as having 'cocoa in the dorm' in some girls' public school. I began to like life in Germany, and I have liked it ever since. The German Jesuits themselves were efficient, predictable, diligent and kind. If the English-speakers seemed to go out a lot, it was partly because the Germans handed on opportunities to us in their own preference for concentrated study. Not that they seemed to get much of a return on it. I found the philosophical studies no problem, once I was used to the Teutonic Latin. The studies were, after all, a continuation of the same kind of proto-theology I had been doing at Heythrop, and they followed precisely the same centrally dictated syllabus. My obvious regret is, of course, that I got no more nearly acquainted with German philosophy and culture than if I had gone to France or Italy or India. I would have dearly loved to study Kant (and Goethe even more) in their native habitat. But I have never managed to get round to them since, and it is too late now. I did well in my final Latin oral examination in front of four seriously Germanic professors, though they seemed suitably baffled by my naming certain minor English philosophers I had airily picked from the England cricket team – Hutton, Washbrook, *et alii huius generis*. They had never heard of them and wrote them off as plainly offering no threat to Kant.

I was ready to make my way back to England. In Frankfurt I saw the very popular film of the Queen's coronation which was showing to packed houses from morning to night. I have never forgotten my shock at hearing Archbishop Geoffrey Fisher speaking in dubbed German. In Koblenz I met Franz-Josef Mohr, who was about to leave for Japan, where he has served the Jesuit mission all his life. Back in Cologne I got pleasantly drunk for the first time on a bottle of cheap hock. I then moved on to Paris to visit the Louvre and other sights. I made the most of my return trip after what had been a fruitful year. Once I was back in England I was at last given permission to go North and visit Leyland for the first time in five years, staying not at home, of course, but at St Wilfrid's Preston. After that, I returned to Heythrop with the aim of buckling down, at long last, to some serious preparation for the next stage of my Jesuit training, four years to be spent reading Classical Moderations and Greats at Campion Hall, Oxford. I had done almost everything except classics for the last five years – and that was on top of my poor start in classics at school. With a few weeks to go before the start of Michaelmas Term 1953, any amount of serious preparation was obviously going to be far too little, far too late.

⟨୭⟩

Despite my academic unreadiness – of the real extent of which I was happily unaware – I was pleased to be going to Oxford. Campion Hall was a 'Permanent Private Hall' owned and run by the Jesuits for their own staff and students; and tiny as it was in comparison with the great Oxford Colleges, it enjoyed considerable prestige, along with full collegial status, in the University. Founded in the 1890s, the new 1930s Campion Hall in Brewer Street, designed by Sir Edwin Lutyens, was the creation of Fr Martin D'Arcy, and it continued to bear his elitist stamp. English Jesuits who had been to Oxford were something of a small and privileged minority in the Province, and those who were sent to read classics even more so. My sense of belonging to the Society I had joined received a strong boost by my being sent there for that purpose. In those days not many 'scholastics' were so singled out. In 1953 only two of us matriculated, thought there were already rather more in the second year and beyond. In all there were usually about a dozen of us at any one time. There were other Jesuits there from abroad, and particularly from the United States. They were already ordained. So in the small community of about thirty there was an international flavour which I found attractive. The other scholastics who were now my contemporaries were a varied, intelligent and very congenial group who provided excellent company. To be frank, I liked the idea of being sent into the elitist world of Oxford, and not least because it was a further development in what had long been my favourite hobby, the pursuit of learning. For all my lack of proper preparation I was determined to do my best.

I was now twenty-two years old – old for an undergraduate from the ordinary world, but, because of the religious world in which I had been living since I left school, still immature. I sometimes wonder what it would now be like to meet myself as I was then. Just whom would I be meeting? – an alien, I fancy, from a world apart, a person who had invested himself entirely, and with more than a touch of arrogant confidence, in a world which, for him and his like, transcended and surpassed the world of ordinary mortals: a metaphysical world which possessed a reality which, far from being transient like that of the ordinary world, was ultimate, even everlasting. I would be meeting someone who actually thought he knew where he stood as he prepared to dip his toe, rather condescendingly perhaps, into the alien world of Oxford; someone who had acquired the mind-set of a system which would, in any case, see him safely through his days on earth and into the life beyond; someone who, despite what he had gone through in the last five years, had experienced no real contact with the ordinary worlds of ordinary people, had had no real responsibility for any other living soul, and no real control over his own life. There this someone would have stood, dressed in his permanent black and his shining dog-collar, tall, pale, somewhat remote but affable enough – but in reality, just who and what did he amount to? A religious prig? More, I think, of a misleadingly real-looking zombie who lived with similar creatures in a world of their own. I do not think I would now find an encounter with my undergraduate self anything but deeply embarrassing. But would Oxford challenge and change such a creature of abstractions? Or would it, in its gentlemanly, centuries-old, ironic way, confidently let him pass through and smilingly wave him on his doomed way? To the first question I would now answer 'No, but then again in time, Yes'; and to the second 'Yes, but then again in time, No'. Oxford was to plant its own time-bomb in me, a bomb with a very slow fuse.

It will be obvious that in many ways being a Jesuit undergraduate at Campion Hall restricted our participation in the more social aspects of Oxford life, though in surprisingly few of them. Sports were permissible and encouraged, whereas wilder parties and mixing with the opposite sex were naturally out of the question. But one of our advantages was that we were farmed out to tutors in the other colleges. There would have been little point in going up to Oxford to be taught by other Jesuits, even if there had been the staff at Campion Hall to cover the wide range of courses we studied. Because of the Hall's high reputation we had access to many of the best tutors around. The first tutor to whom I was assigned was Colin Hardie, Fellow of Magdalen and later the University's Public Orator. Son of a great Edinburgh classicist and brother of the President of Corpus, Hardie was a superb product of the Oxford classics system. His *forte* was Virgil. He was also a notable expert on Dante. It was to him that I had to present my weekly prose compositions, alternately in Latin and Greek. I think his initial reaction must have been acute disappointment, but he was fairly tactful, gently demanding, and not too discouraging. I simply had to learn to live off my wits as I picked up prose writing almost from cold. My first efforts were clumsy and inaccurate, embarrassing to lay before him. But Hardie represented for me an ideal in classical scholarship to which I know I would have loved to have been able to aspire, however unrealistic such aspirations were. Gradually I began to improve. I paid close attention to all the right things: grammar, syntax, word-order, rhythm, sound sentence construction, authentic *clausulae* at the end of sentences, that judicious use of Greek particles without which the language is dead. I started to work quite hard, in my way, and I began slowly to survive the initial pressure and enjoy myself. I remember well the first time Hardie gave me an 'alpha' for a Greek prose – the walk back up the High Street from Rose Lane near the Botanic Garden on a cold winter's evening (I was now in my second year), the toned-down Oxford street lighting, very little traffic apart from bicycles, the undergraduates hurrying to dine in hall at Univ. and Queen's, and myself feeling blessedly content. A pity, though, that I had made such a poor, late start.

All lectures were optional, but it was wise, in view of future examinations, to attend those lectures which dealt with one's choice of set books and other Classical Mods. courses. Oxford was fortunate in the range and depth of classical learning on offer in the 1950s. Apart from attending Hardie on Virgil, I went to E.R. Dodds, the sharp-minded Regius Professor of Greek, on Homer and Aeschylus' *Agamemnon*, and to the world-class Eduard Fraenkel, Corpus Professor of Latin, on Horace. There were excellent lectures on the textual problems of Aristophanes' *Acharnians* (D. Mervyn Jones) and on Lucretius (A.F. Wells). For more general interest I went to E.S.G. Robinson on Greek coins and to the great Sir John Beazley on Greek vases. It was all a feast of learning I greatly relished. It satisfied a taste I had discovered in myself – never a very discriminating or well developed taste – for the apparatus and intricacies of scholarship and the delights of learning as such. The satisfaction I derived from them was quite as much aesthetic as intellectual. My admiration for first-class academic work in both lectures and books became acute to the point of running the risk of being uncritical. I never deluded myself that I could produce anything comparable, but this never dimmed its attraction for me. From time to time I have laboriously worked out and published a few minor contributions to learning; but I have never misled myself into thinking that they are the real thing, even though I still get much pleasure even out of my flawed attempts. This fact does not make me unhappy or envious or resentful in the slightest. I know I have a fairly good mind and perhaps a better imagination. I do not lack the intelligence or the ability to appreciate the true learning I love. But I do not have the sustained acumen, industry, objectivity, curiosity and ambition which provide the motives for learning as such and for its own sake. As I have already said, from an early age learning – and quite indiscriminate learning – was for me more of a means of self-identification, perhaps, or at any rate a means of being different, of being accepted, of being recognized as belonging to an elite, of feeling that I am in 'in the know'. Throughout my four years at Oxford – and later – I could never shed the bad habit of becoming too learned. The acquisition of learning was no problem: the problem was the fast and intelligent deployment of what I had learned; and it was this that Oxford prized. My shortcomings were to show up very precisely in my results.

Jesuit scholastics at Campion Hall were not allowed to stay up at Oxford during the vacations. The Oxford terms were only eight weeks long (but eight very hard-working weeks they were) and we dispersed to spend the vacations in some other Jesuit house, where we could get on with the thirty hours per week study we were expected to do. I took to spending my Christmases at Heythrop, where there was a familiar programme of entertainments, and from where I could get back into Oxford quite easily. At Easter, or at other times, I might go back to Roehampton or to Stonyhurst in Lancashire, from where I could visit my family in Leyland. In summer the Campion Hall community would join up with other scholastics from various Jesuit schools, and hire a seaside holiday house, often in the West country, near Newton Abbot or Barnstaple. In these ways I found I was spending all year in the congenial company of familiar people, whilst getting on with the demanding Oxford syllabus, with its many set books and wider background reading. I generally reached the targets I was set, without stretching myself all that much. I was led on more by the pleasure provided by the kind of reading I had to do than by any ambition to do well. In the Mods. examination I got a very good Second, and I was pleased enough with the result. There were solid elements of alpha-work among the papers I had taken, but not enough to lift me out of the second class. I have always thought this a very fair result, and a creditable one, too, considering my dire lack of preparation. I regretted, of course, not getting a First, as any sensible person would; but I was not disappointed – though perhaps others were. After the examination I went back to familiar Germany in the Easter vacation of 1955, and in the quiet countryside outside Stuttgart I began to prepare for the Greats course by reading the whole of Herodotus and, unforgettably, Plato's *Republic*.

I returned to Oxford for Hilary Term 1955, the five terms of Mods. behind me, and the seven terms of Greats to come. I involved myself in sport, rowing for St Catherine's Second VIII, and playing in the scrum for their Second XV. This was hardly serious sport, and neither sport required much skill at that level; but I was becoming physically quite big and strong, and I enjoyed the exercise and the limited social life that went with it. We had, of course, to keep up with our religious duties at Campion Hall – early rising, an hour's prayer, daily Mass and other exercises during the day and in the evenings – but the authorities seemed happy enough that we should make the most of having been sent to Oxford. Inevitably there were those among the English Jesuits who looked on Oxford and Campion Hall with the suspicion that it encouraged religious laxity. But I found Oxford the nearest thing I had come across to what real knockabout Jesuit life should be like, and where there was least pressure from the dead, systematic Jesuitism we had all picked up in the novitiate. In any case, Oxford certainly represented the first really hard work I had had to do since I joined, and taking some part in games only helped serious study. Tension certainly existed between the training we had been given at the start and the working life we now had to lead. The tension had not arisen at remote Heythrop, or even in Munich, because the novitiate had prepared us well for the second-rate monastic and contemplative life which was led there. It had not prepared us for Oxford; and a number of Jesuit scholastics in my day could not cope with the tension and had to go down. Others, I think – and often the very talented – suppressed the tension and did extremely well at Oxford. They had problems later, sometimes even coming to dislike Oxford, or perhaps themselves, ever afterwards. This meant in effect that the

Jesuits, on the whole, took far more out of Oxford than they ever put back in by way of their undoubted talents, which I find regrettable. Others, possibly more balanced people but surprisingly few in number, coped well, worked hard, experienced success and went back to Campion Hall to live very fruitful lives. But there can be no doubt that Oxford, its life and the work it demanded, was hard to take for many who had been brought up in the Jesuit system and were not ready to come to some practical accommodation with it.

But for the moment my preoccupation with studies gave way to a far more serious concern. My father suffered a serious heart attack and was sent into Preston Royal Infirmary. I asked for permission to go and see him, and it was reluctantly granted on the condition that I had finished my two weekly essays. I had done so, and I went North. It was the last time I was to see my father alive. He recovered in hospital, went home to recuperate and died shortly afterwards on 10 July 1955 at the age of sixty-one. He had not even retired from work. I have already written about his impressive qualities and his conscientious character. I could not have had a better father. I would like to have been able to get to know him better; but when I had been at home I had been too young, and he too reserved, for this to happen. For the last seven years I had barely seen him. His death was a great loss to all of us; and not least, of course, to my mother, who was still only forty-nine years old. She and Barbara and Alan had a difficult time to face after his death. Barbara and Alan were about school-leaving age, but were both soon usefully employed and giving full support at home. My mother had a bad time of it with depression, but Gertie and other relatives worked wonders, and she did well to pull out of it and go back to exercising her remarkable dress-making skills. She was employed by the Holy Child nuns in Preston, and later on she spent much of her time making up-dated habits for the post-Vatican II sisters. It was the saving of her. Meanwhile, of course, I went home for the funeral after the end of my first term of Greats and looked on, feeling rather distant and useless.

The Greats course was a combined studies course in ancient history and in philosophy. This latter was not confined to the ancient world, but, once it had dealt with Plato's *Republic* and Aristotle's *Nicomachean Ethics*, it passed on to modern philosophy, beginning with Descartes and then on to the British empirical tradition which culminated, of course, in so-called 'Oxford philosophy'. All of this was completely different from the 'proto-theology' I had studied in Heythrop and Munich, and there did not seem to me, at that time, to be any point at which the two concepts of philosophy usefully met. I began in Oxford by taking Plato and Aristotle with Basil Mitchell at Keble. He was a thoroughly pleasant man who later became Professor of the Philosophy of Religion at Oxford. I had joint tutorials at first with a Chicago Jesuit priest, John N. Felten, a humane character who became a good friend. Mitchell treated us with kid gloves, which was perhaps a pity. The Catholic 'philosophy' we had both imbibed, with its determination to instil the right ideas into us once and for all, badly needed challenging. We should not have been allowed to get away with what would nowadays be called our 'ecclesiastically correct' views. We had had the worst possible preparation imaginable for the kind of philosophical stance that was now required: open, curious, exploring the real issues regarding justice and virtue raised by Plato and Aristotle, and all without the preconceptions of a religious doctrinal system to guide and control the exploration.

No allowance was made for our strange kind of philosophy, however, in the outstanding and entertaining lectures that were on offer. The urbane Gilbert Ryle used Jane Austen's *Emma* more or less as a philosophical text-book. J.L. Austin, devastatingly witty and clever, gave a course on 'Sense and Sensibilia' to a packed out lecture-hall. Richard Hare lectured on Plato's moral philosophy. I enjoyed these courses very much, though I have to admit that the diet was all rather too rich for my scholastically dehydrated stomach. I had difficulty holding the material down, and I doubt if I ever quite cottoned on to the nature of the game that was being played – not even when I was sent to Anthony Quinton at New College for further tutoring in modern philosophy. Excellent tutor as he was, urbane brilliance was not quite what I needed. I could have done with much cruder treatment from someone not afraid to point out that I was in danger of becoming an ignorant and bigoted cleric who should try to get to grips with some real philosophical questions for a change. But such is not Oxford's way. I managed to do fairly well in my philosophy essays and examinations; but without much conscious appreciation of the nature of philosophical study, I found that my heart was not it. Oxford's methods, as I was to discover much later, are far more subtle and effective. But vitally, when I needed help from philosophy later, I had retained enough of the philosophy I had been taught at Oxford to know where to turn with the acute critical problems that teaching theology naturally raised. I was then deeply grateful for what I had learnt in the philosophy part of Greats.

With the ancient history part of Greats, it was completely different. History suited my gift for learning better than philosophy did. I was very well tutored by dons who, in their very different ways, made personal demands on me to buckle down and take the history game seriously. For Greek history I was sent to Alfred Holladay at Trinity, a tall, languorous, unaffable, effortlessly clever man who wasted no time in tutorials, gave out sharp but well-considered criticism in response to the essays I read out to him, and then delivered crisp instructions, including bibliography, for the writing of next week's contribution. End of tutorial. Little or no chat, but sometimes a functional glass of sherry and a few words. Pretty well the perfect tutor, I would say; and I worked very hard during the year I had under his direction. In my finals I had an Alpha in Greek history, and all the credit goes to Holladay.

In Roman history I finished up with an ambiguous mark – Beta/Alpha – and the credit for this goes to the year I spent under the strong influence of one of Oxford's all-time great tutors, C.E. (Tom) Stevens at Magdalen. My eventual result might not have been quite high enough, and it may have cost me a First, but my time with Stevens was worth it all. He was a very clever Wykehamist who had been appointed a Fellow of Magdalen in the 1930s. He had started academic life as a historian with a leaning towards archaeology – his own Oxford mentor had been R.G. Collingwood – but his career in Romano-British and Celtic studies was interrupted by the war. His *Times* obituary (2 September 1976), obviously penned by someone who had enjoyed his teaching as much as all his students, says of his war-work: 'His sharp intelligence and imagination, devious cleverness and inventiveness, here found ideal employment.' In the course of his work, Stevens it was who had suggested the adoption of the four opening notes of Beethoven's Fifth Symphony as the most famous broadcasting theme of the war, the Morse Code 'V' signal. In fact, you could believe almost anything of Stevens. In my view, he never quite got over his experience of being a brilliantly creative black propagandist in the war, and his reading (and very much his teaching) of Roman history became highly coloured by his idea that all history and all historical texts (even, or especially, the most fragmentary and esoteric) were essentially products of the propagandist's art. Apart from its being tenable and respectable, this view, as expressed by the master, made his tutorials and his very popular lectures exhilarating, not to say hilarious, experiences. His knowledge of texts and obscure facts was legendary. He lived his tutorial work day in and day out. He is said to have done, at one time, between fifty and seventy hours tutoring a week, and no doubt every minute of this incredible load was packed with his irrepressible enthusiasm. He – and his students – drank a lot, as he filled up his and their tankards from a beer barrel which was perched astride his bath. Earlier on, he had published a basic book, *Sidonius Apollinaris and his Age* (Oxford 1933), and he wrote a surprisingly large number of learned papers. But tutoring was his life and his greatest achievement. His *Times* obituarist remarks, rightly, that his work was marred by over-ingeniousness and a delight in cleverness for its own sake – 'like Stanley Matthews, his footwork was a joy to behold, but he did not often score goals'. I would point out that Tom Finney, our Preston North End legend, both displayed wonderful footwork and scored goals as well.

Tom Stevens and I got on very well indeed, and I worked extremely hard for him. He was obviously set on grooming me for a career in ancient history. One tutorial I had with him began after dinner at 8.00 p.m., was adjourned over a drink in the Magdalen Senior Common Room at 11.30 p.m., after which I was let out of the College by the side-gate, and was resumed the following morning at 7.30 a.m., when I was given breakfast. It ended at 9.00 a.m., when his next student came. He cannot possibly have treated all his students in this way, but if a student showed promise (as apparently I did) nothing was too much trouble for him in his ceaseless crusade to outwit the eventual examiners. At long last I became seriously interested in study and firmly committed to learning. He was mightily encouraging, and I responded – no doubt to the neglect of the some of the philosophy I was also supposed to be studying. The Oxford Greats course did not cater for the kind of specialization Stevens was quite prepared to demand. Every week two essays had to be written and read to the two tutors, one in philosophy and one in history. But inevitably I put more work into the one than into the other. With Stevens I covered the later Roman Republic, his favourite period, and I am glad I had the sense to take as much as I could of the marvellous teaching he offered. Since then it has always represented for me the ideal form of serious education in the humanities. Here was a teacher with ideas of his own, an immensely learned enthusiasm for his subject, and an outstanding gift for imparting knowledge in an academic and critical way.

I only hope that later on I managed, at least sometimes, to be something of a worthy, if dim, product of Tom Stevens of Magdalen.

Not that Stevens was the only ancient history teacher from whom I benefitted. In Greek history, the Wykeham Professor, Anthony Andrewes reigned supreme. Large and untidy-looking, he delivered his lectures lounging about on the high table in New College hall. They were models of erudition on such tricky subjects as the early history of Sparta, with much use of Jacoby's *Fragments*. At Balliol Russell Meiggs was a very informative entertainer of the highest class. At Brasenose there was the inimitable Ronald Syme, the Camden Professor, lecturing in the exact style of Tacitus on – Tacitus. Even the then lesser lights were excellent lecturers: David Stockton, Peter Brunt, and the elegant J.P.V.D. Balsdon. Considering I did not have to go to any lectures, memory tells me that I must have gone to a great number of them. But the quality was there, and I am glad I took advantage of it.

Meanwhile Jesuit life went on as usual at Campion Hall. I was the sole scholastic in my fourth year, though a solid supply of bright colleagues was filling up the house from below. The Hall remained a good base for studies. The authorities were generally benign, and life, both in term-time and the vacations, was hard-working and absorbing. Our religious lives had, by this time, to take care of themselves, helped along by the normal daily and annual exercises. Socially I got about Oxford a little, and a stream of Catholic notables came to stay with us: Evelyn Waugh, Ronald Knox, Lord Longford. Guest-nights produced other remarkable people: Isaiah Berlin, C.S. Lewis, J.R.R. Tolkien. It was interesting and encouraging to see such people close up, and even to get to speak to them. But my time at Oxford was beginning to come to an end. I continued to take a good deal of physical exercise, chiefly cycling and walking, though in a less organized way than earlier on.

I took my Final Schools in the summer of 1957. It was hot, and we had to take ten or so three-hour papers, morning and afternoon, one after another. I enjoyed formal three-hour written examinations, and I still think that this is quite the best way of being examined and getting examinations done with and out of the way. It was now over two years since I had sat an examination. I simply cannot understand the modern taste for the frequent examination of 'course-units', and still less for the nerve-racking threat of 'continuous assessment'. Later experience in university teaching demonstrated to me that many students

hardly ever draw an unexamined breath, but seem quite happy
not to do so. How they ever get any serious work done, or get
enjoyably involved in sports and other social activities, or even
just enjoy their student lives, I do not know. Much is made of the
argument that, if three-hour papers are set at the end of a degree
course, too much rests on the one and only chance which this
arrangement gives the candidate. But I fancy that behind this
argument lies some problem with how students are taught to
approach examinations. Many of them insist on looking at examinations as if they were blind dates, preparation for which
consists of learning answers to questions which then, of course,
fail to show up on the examination paper. Then there is blind
panic. I do not know why, in my day, we were confident enough
to suppose that we could actually think in the examination room,
and work out how best to respond to any set paper. Stevens' view
of examinations was that they were a game in which you had to
outwit the examiners by convincing them that you knew far more
than you actually did – a form of propaganda, if you like. He even
produced, annually, two or three cyclostyled sheets entitled
'Stevens' Muck' – a list of hopelessly erudite points which you
were challenged (that is, dared) to introduce into your written
answers. We must have been very confident; but then we were
not exam-ridden – and we had, of course, worked very hard at
the syllabus anyway. I rested for a full week in Bristol away from
all books before the Greats examination began.

I had no problem with any of the papers. I later had a
prolonged Viva – over an hour – after which I was awarded
another top Second, just short of a First. My philosophy papers
had been predictably ordinary, and the impressive row of philosophy examiners had obviously seen all they wanted to know. The
problem was the Roman history paper. In Greek history, there
was no problem. Holladay was an examiner that year, and he told
me how pleased he was as he left the room before my Viva. In
Roman history, as I have said, I was parked on the borderline
between a Second and a First. The problem was of my own
making. I had written very extensively (as the rules permitted me
to do) and very learnedly on one relatively minute point on a
Latin inscription to do with Claudius and the granting of the
Roman citizenship. The examiners were happy enough with this,
even though I had flatly disagreed with one of them, A.N.
Sherwin-White, in an area where he was the reigning expert.
Benign as ever, all they asked me to do was to find another question on the paper and let them hear how I would have answered

it. Mistakenly I thought I would show off, and I chose a relatively difficult question, when there were far easier ones staring me in the face. I sketched out my answer to it, and simply failed to impress. I was left with a Second. It was entirely my own fault. The examiners did their level best to give me a First on a plate. I instantly knew I had failed, and from that moment I have admired Oxford and its standards all the more. In the end I had not been intelligent enough to cope, and they had rightly not fudged matters in favour of someone who did not have the wit to help himself. Their judgement was rigorous, perhaps: but that kind of rigour is the only way to maintain the standards expected of a world-class academic institution.

෴

In late August 1957, as instructed, I followed my old trunk to Liverpool where I had been sent to teach at St Francis Xavier's College in Salisbury Street. In the Jesuit house I installed myself in an attic room looking down over the city centre through the smoke and frequent fogs to the Liver Building, the Mersey, the docks and Birkenhead beyond. Although battered in the war, Liverpool was not much changed. The docks were still fairly active, the Overhead Railway had only just been taken out of service, and there were still some trams running up and down the cobbled main roads and turning round at the Pierhead. The ferries were running back and forth across the river. There were still wide bare patches among the houses where the German bombs had fallen. There was still no Catholic Cathedral, only the Lutyens crypt for one that would never be built. The Anglican Cathedral rose in solitary dignity and in all its cold academic beauty. Close to the College next door were the Walker Art Gallery, St George's Hall, the Picton Library, the University with all its facilities, the Philharmonic Hall with its excellent orchestra, then under John Pritchard, the big railway stations and the shopping streets. The place was noisy and dirty, and everywhere there was the push and hurry of busy, witty, money-making people. I soon came to realize that I had never in my life lived in the centre of a big city. I took to it all very quickly.

There were a large number of Catholic parishes and schools in Liverpool. St Francis Xavier's, near the top of Islington and about ten minutes' walk from the city centre, was the largest Roman Catholic encampment in the city – a big Gothic church and a once very populous and poor parish (where Gerard Manley Hopkins had spent yet another of his unhappy postings to parish work), a big primary school, and, alongside all this, the huge brick pile of

the city's leading Catholic grammar school – S.F.X., as the place
was always called. It had been the Jesuit stronghold in Liverpool
since it had been started in the nineteenth century. In the past it
had enjoyed a formidable academic reputation, chiefly in classics,
and it had an equally good name for soccer among the Liverpool
schools. I was to spend two enjoyable years here. The Jesuit house
was wedged between the church and the college. It was spacious
inside and well enough appointed. The individual rooms (but not
my attic room) had their own coal fires. The house seemed dark,
even in summer. I remember it all, and its surroundings, as grey
and grubby and slightly damp. But what gave colour and interest
to my time in Liverpool were some of the people with whom I
lived and worked. The city and the church seemed their perfect
habitat and foil, and, in their different ways, they made my stay
almost continuously entertaining. Whatever else Liverpool did
for me, it provided a very welcome break from the solemnities of
study; and this, I suppose, was one of the reasons for sending
Jesuit scholastics into the colleges on what was called their
'regency' in the middle of their protracted training. I had had
nine years of more or less spiritual and intellectual education so
far. Apart from Oxford, it had perhaps been not particularly
intense. But some respite was advisable; and Liverpool provided
a wise and helpful contrast, with its big-city feel, its quick-witted,
no-nonsense people, the completely unfamiliar work I had to do,
and with the general knockabout character of life in a lively
school among colleagues, the like of whom I had never yet
encountered in the Society, and most of whom I did not know.

   Perhaps only a separate and lengthy study would do anything
like justice to the Jesuit community at S.F.X.; or perhaps, once
again, a well-observed account by a first-rate satirical novelist. I
shall confess straight away that in describing community life at
Liverpool I am risking being unfair. I am ignoring the good work
that many of them, now somewhat faded caricatures of their
former selves, had done in the past, and were in some cases still
doing in the present. But to me they seemed a fascinating, far
from unlikeable collection of variegated misfits. Again, I must
make it clear that up to this point I had been used to homoge-
neous and congenial communities of students of my own kind.
Now I was thrown among much older men with lifetimes of
varied and sometimes unhappy experiences behind them. They
had been washed up into the same Liverpool house, with little in
common from their varied pasts, and little to hope for from a
bleak future. Some were disillusioned, some burnt out, some

perhaps slightly crazed. Not that any of them was unpleasant – we all got along cheerily enough. But encountering this community was for me an eye-opener on what life in the Jesuits could, and perhaps inevitably would, become. I do not wish to be as unkind as a certain Jesuit Superior who described the community in his care elsewhere as 'a crate of returned empties'. This may have described some, but surely not all of them. All the same, my introduction into the Liverpool community came as quite a shock.

But again, it could be argued that it was time I got a bit of a shock that would bring me down from the academic heights to life in a religious world which was closer to the world of ordinary people. Maybe this is what the 'regency' was all about. Jesuits are not meant to live community lives based on the monastic model. Indeed, the Order was founded at least partly to get away from the monastic ideal of the family under its Father Abbot, and with its regular round of divine office sung in choir. Jesuit houses tend to be run more like rather seedy gentlemen's clubs which house individuals who are meant to be getting on with the work in hand. There is no family atmosphere, and a Jesuit lives there only as long as his work is there. And since there is only a poorly developed concept of retirement (since you are a 'priest for ever according to the order of Melchisedech') ageing Jesuits, who have really done nothing in the past but work at whatever they were given to do, find they must maintain some pretence of continuing to work until they drop. They have nothing else – and nowhere else – to retire to. Individuals and their individuality are not priorities in the Jesuit system, which tends to reduce the person to the job in hand, functionalizing him, rating him little higher than the efficiency with which he is still prepared to operate. When a Jesuit can function no more, or even becomes dysfunctional, there is little further the Jesuit system can offer beyond a decent Requiem and funeral. It turns into a Burial Society.

In relationships within the community there was little room for showing mutual sympathy and understanding. It was not so much that these attentions were formally ruled out, as that they simply had no place in how Jesuits habitually got on together. I suppose there were about a couple of dozen Jesuits in all at S.F.X. One section of these worked on the parish under the Rector, William D'Andria. Willie was an odd little man. Very short, and of grim, rather Mediterranean aspect, he contrived to make the most of his position of authority. He habitually wore a biretta, in order, it was said, to make himself look slightly taller than he was. He had very decided views, and not least on what was expected of young Jesuit priests. For a short while he had had a major role in their training, and he had acquired a reputation for being ultra-rigorous and unsympathetic. In short, he was thoroughly disliked. He endlessly chivvied those he thought were not trying their best, and he corrected those whose Jesuit standards he thought were slipping. He can hardly have been the right man to manage the Liverpool community – unless he had been put there to make life hard for them. He must have been very hard to work with. Although he was not responsible for the workings of the College, the College staff also came under his authority, and they too disliked him.

I am happy to say that I never had a better Superior, and the two or three other scholastics who were on the College staff with me would have agreed. The reason was simple: we were not yet priests, and so not yet suitable targets for Willie's fierce attentions. On the contrary, his dealings with us were marked with the greatest indulgence. He truly fathered us along, feeling responsible for our future in the Society, encouraging and helping us in many ways, taking us out to lavish teas either in the city or over to New Brighton. He would drive us jerkily through the Mersey Tunnel and buy us sticky pastries in deserted seaside cafes in the depths of winter. To my knowledge, he is the only Rector to whom scholastics spontaneously gave a Christmas present – in his case, a box of cigars, to which we all gladly contributed from our exiguous pocket-money. On occasions he could be silly and petty and autocratic. But you could tell him so to his face (as, of course, I did), and he would instantly come off it. Willie was a good and an essentially simple man, whatever others thought, and he remained a good friend. Though he was disliked by so many Jesuit priests, he was, oddly enough, revered as a priest by the diocesan clergy; and more than once they put his name forward in hopes of his being appointed their bishop. This procedure must be extremely rare in the case of a Jesuit.

There was also one other colourful Jesuit on the parish staff who cannot be overlooked – Dan Hughes, very old, and brutally battered by his experiences in the trenches of the 1914–18 war. He had been a chaplain with the Royal Welch Fusiliers and had been buried alive with some of his men in the course of a savage bombardment on the Somme. He had been decorated with the Military Cross and Bar – a rare double distinction. He was left prone to spectacular epileptic fits which he would throw at any time – in the corridor, the refectory, his room, the church. He had to be allowed to come round in private. To be present when he revived was to become his sworn enemy. He was rarely without visible cuts and bruises, either from his fits or from stopping fights between drunken parishioners in his district in the parish. The first time I ever met him, on my first full day in the house, he was bandaged and still bleeding from an attempt to intervene between two old women who had been attacking one another with broken beer bottles. He was ferociously attached to his parish district. He recited the house numbers in his beautifully resonant voice throughout community prayers, and he traipsed round his streets, day in, day out, in all weathers. He disliked all the other priests in the community, but only because he suspected they had come to take his beloved district from him. So, logically enough, once he knew you were only a scholastic, he became friendly and he would embarrassingly enlist you on his side against all-comers and especially against the authorities. You became his ally and the recipient of the loud and pungent criticisms he normally voiced during community meals. Sitting next to him at dinner was a hazard. I caught my first Liverpool flea from him in my first week in the house. He had imported it from some poor house in his beloved district. His language at dinner could be quite foul, and he was characteristically fearless in its use. Sometimes Willie even had to send him to his room like a recalcitrant child. On one occasion, though, he behaved beautifully. Some forty years after the event, Dan was finally sent the citation for his Bar to the Military Cross. Willie ordered a special dinner to mark the event, and – wearing his biretta – solemnly read out the citation which detailed Dan's awesome exploits as a chaplain all those years before. It was a touching occasion, crowned with a most gracious and completely untypical speech from Dan himself. He was a priest worth remembering.

On the College staff there were eight or nine Jesuits who taught at all levels. The Headmaster, Edward Warner, was another distinguished ex-chaplain, highly intelligent, a fine English scholar and a most efficient teacher. But his *forte* was undoubtedly administration, and this suited his extremely distant personality. He gave up teaching and came over as a super-efficient bureaucrat, highly conscientious in his religious life, but seemingly without a spark of human interest or involvement in other people's lives. Even the memory of him engenders an air of depression and a feeling that he cannot have been 'really' like that. I never knew him to encourage anyone in their work in the school, or to try to cheer them up if things were going wrong. His

habitual emphasis, in human affairs, was on their negative possibilities – indeed, probabilities; and if someone was putting in
extra work (such as taking groups of boys to the Philharmonic
concerts or to camp in Scotland) he would dismiss it scornfully as
beneath his praise, and he would snap: 'He only does it because
he likes it.' In my two years at Liverpool I suppose I never really
had a conversation with him. I received neither advice nor
encouragement from him; nor, to my face, any criticism. He was
reckoned, of course, a very observant religious, and I am
prepared to concede that he was. I cannot help thinking that I
may be getting him wrong; that there must have been more to
him than that. In fact, I believe that there was much more, and
that he was a man of real quality; but he remains to my mind a
classic – but by no means unique – case of someone who has
successfully hidden his humanity under the cloak of what he
fancied was devout religion. He was, I would say, a notable
victim of the Jesuit system.

The rest of the priests on the staff were a mixed bag. Some of
them were still fairly new to teaching, others had been in teaching
too long. They were generally good and devoted men, men who
had their little idiosyncrasies – this one specialized in discipline,
this one in sport, this one frightened boys into submission, this
one liked dealing with the small ones, but in obviously innocuous
ways. All in all I found them uninteresting. But there was a
general quality that I think seemed to hang about them all: an air
of disappointment, even disillusion. They did not often seem
happy. Some of them were academically well qualified for far
higher posts, but had finished up teaching well below their
potential. Others resented the fact that, able as they were, they
had never, long ago, been sent to Oxford. They seemed frustrated, almost defeated, by the demands the system had made on
them. Their novitiate spirituality had led them into a form of self-
denying, passive, negative compliance which, frankly, had done
them harm. I began, in Liverpool, to get unambiguous glimpses
of what the Jesuit system could produce in those whose lives it
demanded. Not that I dwelt on such uncomfortable thoughts, if
only because life and work as a scholastic at S.F.X. were continuously lubricated by the presence of fellow-scholastics who just
happened – and it was sheer luck that governed my fate – to be
highly congenial.

The three of us together – with, of course, the support of Willie,
our indulgent Rector – turned S.F.X. into an enjoyable, even hilarious, interlude in our training. We found we could largely ignore

the older community who were either uninterested in us or unable to prevent our multitudinous activities in and around the school. When I arrived in Liverpool George Sandham and Paddy Cooper were already starting their second year, so I was in a good position to pick up their established ways. George was a Preston Catholic College product: awkward, intelligent, with wide interests and very keen on out-of-school activities – scouting, soccer, cricket (his uncle was the great Andrew Sandham of Surrey and England), music, and so forth. Paddy was quite different. He was a product of the Jesuit College in Wimbledon, where he died a few years ago as Headmaster. He had no particular interest in games, but he loved organizing and managing things for the boys – the College tuck-shop, trips to London, trips to Scotland, anything that made the most of his entrepreneurial skills. He drove the College van, eventually teaching me to drive, so that the van became virtually the private transport of the scholastics. No one else drove. Paddy was a superb teacher, patient and relentless both inside and outside the classroom. So I had two role models in my first year. I could not have been luckier. We stood like musketeers against an alien world.

We got up to everything, doing, as I believe, a great deal of good for the boys. We set aside profits from the tuck-shop which Paddy had astutely turned into a small private gold-mine. We used the money to fund boys from poor families on trips and holidays. We ran football and cricket teams all year round. The more talented players came under George, and I ran the College Second XIs in both soccer and cricket for two whole years, and with surprising success. I have long thought this was probably the best thing I did in Liverpool. I have little skill in either game, but I am a good team manager, using discipline and routine both on and off the field. On our Scotland trips we took as many as forty boys to a centre near Pitlochrie, and toured around in our own coach. We took the same number to London and stayed in Sussex Gardens. Once George and Paddy had moved on at the end of my first year, they were replaced by Bill Crooks, himself an old S.F.X. boy, and we kept up what had by now become the traditional occupations for scholastics. There was a great deal to do in Liverpool, both with and without the boys – the Philharmonic gave wonderful concerts, and I could use the University Library when I felt I needed to. Then, of course, there was Anfield and Goodison Park for top soccer matches. It is easy to see how much I owe to my fellow-scholastics at S.F.X. They made what could have been a depressing experience into a very lively one indeed.

However I was not in Liverpool to run sideshows, but to teach in the College. I had a full timetable, and almost all my teaching was in the Classical Sixth. I was, of course, not well prepared for this. True, I had my degree, but I had no Teaching Certificate and no experience of teaching whatever. That an untried Jesuit should be able to walk into what was clearly a plum job at S.F.X., whilst laymen, both experienced and well-qualified, were kept teaching lower down the school, was simply a scandal. I very much enjoyed the challenge of teaching, though I received no advice or help from anyone. I think I made a pretty poor job of it. The clever boys I was given to teach were on the brink of university entrance, and they needed careful and wise coaching from some old classics hand long accustomed to the entrance system and the ways of getting boys into the right university places. Instead they got me. This was unfair on the other masters who had taught them, and especially on the boys, a good number of whom were exceptionally bright and should have gone much further than they did. They were being used as nothing better than guinea-pigs, to test out the potential of whatever Jesuit scholastic was next put in charge of them. But I got on very well with them, much helped by the fact that they actively disliked the two older Jesuits who also taught Latin and Greek. One of them, a burnt-out case if ever I saw one, was teaching Euripides' *Hecuba* for the fourteenth year running, and chiefly as an exercise in grammar. The other had been reduced to a state of savage indignation about life in general and teaching in particular. I always prepared my classes very carefully, and I was diligent in marking homework. I simply lacked appropriate training and experience. But the boys presented me with book tokens at the end of each of my years there; and I presented them with several large bottles of Guinness, their favourite tipple. Some of them got into university and did well. But I do wish I had been up to the standard they deserved.

So, all in all, the two years at Liverpool passed pleasantly. I worked hard and played hard, and my teaching was as good as I could make it at the time. Perhaps most importantly, though, I had now been introduced to Jesuit life in the raw, and I was not at all sure that I liked much of what I saw. As a glimpse of what my future might be, it was not reassuring; though when, later, I was asked if I would like to go back into one of the Colleges as a Headmaster, I said that I would – but on condition that I could choose the other Jesuits I had on my staff. An impossible condition, of course. More worrying, however, was the glimpse I got of what a friend of mine memorably called 'the arrogant mediocrity' of the Jesuits. At the time I thought this a harsh description of the attitudes I had seen displayed at S.F.X.; but there is certainly some point to it. Liverpool had raised questions in my mind. It had fed my already critical tendencies. It had opened my eyes to what could happen if you became 'like them'.

By July 1959 I had been given clearance to embark on the next stage of my Jesuit training. Clearance consisted in getting positive approval from four older Jesuits who had been detailed to fill in the *informationes* – the Latin questionnaires that had to be returned to the Provincial with reports on religious life and observance, attitudes and performance in whatever situation was current. This was a secret process, but there was nothing at all sinister about it. Later on, I became a consultor to the Vice-Provincial in charge of scholastics, and it was one of my tasks to read *informationes* (by then in English) on scholastics who were making their way through the system. I was struck by the general honesty, fairness and helpfulness of what older Jesuits were prepared to say about younger ones even behind their backs. It was impressive, and I think the system of reporting back ran on sensible lines. I was now at a key juncture in the system, since clearance to go on to study theology more or less entailed clearance to be ordained to the priesthood in another three years' time. In my case clearance was given, though someone (I think I can guess who it was, since my old Headmaster, John Duggan, had been on the S.F.X. staff with me) did note that I tended to be 'un peu difficile'. It was probably this negative mark that stopped my being sent to the rather avant-garde Jesuit theologate in Lyons, where I had asked to be sent. I was a kind of 'export reject', in other words; but I was not unduly bothered. In any case, I knew well enough that I could not possibly have pleased everybody at S.F.X. So I moved in August 1959 back to Heythrop for four years' theology – a move that was to determine the rest of my life in ways I could not then have begun to imagine.

None of the worlds in which I had lived in the last eleven years, not even the world of Oxford or that of S.F.X., had been anything much like an ordinary world. They had all been worlds apart, and most of them remote, religious constructs, custom-built to accommodate and facilitate the devout aspirations that belonged to a religious life professedly superior to the lives of ordinary folk. In the serious study of Catholic theology I was, as I thought, going to be taken more deeply into whatever it was that was supposed to lie behind these religious worlds. What I was still too immature to realize was that I was going to finish up even more sealed off from human normality than I already was.

Chapter 5

The World Beyond

It was now eleven years since I had joined the Jesuits and ordination to the priesthood was still at least another three years off. It could scarcely cause surprise if, despite reminders of the priesthood at daily Mass and from the presence of priestly colleagues, the priesthood might have lost something of whatever glow it may have had as a personal goal. Then again, as I have said, in my own case the priesthood had always been more a part of the Jesuit package than a personal goal anyway. Indeed, it would be possible to go further and say that over the past eleven years I had been kept so busy, so much on my toes finishing off one stage of training and then, without adequate preparation, picking up the next and completely different stage, that being a Jesuit was becoming more a matter of habit and performance than of deeply conscious attention. It may seem strange to say this, considering the extent to which the whole system of Jesuitism bore down on daily existence; but any way of life contains, I suppose, the possibility of just going on under its own momentum, of becoming routine and run-of-the-mill. It is part of the process of institutionalization. And this is what had been happening in my case. I had been happy enough doing all the various jobs I had been called on to do. In the eyes of the authorities I seemed to be functioning up to standard. I was, in other words, being turned into the sort of Jesuit the system required: a viable operative who looked as though he could cope with whatever he might be called on to do. Beyond my practical contentedness and my Superiors' satisfaction at my functional potential, a deeper personal relationship with God or with the spirit of my native Catholicism or even of the Society was not really developing. I was reasonably faithful in performing the duties of religious life, but my performance was as functionally pragmatic as the rest of my activities. A spiritual deadness had set in, but far from being alarmed at this, I was almost inclined to justify it as naturally due to my exemplary

conformity with the system – and this, after all, was what we had
been taught should be our religious priority. Of course, these
were times, pre-Vatican II, before talk about personal attitudes
and commitments and relationships was brought into the open;
and an impersonal functionality, a practical viability, was
allowed to be what really counted. So no serious personal questions were raised, either on my side or by the Jesuit authorities,
about what might be called the state of my soul – my spiritual
development, my growth in wisdom, even in holiness. Such questions would have embarrassed both of us. Jesuit life was not
conducted at that level, not even in one's annual interview with
the Provincial, who, more often than not, was an able but harried
individual, happy enough to be keeping the show on the road,
until, after his six years of office were up, he could hand the
whole circus over to somebody else. What mattered was the
extent to which you were prepared to function, and whether you
could keep up with the practical demands of the system. Other
more personal matters were best left to look after themselves.
They were between you and God, though every house had a
'spiritual father' who was on call to help. More often than not, he
would be a retired Jesuit with little, if anything, else to do. An
occasional perfunctory visit to him was largely a matter of cour-
tesy, to make him feel he was still employed. This pragmatic attitude – again on both sides – spread to the priesthood, which
became more or less just another function that you would eventually have to take on, if you managed to pass all the tests that
still lay ahead. Taking all the necessary tests was what we called
'theology'.

    In the Jesuit scheme of studies of those days, theology lasted
for four years. According to their already known abilities, all
Jesuits scholastics began either on the Long Course or the Short
Course – partly different courses of study which were,
perversely, of exactly the same length. The contents of both of
them were centrally dictated and controlled from Rome, at
Heythrop as at any other of the many Jesuit theologates round the
world. 'Longs' was meant to be more academic than 'Shorts', at
least in the key area of dogmatic theology. For other areas considered less important – biblical studies, Church history, Canon Law
– no distinction was made; and for all a severely equal emphasis
was placed on moral theology. Perhaps the most formidable
examination in the course had to do with the candidate's ability
to hear confessions with the kind of efficient clarity and casuistry
the faithful were thought to have a right to expect from a Jesuit

confessor. This emphasis seriously distorted the shape of our theological studies, and dominated a student's interests, since without success in the examination *ad audiendas confessiones* there could, of course, be no question of being ordained priest. It was our Driving Test, and until you passed it you were not a viable priest. But then this was only another way in which our study of theology seemed to have been reduced to a series of tests, or an obstacle course leading, if surmounted, to the trophy of the priesthood. Witholding or granting permission to be an ordained priest became the stick or the carrot which Superiors used to help us over all the hurdles.

We had already been pre-conditioned and partly trained for the obstacle course by 'philosophy', our proto-theology, as I have tried to explain. We were not embarking on anything remotely like a university course in theology, no more than our philosophy had anything to do with university philosophy. In the normal university course in theology, at least in one shaped by the Christian tradition, there is, in first place, understandable emphasis given to the Bible; students would learn to appreciate the historical background of the biblical books, and to master the best available methods of interpreting them. Due place would be given to the study of Hebrew and Greek as the biblical languages. As for the Christian tradition itself, the work of the early Christian councils and theologians would be examined; and then, probably omitting the medieval presentation of the Christian faith, attention would be given to the modern period as represented by the great Protestant divines, Schleiermacher, Tillich, Karl Barth, and the like. Church history, Christian ethics, and some introduction to non-Christian religions would be taught. There would also be an important course in the philosophy of religion (a difficult but key subject which, interestingly, played little part as such in our Jesuit training). A university theology course such as this would be taught without requiring any prior commitment to its truth. As far as belief in Christianity was concerned, the syllabus would neither depend on it nor lead to it. The tone of the studies would be academic and critical, with proper stress on meaning and interpretation. It is this attempt at scholarly objectivity which gives theology its rightful place as a subject to be studied at university.

There was little similarity between university theology and what we had to learn as 'theology' at Heythrop. We were embarked on a course of heavily systematic indoctrination in strict preparation for working as an efficiently trained Jesuit from whom the faithful Catholic had a right to expect answers to any doctrinal or pastoral query or theological conundrum which might occur to them. Our theology was meant to produce the Compleat Apologist for the Roman system of belief and morality. We were to become fully-armed Defenders of the Faith. From the dismal course in Apologetics with which we began, and throughout the whole cycle of courses in dogma, we cultivated a defensive mind-set, never thereafter to be abandoned. We were to man the barricades against all-comers, fending off objections against the doctrinal system of Catholicism, proving beyond possible doubt that all of it had impeccably divine origins, that it had been prophetically foretold in the Old Testament and indubitably instituted in the New by One who was no less than God in person; and that there were no historical or philosophical objections to such a system that could be made to stick, or that could undermine its absolute certainties. This comprehensive apologia for the Catholic religion was extended in particular to the Roman Church itself, which had the divine right to demand the same faith in itself as in any other of the mainline doctrines of the system, such as the Incarnation or the Trinity. These doctrines: the One God, the Triune God, Creation and Fall, the Word Incarnate, Sin, Grace, the Sacraments, Mary, 'the Last Things' were taught as separate and elaborate 'treatises' which followed one another round a three-year orbit. No particular attention was given to any kind of structural or material coherence or the deeper connections which might exist among them. The system simply spoke for itself. The student jumped on the roundabout when it was time for him to do so, and he got off once he had successfully completed the circuit. As I have said, biblical studies, though they were intelligently taught in my time, were ranked below dogma, since the chief role assigned by the system to the two Testaments was to serve as sources from which Catholic dogmas could be 'proved'. Church history was similarly downgraded, because historical considerations were not what counted in assessing the truth of a dogma. What counted was the degree of infallible authority with which a dogma had been defined or consistently taught by the Church. Moral theology, on the other hand, demanded, for reasons I have given, a disproportionate amount of time and attention. Any suspicion that we did not know, or could not express, the Church's moral teaching, not least in sexual matters, meant no ordination to the priesthood. The whole theology course was aimed at the production of informed and indoctrinated priests who were 'safe', in the sense that they could be trusted not to deviate from the doctrinal and moral certainties infallibly defined and taught by the Roman Church. Grim as this description must make our study of theology sound, it has to be remembered that we had willingly committed ourselves to life in a particular religious world which worked along the lines of a logic and a system of its own, and one that saw no need to keep looking over its shoulder at the ordinary, or even the academic, world. As for science, was not theology the queen of all the sciences? For life and work in that religious world a particular training was required, and theology was the final and foremost part of that training.

The method used in learning our doctrinal (or dogmatic) theology followed the totalitarian logic demanded by the special world whose structure and contents it was the aim of the theology to describe and defend. A series of 'theses' or propositions, about fifteen or twenty to each major treatise, had to be 'proved': that is, propounded, supported by various arguments, and defended from benign objections. First, the significance and purpose of the proposition was stated (the *Status Quaestionis*), and its chief opponents (the *Adversarii*), usually familiar and well-demonized heretics, were identified. Then the precise status or degree of certainty within the Church's doctrinal system that was being claimed for the proposition was made clear (the *Nota Theseos*) – was it a formally defined doctrine? Or did its certainty rest only on its being the view of some theological school or prominent Catholic theologian? Here references to conciliar and papal declarations, or to the theologians in question had to be furnished. With such preliminaries out of the way, it was time to move on to the arguments that were supposed to establish the thesis without leaving any room for doubt (the *Probatio Theseos*).

The first line of argument usually came from the biblical texts. A verse or passage would be taken, normally with no regard to its context, and interpreted, often ingeniously, so that it could be used as a premise in a syllogism which led to a conclusion that was then considered proven on scriptural grounds. The second line of argument usually came from the Church's tradition itself, from a Church council or an early 'Father' with weight and authority. In the third place, there could be an argument from 'reason' – a line of argument, that is, that purported to show the apparently rational fittingness of what was being proposed in the general scheme of things as seen, of course, from an already Christian perspective. In this pick'n'mix way, the proponent of the thesis presented it as certain and declared it proof against all objections. As a final flourish, fictitious objections, in syllogistic form, would be brought against it and would be stoutly and slickly refuted.

In this way, more or less, the theological student had to proceed through all the material contained in the doctrinal treatises. The whole operation – teaching, learning and the oral examinations at the end of each year – was conducted in dog-Latin. Considerable feats of memory and of mental and linguistic dexterity were demanded. I recall that for my final two-hour oral examination on the whole range of the theology (and some of the old scholastic philosophy) which I had learnt, I had to revise over a hundred and twenty theses or propositions and be prepared to expound and defend each of them, as my four examiners requested, in the manner described here. There was nothing exceptional about this. Everyone still on the 'Long' course had to do it. Whatever a man's academic past or, even more importantly, his personal talents or taste, he had to be ground through the same mill. It was hardly surprising that some of the most intelligent students around wisely gave up the struggle and descended to the 'Short' course, where standards were said to be lower and the final ordeal was considerably less testing.

Once again, our survival during four years of all this was greatly helped by such light relief as we could derive from one another's company, and on seeing the comic side of things. Only one of our courses set out to entertain us – unlikely as it may seem, the course in Canon Law. Given the dominance of the institutional structures of the Church in Catholic life, the study of Canon Law is obviously important. As an academic subject looked at from a historical point of view it is also a richly fascinating and rewarding pursuit. The Church's 1918 Code of Canon Law (now superseded) is surely one of the masterpieces of the legal craft. Far more should have been made of Canon Law than was possible in the scrappy course to which it was reduced in our scheme of study. But at least we derived constant amusement from the lecturer, Fr V. Paul Brassell. Brassell, with whom I got on well, was a large, squat figure with a huge head and a much-imitated fruity voice. His gifts were those of a late Victorian actor-manager, a sort of run-down Henry Irving, who had devoted his life to melodrama. He lived, and claimed to work, in a world of lurid problem cases, many of them with some sexual dimension. Of irony and understatement he knew nothing. He was a good lawyer, however, and had real histrionic gifts of a high order. He would have made a fortune in the secular courts, or indeed in the theatre. We were fortunate that he was also given the job (though I fancy wild horses could not have dragged it away from him) of training us in the technique of hearing confessions. For this purpose, he had a confessional grille built into his room, and he always played, with truly alarming realism, the impossible penitent; whilst a small group of us, each in turn, had to play the hapless confessor. This was brilliant role-play long before it became a fad of group psychology or corporate motivation. His impersonations were minor masterpieces of instant dramatization, clearly based on years of closely observed confessional experience. They were also very funny. I would not be alone in saying that these classes were probably the best, and certainly the most practical, we attended at Heythrop. But comedy as they were, and of a high order, they had a sting in the tail. The shock came, of course, after ordination, when we discovered that the characters portrayed by Brassell actually existed in large numbers and habitually thronged the confessionals in the churches and convents where we had to work. He did us all a great favour in making his work a matter of light relief amid the oppressive weight of the theology course as a whole.

Another source of relief was the invention of a trio of us who began to collect, from sundry sources, accounts of institutional and other forms of organized human life which cast a measure of humorous light on the situation in which we found ourselves. The collection became known as the 'Grey Book'. There is one copy, and I have it still. It is, in fact, no more than a thin sheaf of cuttings and quotations from books and newspapers. A small number of our like-minded colleagues were privy to it and made their contributions. It could make no sense nowadays, when the system of studies (if there still is one) has been changed, I hope, for the better. Our sources came from afar – pious clerical obituaries, John Henry Newman, Tacitus, J.K. Galbraith, Michael Frayn, Kurt Vonnegut, Evelyn Waugh, Iris Murdoch, Danilo Dolce, and especially newspaper reports on mental health, prisons and concentration camps. We would read our extracts to one another and roar at the uncovenanted appositeness of what was said. Was this puerile? I think not. It helped some of us to cope with our situation and persevere in our vocations. To give a taste of the whole I quote from Geoffrey Ashe's *King Arthur's Avalon* (Collins 1957, p. 30). He is speaking of Druids and their training:

'Druid' is a word of uncertain derivation. An alluring theory connects it with two root-syllables which would give it the meaning of 'One Who Knows' ... The druids ... [professed] to be a band of initiates. Their solidarity was intense ... They monopolised education, and planned it so that its main function was the recruitment and development and glorification of their own caste. Any youth could secure exception from military service by enrolling for the full course leading to druidical status. The inducement was powerful, but the course was intimidating. It lasted twenty years. Failure must have meant a wrecked life. The students gathered in remote fastnesses and consecrated groves. They received a tonsure, acquired the magic arts, learnt secret formulae, and rose through the grades of initiation. Lectures expounded the druidical doctrines, such a metempsychosis, the transmigration of souls. The final tests included answering complicated riddles before a committee, and composing verses while under water. Success, however, was worth attaining ... Every member could aspire to the position of Supreme Druid, with jurisdiction over the order and indirectly over society as a whole. It was a fine thing to be One Who Knew, especially since no layman could ask you what your knowledge consisted in.

I have already said enough about the theology at Heythrop to make the relevance of this account quite obvious. But the important point to make is that some of us, at least, were by now becoming quite consciously critical of the limitations of the system we were involved in, whilst remaining completely unable to do anything about it. For the time being, at least, we had to stay committed to going along with it.

☙

The class of '59 numbered about twenty. A few came from abroad, but the bulk of the year were scholastics from the English Province. No one, I think, came to theology with any intellectual ambitions. We were fulfilling the requirements of the system of training, were keen to get on with it, get ordained, get out and, at long last, get down to some work. In the ordinary world the members of this group – the average age would have been perhaps slightly over thirty – would already have been husbands of intelligent wives, fathers of growing families, holding down responsible jobs – managers, dons, head teachers, lawyers, doctors, and the like. As it was, we were stuck back in the school-room, learning the rules and the ropes that controlled a doctrinal and moral system with which most of us had been familiar since childhood. But what we were not doing was getting to any deeper grips with it – any deeper understanding of it which might enable and encourage us to interpret its meaning and truth as the systematization of a spiritual religion. We had our frustrations with the system of training, and they could perhaps be discounted as petty or inevitable; but behind them lay the larger fact that no amount of the kind of training we were being required to undertake would engage us in a closer, more enlightened and enlightening encounter with the Catholic religion which we already knew and devoutly practised. Quantitative increase was what counted. All we were being required to do was to amass, like our Druidical forebears, more and more of the same kind of esoteric knowledge, the sheer amount of which would equip us to outshine the more ignorant layfolk. For all the more sophisticated modes and habits of understanding which our lengthening experience or our university degree courses might have begun to engender in us, when it came to our Catholicism we were deemed to have made little or no progress at all.

We were still meant to accept whatever theological or doctrinal learning we had to acquire in the same old equiliteral sense in which most of us had understood it in 'Mixed Infants'. What we were learning was simply a much more detailed description of an invisible world, different from the ordinary, visible world, but somehow, somewhere, 'real' in just the same sense. We might now take in what was being said more readily, and in greater detail, but I do not think that we understood it any differently, any more imaginatively – that is, in a different, non-literal way or at a different, symbolic or metaphorical or religious level. Perhaps on the contrary: the increased amounts of theological lore that we were required to learn may well have deepened the impression that it was all literally true; and we mindlessly reified what were mere theological concepts into actual things. Far from there being any attempt to achieve some deeper understanding of the riches of the Catholic tradition, such attempts would have been dismissed in the name of the overriding orthodoxy which we had to acquire. It was somehow just all the more literally true.

I am here prodding away at what I now see as the crucial defect in our theological training. We had easy and leisurely access to the Catholic doctrinal system. Now whatever may be thought to be its religious function or value – and I have no doubts about it on this score – it seems to me to be undeniable that it is one of the most brilliant cultural artefacts of the Western world, inspiring art and architecture, literature and poetry and philosophy, not to mention people's lives, in ways that make its formative influence virtually inescapable. Simply on those secondary grounds it

merits penetrating study and exploration. Yet our studies did
nothing to open it up to intelligently imaginative interpretation.
It was taken to be certain and true simply as it stood. I am not
thinking of the kind of interpretation which would have understood a primarily religious system in terms of something else
altogether – say, simply as an elaborate expression of delusory
wishful thinking; or which would have reduced it to something
quite different from what it was – say, a way of satisfying some
psychological itch. But I have in mind the kind of interpretation
that would take proper account of the Church's doctrinal tradition as a developing attempt to give religious and theological
(and therefore necessarily metaphorical) expression to the
meaning and truth of Catholicism. If there was to be any advance
in understanding, there had to be room for interpretation somewhere. Of course what I am now saying about our theological
training was, I quite realize, unthinkable at the time; and in any
case, even if thought, certainly unsayable. The problem would
have to remain latent, another time-bomb set to explode later for
those who might eventually turn their minds to it. But need this
have been so? If I should seem over-critical of our theological
studies, it is because, far from any attempt being made to defuse
that bomb, our studies consisted in unwittingly packing more
and more explosive material into it.

Here I consider the teaching staff both responsible and excused:
responsible because they should have been in a position to give at
least the brighter students some awareness of the interpretative
problems that attend the proper study of theology; but excused
because they were all as much victims of the Jesuit system as we
were. My interest in criticizing the staff relates as much to myself as
to them. This is because I was later to join them, and I shared fully
both their shortcomings and their predicament. They had their
various jobs to do on the priest production line. We students were
transient beings, due to be out of the place after our four-year
stretch was over. Many of the staff had been in the place since the
'30s and '40s, faithfully teaching the same round of subjects.
Newcomers to the staff – and new talent had begun to filter back to
Heythrop in the '50s – had little chance of introducing the helpful
innovations which they could see were needed. There was the
weighty presence of the older staff who were still in post; and, far
more inhibiting, a system of studies – the *ratio studiorum* – which
was still unadapted to the changes which even the world of theology was having to undergo. New staff were naturally tempted to
succumb to the pressure of the old.

Some cosmetic alterations to the way we studied were introduced in my time, and we were all very grateful for them. In brief, they amounted to reducing the crazy emphasis on listening to lectures by dropping Saturday as a full lecture day (nothing in my experience of depressing tedium surpasses that which was induced by a Latin lecture on the medieval distinction between attrition and contrition on a dark winter evening while the ordinary world was digesting the football results); and by cutting out lectures on Wednesdays and making Wednesday a 'Study Day' – a give-away phrase which casts doubt on what we were supposed to be doing for the rest of the time. Someone had had the imagination to notice that we could actually read real books. So the younger staff made what changes they could to alleviate our condition, and I am sure far more intelligent work was done as a result. Increased scope and importance was also given to writing essays and papers – something that many of us were already well used to doing as part of our method of study. Cosmetic these changes might have been, but they in fact heralded the demise of the old system of studies, though it took an Ecumenical Council of the Church – Vatican II – to kill it off, and even then inadvertently. By the time I joined the staff at Heythrop, and the place had opened itself up to non-Jesuits, the old system survived only in rusting fragments. Nothing, it seems to me, is more telling than the amazing speed with which a cast-iron system which had the backing of the highest authority simply collapsed in on itself when given a firm push. But then the logic of any totalitarian mind-set is always particularly vulnerable – it takes only one of its axioms to be challenged, and the whole business is threatened with ruin. Our system of studies must have been highly vulnerable to any telling criticism. But in my time the 'professors' did what they could with it, and they deserve some gratitude for getting us through. Perhaps the only effective move towards the required improvement would have been to scrap the examination system – the annual one-hour Latin orals with four examiners which served as hurdles to be surmounted and to allow passage into the next stage. This system meant that however well or imaginatively one had worked at the set material during the year, one's efforts, expressed in crude Latin, had to be heard and scrutinized and questioned by a board of examiners who understood their primary responsibility to be the establishment of flat Jesuit orthodoxy, and had no interest whatever in what one might think it all meant. It would surely have been possible to substitute forms of written assessment, perhaps with some oral element as well (but in English), for this tedious ordeal.

But I am still left wondering just why we continued to be taught our theology in such an uncritical way. I quite understand that this was our first close encounter with the theology of a system which, as I have said, most of us had known about since just after infancy. But surely we could have expected courses which, for all their Latin frippery, made intellectual demands a little higher than G.C.S.E. O-level. We were, after all, engaged on a four-year degree course leading to a Roman Licentiate in Theology. We were not even in a run-of-the-mill diocesan seminary. A certain depth of critical treatment – some clear awareness of the special nature of theology, of its epistemological limitations, of the peculiar logic of its language, of its inevitably symbolic or metaphorical quality, of the difficulty and yet the importance of playing the theological 'game' correctly – all these should have had a defining part to play in the way we applied ourselves to the study of theology. Not to approach theology at this depth, it seems to me, is either to store up trouble for the future, or (much more commonly) permanently to anaesthetize the critical faculty regarding religious and spiritual truth. Either way, whether there follows some later rejection of the Church's doctrinal tradition as simply untenable, or an unthinking acceptance of its certainties, neither the real good of Catholicism nor of the individual is being served.

As it was, however, some of the first year teaching was abysmal. Apologetics, on the 'foundations' of Catholicism, was read out in Latin from an ageing Spanish textbook that each of us had in front of us, a book that was ill-informed, out-of-date, and lacking all historical sense. However bad it was, though, we had to remember that it was the sole basis for our end-of-year oral examination, so it could not be ignored. And it did not help that the course was taught by a man who had considerable ability and charm, but who had been steadily reduced to being a universal charlatan by a system in which he had been called on to teach virtually every subject in theology and philosophy, all equally badly. It gave us all a clear signal that we were worth nothing better. Not a single book was recommended for our reading, and one lecture, on the important topic of Christ's resurrection, was based on a piece written by the lecturer for a family magazine of popular piety. In ecclesiology, the case was quite different. Here we were in the hands of a fine scholar, an acknowledged expert in the tradition of the manuscripts of Cyprian of Carthage, and a theological *peritus* at Vatican II. I got to know Maurice Bévenot better later on, and I had the highest regard for his learning. Here was a man who had long been, in far more difficult times, a respected ecumenist. He was the author of judiciously expert articles on major issues relating to the Church and its traditions. He could have taught us an excellent course on the Church off the cuff and in his spare time. But no: the course he gave us in 1959–60, on the very eve of the Council, was based in the main on grubbily cyclostyled Latin notes written a quarter of a century before. All the same, they were probably better than any Roman textbook. But he was a victim of the system to which he was devoted – a system that he knew would have rejected him, had he deviated from its strict requirements. He once told me that around 1950 he had been researching, with no doubt typically penetrating assiduity, the origins of the Inquisition. Then Rome published the encyclical *Humani Generis* (12 August 1950) which severely criticized certain new tendencies in the teaching of Catholic theology – none of which had anything to do with purely historical research. Immediately he had thought it his duty to stop his work and to go back to the safety of tracking the manuscript transmission of the text of Cyprian. In terms of an overheating theological climate, Fr Bévenot was perhaps right to seek the shade; but the point of the tale is that the system kept a complete stranglehold on the most loyal of its workers. But we were the losers, and we were unprepared for the broader type of ecclesiology propounded at Vatican II a couple of years later.

But the whole staff were losers, too. What was true of those who taught us in our first year was largely true of those who taught us for the rest of our time at Heythrop. Their depressingly limited role was to peddle the certainties which constituted the Church's system of beliefs without subjecting them to critical assessment: without trying to examine in what precise sense they might be meaningful and true. They were good, intelligent men who had devoted their lives to not putting a theological foot wrong. In this negative way, they had helped to turn Catholic theology into an intellectual desert. There was no regular irrigation from current scholarship. The tap on the deep and capacious reservoir of the Church's tradition was screwed down so tightly that all it was providing us with was a rusty trickle of recycled catechism answers. And yet it is supposed to be the case that 'every scribe who has been trained for the kingdom of heaven is like the master of a household who brings out of his treasure what is new and what is old' (Matthew 13.52 NRSV). But we were not given even what was truly old from the Church's tradition, never mind anything new: just more stones instead of the bread we needed. When you consider the replication of the Heythrop situation in far inferior Catholic seminaries around the world, it is easy to see that in all this there must have been massive all round loss to the Church, loss to the respectability of Catholic scholarship, loss to the future priesthood, loss to the Catholic faithful, deprived of a proper understanding of their Catholic faith in God.

❧

Still, for the moment, There was No Alternative. So we buckled down to what we had to do to survive and to emerge as unscathed as possible from the continuing obstacle course. In this I was much helped by friendships and alliances I had formed earlier with certain fellow-scholastics. Then there were the traditional Heythrop pursuits that brought us together, most of all the huts, which were in daily use on the theologians' side of the College. Every afternoon many of us sat in one or other congenial group over a smoking wood fire, consuming slabs of buttered and jammed toast and drinking dark stewed tea. We talked on and on until it was time to wash up and make our way back through the woods to the College we had managed to forget for an hour or two, to face our evening lectures. At one time a select group of us formed a Sunday morning club which took to the huts and ate a secret full English breakfast which helped to pass the barren Sabbath hours. It helped if the wind was in the right direction, and the wood smoke did not curl over the main drive and give our illicit presence away. Or perhaps it did anyway, and wise Superiors turned a blind eye. There was also a lot of sport: soccer, rugby, cricket, and golf, which I now began to play, sometimes not too badly. There was also beekeeping and walking and other rural pursuits; and, of course, our traditional hitch-hiking. I did trips to Oxford about once a fortnight, with other excursions to Stratford, Cheltenham, London, and once, on a Saturday, to Wolverhampton to see Wolves play Tottenham Hotspur. A tiny amount of money – perhaps half-a-crown or five shillings – might be privily hoarded and spent on our secret trips. A kind lift into Oxford (those who stopped for us were invariably good and interesting people who cannot possibly have known the amount of good they were doing) and then it cost little to get a basic lunch at the Municipal Restaurant and go to the cinema before hitching back. Some trips were legal, in my case those to the Oxfordshire County Library in Norham Gardens, where I first found interesting books on theology that I could read on my own like a grown-up. They were almost all by Anglican or Protestant divines – L.S. Thornton, A.M. Ramsey, Karl Barth – and I began to find well-written theology attractive.

Among the new Jesuit friends I made in the theology years at Heythrop was Kevin McHugh. Slightly older than I, lively and amusing, he was socially adept in ways well beyond me. He was no dry intellectual, just very intelligent, and we seemed to complement one another well. I played the slower Northerner to his much quicker North London Celt. He was a good planner and organizer, with a practical imagination, and one of his abiding interests was in helping handicapped children. He had taught as a scholastic at St John's Beaumont (now the southern preparatory school for Stonyhurst), and it was back there that some of us helped him to run summer holidays for groups of these children. Back at Heythrop the two of us spent much time together at an obvious afternoon pastime which, as far as I know, no one else had ever thought of taking up – coarse fishing. Many afternoons would find us on our *Pequod*, a rickety oil-drum raft, Captain Ahab and Queequeg aboard, compulsively hunting the Moby Dick of pikes that we firmly believed haunted the depths of the theologians' pond. We were not deluded. We got him only once, by illegally dead-baiting with herring and piano-wire, and we hauled him alongside, a long-jawed, twenty-pound monster, one flat, glazed eye glaring up at us – *monstrum horrendum, informe, ingens, cui lumen ademptum* (Virgil, *Aeneid* 3.658). All we had with us was a small folding trout-net, no use at all for bringing him on board. We committed the elementary error of trying to lift him. The old line broke, of course, and he swam away with a lazy swing of his great tail, disdainfully trailing a yard of piano-wire behind him, to spit it out back in his kingdom in the murky depths. Pike, properly cooked, can be a delicacy, but he was far bigger than any cooking facilities we could have laid our hands on. We would have returned him to the pond anyway. But we had proved, even if only to our own satisfaction, that he was really there. I doubt if anyone believed us. After all, we normally caught large numbers of four-ounce perch.

Kevin went back to St John's after ordination, became Headmaster, and ran the school with typical flair. After a number of very successful years, he had a disagreement with the Jesuit authorities, left the Jesuits, and was wisely snapped up by the diocese of Arundel and Brighton. He worked with all his usual skill as a curate at Hersham, near Weybridge, and I used to stand in for him from time to time in my later long vacations. In time he was seconded to the diocese's efforts in Peru, where, once again, he was amazingly successful. In the suburbs of Lima he custom-built a state-of-the-art therapy and work centre for handicapped children, and bred guinea-pigs for (I'm afraid) culinary purposes. This work was later extended to an equally splendid residential centre for the handicapped, beautifully designed, not far north of Lima in the fertile valley of the Chillón. Here he bred goats and made cheese to fund the enterprise. Kevin was solely responsible for these remarkably imaginative, practical and effective ventures. I managed to get out to Peru twice to see him, and we toured the country – Cuzco, Machu Picchu (spending the night there to see it at dawn, magically folded in mist after a violent night storm), Puno, Arequipa (one of my favourite places), and, on my second visit, north into Ancash and over to Iquitos, deep in the Amazonian jungle, then down south to Arequipa again and from there over into the remote Colca valley, where we went to see condors and where I never saw a single one. After well over a decade in Peru, Kevin came back to work in a number of parishes in his home diocese. It is difficult to see how any of this would have been accomplished if he had stayed dependent on Jesuitism. I mention him here because more than anyone else in those days he showed me how a human – and priestly – life could and should be lived by someone with gifts like his; and about how deadly the infantile paralysis so often induced by dependence on a religious system can be. I did not have his gifts at all; but he alerted me to the limitations of religious institutions and systems; and unwittingly of course, he was pointing me in the direction of my achieving eventual freedom and happiness without having to reject my native faith. For that I shall always remain very grateful to him.

Inside Heythrop there was the usual wooden round of religious duties and activities: early rise, meditation, Mass, meals, recreation periods after dinner and supper, night prayers. Twice a year we had a brief retreat or triduum, after which we devotionally 'renewed' our vows. Once a year we had an eight-day retreat, the talks given by some worthy father who was thought to have a message to preach, or an approach to the religious life, which was worth hearing. These spiritual exercises were almost all uniformly dreadful. I can recall only one of the many triduums as at all helpful. It was given by Fr Cuthbert ('Ma') King, the very picture of a crazy scholar, a retired expert in Christian archaeology, liturgy and spirituality, and a hero of mine, whom I got to know quite well later on. His triduum had a message, and one which he proceeded to put across loud and clear – the inadequacies of the spirituality of Jesuitism in comparison with the teachings of St Francis de Sales. His valid point, which he may have slightly overstated, was that Francis de Sales was a thoroughly humane character, whereas Ignatius, a man of the late medieval world, was not. It was a convincing performance which he was never invited to repeat. Of course, what he said was instantly dismissed on the grounds that Ma was mad. But we could have done with much more instruction on different schools of Catholic spirituality. Our general spiritual diet was as thin as our intellectual one, and we were left to our own devices. There persisted a general view that spiritual growth was something that the system and the Jesuit mode of life would automatically promote. This I was finding not to be the case.

But despite my increasingly critical attitude, before my third year I was, paradoxically, beginning to be groomed for returning to the Heythrop staff – for becoming even more deeply embedded in the very system which I was finding so unrewarding. I think I shot myself in the foot in this manner: I was still completely committed to being a Jesuit, and doggedly determined to do my very best. I worked hard, got on well with my mentors and did well in the examinations. At the very same time I was showing signs of acute critical stroppiness, and I was also getting physically run down. It was all reminiscent of my school days, when I was given an Excellent mark for work side by side with a Bad mark for conduct; or when I was made a prefect as a way of containing me and bringing me to heel. I had one important row with a teacher whom I in fact much admired – John Bligh, brilliant classicist, an Oxford prizeman of the first rank, newly returned to Heythrop to lecture on the New Testament. I disliked what I considered his over-didactic methods intensely. Questions were not allowed. No doubt he was very uncomfortable with the job he had been given to do, but I took no account of this and refused to attend his meticulous lectures. For this I was punished. I was given a spell of detention at Heythrop in the summer vacation and made to produce six essays, set by Bligh, on St John's Gospel. Bloodymindedly and out to show them what I was worth, I worked very hard at them, sent them off to the United States, where Bligh happened to be lecturing, and got back a kindly letter (I have it still) which ended: 'after a quick look through them, I cannot help suspecting that you have learned much more this way than you would have gained by attending my lectures. That is one of the sad things about being a professor'. The essays were in fact the best thing I had ever written, and a somewhat perverse proof of what was wrong with the whole system. But I was touched by Bligh's gracious reply and very grateful for it. He was equally kind to me when I finished up on the Heythrop staff with him. Then early one morning in the late 1960s he simply dropped everything and walked out of the Jesuits. Feeling I was somehow still in his debt, I tracked him down to North Oxford where he was temporarily living, and we cheerily drank lemonade together in the garden. He later went on, I believe, to Canada to live the academic life for which he was so well fitted. He was one of a number of big losses that the Jesuits just shrugged off.

I have often wondered since why those with whom I found I had most sympathy in those days eventually finished up outside the Society – Barney McCann, Kevin McHugh, John Bligh – and there were to be a number of others later. Perhaps if I had had the wit and the experience (or guidance – which was non-existent) I might have been led to see that I could have been developing some kind of latent unease with the Jesuits. But I cannot recall that I was. Superficially at least, I felt completely unaffected. Fatally, I also think I felt flattered by being considered for a job on the Heythrop staff. I was certainly being treated with nothing but kindness. After I had taken my deserved punishment for my bad behaviour towards Bligh, I was sent for three or four weeks to the South of France by a decent Provincial (John Coventry) to stay in Avignon and visit Roman archaeological remains in Provence. So I was in good order to begin my third year.

I continued to work hard. For one thing, work was a great help in combatting the increasing boredom of rural life and the undemanding course of studies. There was just one theology lecturer who, to my mind, stood out from all the others and suited my theological tastes: Fr Hugh Lyons, who dealt with the central topics of the Incarnation and the Eucharist. He struck people as a prayerful, spiritual person. For a short time he had been novice-master, but his true gift was for the delicately nuanced presentation of orthodox dogmatic theology – nuanced, I would say, with a feel for the spiritual values enshrined in the Church's doctrinal tradition. No other lecturer seemed able to get this feel across. The price he seemed to pay for the possession of this gift was very high. He was shy, neurotic, over-sensitive, living mostly *incommunicado* in his room in the Heythrop cellar, racked with migraine and mocked by the more robust members of staff. He also needed to spend long periods away from the place, and to be carefully nursed by understanding nuns in Hampstead. But in him I seemed to recognize what the gift for theology might amount to. He had, I would say, a way of actually 'believing' the doctrines he taught which was intelligent and not at all uncritical, and which afforded a glimpse of the deep Catholic vision which they exist to express. There was nothing in his teaching which was explicitly along these lines, but the feel and the taste of it was certainly there. Not surprisingly, most dismissed him as having only one idea – even though that idea happened to be, as I thought, close to what Catholicism could be said to be about. And it should be remembered that if every lecturer had possessed only one such idea, we would have been in theological clover. In the course of the third year there was much discussion among the authorities about which subjects in theology a trio of us would be asked to teach back at Heythrop. The jobs on offer were dogmatic theology, moral theology and Canon Law. I was assigned the first of these, and I was happy that this lot fell to me. I still disliked the whole system of studies, but among the limited range of possible jobs dogmatic theology began to sound not too bad. So it looked as though my future was settled.

My theological interests were further stimulated by an encounter with a venerable figure from the past history of Anglican theology. This was Dr Henry Major, the arch-modernist from the early years of the century, founder of Ripon Hall Oxford and of 'The Modern Churchman', the learned journal of the Modern Churchman's Union. Dr Major had been formally arraigned for heresy, and acquitted, in 1931; the last Anglican, I think, to be so. The official Anglican judgement on his view of the resurrection had been that it was 'temerarious'. He was the maternal grandfather of two Jesuit colleagues of mine, Mick and Billy Hewett. With their mother, Molly, they would take me over to Merton-on-Otmoor, north of Oxford, where Dr Major, now aged 90-plus, had been Rector since his time in Oxford early in the century. At one time he had been a Fellow of Exeter College. While the rest of the family talked, I had long theological conversations with him through his primitive hearing aid. He seemed pretty orthodox to me, though on occasions theologically naughty. He had a twinkle in his eye as he teased me, I think, with his views, say, on baptism, first quoting Matthew 28.19 and giving what seemed to me a sound exegesis of it, then adding: 'Of course, brother, I do not believe that our dear Lord ever used those words.' I only wish I had known then as much as I do now about Roman Catholic Modernism and George Tyrrell. Henry Major had known Tyrrell quite well, along with other Roman and Anglican worthies on the Modernist scene; and I would have been able to get some wonderful vignettes of that period from him. His memory for the past – say, from 1900–20 – was very strong, and he would even confuse me occasionally with figures from that time. He was a charming and fascinating man to know.

&

My rather dormant interest in being ordained priest quickened as my third year of theology went on. This was the next step in progressing through the Jesuit system. I passed the most important practical test which had to do directly with proceeding to the priesthood – the Driving Test for hearing confessions – as well as the hurdle of further *informationes*, those four private questionnaires on my general and particular suitability. Despite the problems I had caused at Heythrop, I do not recall that this time I was even said to be 'un peu difficile'. Perhaps the goalposts had been shifted in view of the fact that I was wanted back on the staff. Or again, it might even be the case that since I wanted to be ordained, my behaviour actually had improved just in time. Superiors, I know, took the credit for my improvement, but with little justification. The fact was that I wanted to be ordained because the priesthood was a part of the Jesuit vocation on which I had embarked. As I have already said, I do not think I would have wanted to be a priest in any other context. The priesthood was a *sine qua non* of what I wanted to be. Pastorally speaking, I had no personal experience of what it might be like to be a working priest; and I still had not met such a priest, save in passing, in my time in the Jesuits. Such ideas of the working priesthood as I had came chiefly from novels or clerical anecdote. Before ordination the possibility of real experience of the working priesthood was in any case ruled out. We were busy with our studies, and in those days in the Jesuits the diaconate, much used these days for the acquisition of pastoral experience, was conferred only forty-eight hours before the priesthood itself. Whatever one's personal aspirations, the Jesuit attitude to the priesthood was pretty functional. Given the range of likely occupations once the training was over, opportunities of exercising the priesthood would, in most cases, be limited to possible supply work during the school or academic vacations. Parish work usually came much later on, with late middle age or retirement. Provided that we turned out to be reliable confessors, and appreciated the need for efficient church services to start on time when we were called on to perform them, we would be satisfactory Jesuit priests. It must be remembered that pastoral theology and pastoral training in the modern mode were both still in their infancy. We did have to attend dismal sessions on Sunday mornings in which one of us had to preach a mock sermon to his fellows – an exercise called 'Tones' – and have it criticized afterwards. There was also an even more meaningless annual ordeal in which each one had to preach in the refectory to the whole community as they ate their supper. Supremely artificial as these situations were, they might possibly have been better than nothing by way of learning to preach. Whether any of these sermons would have been understood by the normal faithful never became clear. Of any particular spirituality of the priesthood, as distinct from the kind of Jesuit spirituality I had been assimilating for the last fourteen years, I knew nothing. Thus, for instance, priestly celibacy as such had no relevance alongside the religious chastity to which I was already vowed. The priesthood, its spirituality and its practice were somehow taken for granted: largely taken as read. But without it there was no possibility of progressing further in the Society.

Preparations for ordination gathered speed. Once more Paul Brassell took the stage to instruct us in administering the sacraments. Theatrical to the last, he made us baptize and anoint large baby dolls which lay in his bed – but we had to do it very gingerly, because he had covered them, as an added hazard, with the large, livid spots of what can only have been terminal measles or chicken-pox. We also had to learn to celebrate Mass with exaggerated care – the Latin Tridentine Mass, of course – until we were word, gesture and vesture perfect. Vatican II was still considering the use of the vernacular in the liturgy, but no changes had been introduced by the time I was ordained. The rigid form of the Latin Low Mass invited a scrupulous perfectionism in its performance that was strongly recommended to us. You could tell a Jesuit, they said, by the meticulous attention he gave to detail in his celebration of Mass, by his reverent bearing, and by his timing – he started spot on time and took precisely thirty minutes. At the end of my Mass examination I received a single phrase of criticism in a brief note from my examiner, Francis Clark, now retired as Reader in Religious Studies at the Open University, a post he took on his own retirement from the Jesuits. The note read: 'Tilting head when doffing biretta'. A bookable offence, but I had passed.

I was ordained to the priesthood on 31 July 1962. On two previous days I had been ordained sub-deacon and deacon. The ordaining prelate was the Archbishop of Birmingham, Francis Grimshaw. A few of the class of '59 were ordained in London, but the dozen or so of us ordained at Heythrop were each allowed the statutory twelve guests only. With a complex family background like mine this made for great (and lasting) problems to do with who should be invited. To avoid offending more people than was strictly necessary, I made do with 11 guests, and we had a very pleasant and memorable day. I celebrated my first Mass in Oxford the next day in the chapel of Campion Hall, with my brother Alan serving. We repaired to the Golden Cross near Carfax for lunch, and then dispersed. I went back with my mother, Alan and Barbara to Leyland, and I stayed at St Wilfrid's Preston for a few days' holiday. My family had given me unstinting support in the fourteen years it had taken me to get to ordination – little did they know that they were to prove an even greater support in the years ahead. Then I went to the inescapable community villa at Barmouth, and eventually back to Heythrop, very freshly ordained and no doubt full of my new priestly self, but still with several years of study to come before I could actually start work.

෨

By now I was happy enough with the idea that I was to teach theology. I realized it could be an almost ideal time to be starting to do so. I was rigorously schooled in the old scholastic methods, yet Vatican II was just about to try to open up the theological field with certain modern insights and some much-needed emphasis on the pastoral needs of the Church. An age of transition was just about to dawn, and I would be in a good position where I would have to keep up with current theological thinking. This I tried hard to do, not without success, until I was overtaken by problems arising from the nature of theological thinking itself.

But for the moment everything remained the same. The first Vatican II document *Sacrosanctum Concilium* (The Constitution on the Sacred Liturgy) was published on 4 December 1963, more than a year after my ordination. I gladly fell in with the custom by which the 'fourth-year Fathers', as we were called, might take on the running of a small 'parish' somewhere among the North Oxfordshire villages. There must have ten or more outlying villages where the sparse Catholic families were visited, and where Mass was said on Sundays and feast-days. I took on the village of Ramsden, not far from the town of Witney. An old cowshed in the middle of the village had been donated and converted the year before into a pleasant little chapel to which thirty or forty of the faithful could come to Mass. Running this little 'parish' I found very enjoyable, and it made a good change from an uninterrupted regime of study. I got there by ageing motor-bike over country lanes in all weathers – the start of the dalliance I enjoyed with several motor-bikes over the next twenty years. We had Latin Mass on Sundays, of course, except that the readings were in English and the congregation made all the responses to the priest – the 'Dialogue' Mass. I heard confessions before Mass, and on Thursdays I could visit houses and farms to see Catholics who did not mind being visited. The people were friendly and tolerant, and as far as I know, I did not do any positive harm. But I must have seemed – and in fact felt – a wondrously remote figure as I putt-putted around the Oxfordshire countryside. I had had virtually no contact with the ordinary world as I had orbited round it in my religious and largely academic capsule for the last fourteen years, and my brief and happy experience of Ramsden hardly provided much of a splashdown. I would need to go through some quite severe re-entry problems before I could claim to have re-contacted the human race. Ordination was, of course, no panacea for the amazing innocence, sheer inexperience, and scary naivety of judgement that I began to discover in myself.

For the moment there was nothing I could do about it, since the cycle of our doctrinal treatises was moving on again, and there was still a lot of work for me to do. Early in 1963 formal lectures came to an end for me, and it was time to begin my last revision for the final examination in June. This was the so-called 'Points' examination – the two-hour Latin oral I mentioned previously, in which the main theses in philosophy and theology had to be offered to a board of four examiners who would select those they wished to hear defended. On the result of this examination – in Latin, *Ad Gradum* – depended the grade in the Jesuits to which I would be finally assigned. In the event I did very well in the protracted Latin oral – all four examiners gave me maximum marks and I received a congratulatory letter from the Jesuit Provincial. My overall final result was a First, and it was duly reported in *The Times*. I might have thought I had beaten the system, but they were determined, I think, to get me back on the staff.

Thus ended my days of undergraduate theology. It had been a time of personal ups and downs. The system of studies I considered dreadful, but I had tried hard to make the most of it. In my usual way, I had enjoyed the process of learning. And in my usual way, I had wanted to be accepted and to be a leading member of the group to which I belonged, and my desire had been granted. I retained my usual outspokenness, but I was not perceived as a threat to the establishment. I had become too fond of belonging to it for that, and too flattered by the Jesuit authorities' desire to see me back on the Heythrop staff. I was getting dangerously close to becoming thoroughly domesticated in the Jesuit household. I had been well enough trained as a priest who could function with efficiency (and, frankly, not much else) in most areas of the pastoral field, though I was well aware of the danger of seeming to have more experience and practical wisdom than I actually had at my command. For my age, thirty-two, I was still immature. As far as my future field of study was concerned, I felt that I had barely scratched the surface of what the Church's doctrinal tradition had to offer, and that there must be much more to be said about it than had hitherto been revealed. I felt I was faced with a still widely unexplored territory – a land where religious wisdom and insight might reside. With my background in classics, I felt I would be chiefly interested in early Christian theology. So off I headed to St Wilfrid's Preston to do a little parish work, read Thomas Hardy, see my family in Leyland, and, when I was off duty, go on long restorative walks in the Lake District and the Lancashire hills with Barney McCann.

Before I could proceed further along the Jesuit trail, and before I could start work, there were still two more obstacles or tests to be surmounted. I had to do my year of 'tertianship' – meant to be a long spiritual refresher course, including another full round of Ignatius' *Spiritual Exercises*, to brace and tune the interior life of the soul, which was assumed to have, hardly surprisingly, wilted under the ceaseless round of studies. It was also referred to as the *schola affectus* – the place where the young (or now not so young) priest, finished with academic studies, could get back in touch with his religious feelings and his spiritual life – assuming, of course, that he had any left. After that, I would also need to get my doctorate in theology. I had now been fifteen years in the Jesuits, and I had been indulgently fast-tracked to the point at which I had arrived. I would say that I had become pretty self-satisfied. I thought I had weathered those years quite well. But, for all that I now had a well-defined future in the Society, I had also become dissatisfied and critical of its institutional ways, and certainly of the system we had all been so indiscriminately put through. I had not been slow to voice my criticism from time to time, but my petty rebelliousness had been smiled on by my Superiors, particularly during theology, in the justified realization that, once I had ordination to the priesthood in prospect, I would more or less come to heel. More than that: the authorities had convinced me – not perhaps without a touch of cynicism – that I would be better off studying and teaching theology in an academic and scholarly environment, whatever its short-comings, than taking my chances in the knockabout life of school-mastering. I assumed, for once, that they were right; and teaching theology seemed a good way of becoming a useful member of the English Province. I was prepared to ignore the fact that my uneasy past experiences had left certain buried traces of discon-tent that showed no outward signs as yet – certain seeds, not yet adequately fertilized, that still had to strike root and push their shoots up into the light of day. Or, to resort to a more violent imagery, I believe that certain time-bombs had already been planted, and were quietly ticking away deep in the cellars of my mind. The ticking got louder throughout the 1970s, but it was only towards the end of the 1980s that they would begin to explode.

Would the tertianship, perhaps, serve to defuse them? In September 1963 I went to Münster in Westphalia in Germany for what was technically the third year of 'probation' – third, that is, in addition to the two years of novitiate – prior to pronouncing final vows. The Provincial (John Coventry) asked me if I wanted to go there by way of making amends for having deprived me of the opportunity of studying theology in France, and as something of a reward for my hard work at Heythrop. This was typically decent of him, and I did not want to go to the English Province tertianship at St Beuno's in North Wales, a house I instinctively disliked. The tertianship in Münster was German-speaking, and in my year it took Jesuit priests from all the German Provinces, from France, the United States, Holland and Australia, as well as myself from England. We made a good international group of about twenty-four. Some of the Germans had been in the same community as myself in Pullach nearly ten years before. The 'Instructor', as the Jesuit in charge is grimly called, was Fr Walter Stein, a German with a background of work in Brazil, a stern-looking character, but pleasant and honest, with no pretensions (I was delighted to discover) about being a spiritual guru. Münster itself is a neat, attractive North German city with an old centre and a distinguished University which has twin Protestant and Catholic theology faculties. I already had sufficient German to make my regulation stay of ten months there fairly easy going.

Münster was also the centre of the British zone of 'military occupation'; so for an English-speaking priest like myself there was plenty of stand-in chaplaincy work on offer in the various army and air force installations around North Germany. This form of pastoral work came as a welcome and regular weekend relief from daily life in the tertianship, which consisted mainly of a replication of life back in the novitiate. Besides our daily religious exercises, there was domestic cleaning to be done, serving at table, endless washing up, work in the garden and the park which surrounded the house. Somewhat more time was allotted to studying the Jesuit *Constitutions* and those parts of Canon Law which relate to the Society. The priesthood was exercised in frequent supply-work in parishes in the city, and, in my case, in the British and Canadian army camps. It might have been because of this undoubted distraction from the strict purposes of the tertianship that I did not find that my year in Germany had much positive effect on me. But I do not think so. I also found that there was something altogether too factitious, too artificial, about the whole notion of an organized course in spiritual renewal, rigidly planned with a definite form and woodenly imposed at a fixed point in one's development. No doubt the general idea was originally a good one, but it had simply become yet another stage in the propagation of systematic Jesuitism. I am not saying that I did not need spiritual help and renewal – possibly even urgently needed it. But the tertianship failed, I think, to work for me. It left me still spiritually cold.

I cannot conceal the fact that the most memorable part of the year was spent outside the Jesuit house. I had a regular weekend job as Catholic chaplain at the Windsor Boys School in Hamm. There were some stalwart Catholics on the staff, and they gave me great support. An Army Volkswagen would pick me up early on Saturday morning, and return me to the house late on Sunday evening, thus reducing the tertianship to a five-day week. I quite liked the work with the Catholic boys, who were decent kids who had been frequently moved round the world to a number of similar British Army schools as the family tracked the father's career in the armed forces. But I did not enjoy it as much as I had my time as a scholastic in Liverpool. In the meantime I had changed, of course, and I was now a priest. I had, of course, no teaching responsibilities. I had also probably become even more abstractly intellectual than I had been when I left Oxford. I found myself lacking the kind of spontaneity and easy familiarity that is so helpful when dealing with the young. In my dealings with the teachers, with families, and with the other military chaplains, however, I felt more at home. I spent some very happy times with the army chaplains at the retreat centre of Benkhausen, a moated Schloss in Lower Saxony with its own resident ghost, a lady whom I heard but never saw. At Christmas and Easter time extra priests were needed to go out from there to say Mass in the large number of camps around North Germany, and I was not needed at Hamm in the school holidays. On Christmas Day, for instance, I was taken round three or four camps – Hamelin, Minden, Rinteln – to say Mass, preach a brief sermon, and then rush off to the next one. The resident genius of Benkhausen was the unforgettable Fr Sidney Lescher, an Old Stonyhurst boy and distinguished chaplain, confined to a wheelchair by a car accident. He ran the place and everyone in it with enormous vigour and good humour. Later I tried my hand at giving short retreats both to boys and to soldiers, and I was truly grateful to have Sid around in the background. I think it hardly mattered how well or badly I performed. Whatever good was done seemed to emanate from Sid in his wheelchair. For Christmas his friends and family turned up. The moat froze over. We had to devour the stores before 6 January 1964, since the retreat house was then moving lock, stock and barrel to Cologne, and, by some arcane military regulation, the stores could not be transferred. The rest of Christmas and the New Year was, to put it euphemistically, Dickensian, and it all passed in a happy blur. I doubt if this was what the tertianship was meant to be.

Lent was little better. The tradition was that the tertians spent Lent away from Münster doing pastoral work. In my case this was with the Canadian army near Soest, saying Mass, hearing confessions, giving a retreat. I arrived at the large camp on 17 March 1964, when all ranks were celebrating the fiftieth anniversary of the inauguration of their regiment – Princess Patricia's Highland Light Infantry, founded on St Patrick's Day 1914. It was early afternoon, and everyone was already drunk. The retreat was due to start the following day. To pass the time I attended an ill-advised ice hockey match between the sergeants and the men. It was a sheer slaughter. Blood and bandages were everywhere. Next morning, after a very noisy night and just before I went to the chapel to preach my first sermon, I had my breakfast in the officers' mess. My foot caught something under the table – a young lieutenant, out like a light, still in his dress uniform from the celebratory dinner the night before. In chapel I was faced with two or three hundred hung-over faces. I vividly recall the wide scatter of brown, impassive, Native American features. The start of the retreat can only have been a disaster. As usual, I had prepared my material meticulously. It was ornately theological and couched in my best academic style. Fortunately there can have been no one in the chapel who was sufficiently conscious to notice. I improved quickly after that, and the whole three days passed off without incident. I still blush to think what a fool I must have looked and sounded. But the Canadians were friendly, and the Vingt-Deux (the Canadian Black Watch) – fearsomely tough – were particularly kind. I met some delightful Catholic families and I was sorry to leave. At the end of Lent the tertians gathered in Mainz to attend the Pan-German Liturgical Congress, convoked to celebrate the publication of Vatican II's *Constitution on the Sacred Liturgy*. It was moving to sit in the long cathedral and see the Church's great liturgical luminaries – Josef-Andreas Jungmann, Balthasar Fischer, and the like – come forward to be given standing ovations for their foundational work, now finally canonized by the Council.

But all this was outside the tertianship proper. We had made the Long Retreat, the full *Spiritual Exercises* of Ignatius Loyola, before Christmas. It was thirty days of heavy spiritual going, interspersed with two or three rest days, when we were allowed out of the grounds for a brief walk. Fr Stein's daily talks were, I think, competent without being inspiring. The exercitant is led, naturally enough, to pass considerable time reviewing his past life. But this I found a boring exercise, since, frankly, there was still not much of a life to review. My past no doubt contained its share of routine sins and shortcomings, but there was nothing at all lurid in it, whether through lack of motive or lack of opportunity. Amendment, as always, was needed, but nothing all that drastic. Grand conversions, at this late stage, were hardly called for. And in any case, the future now looked as though it was destined to be very similar to the immediate past, and this limited the scope for such amendment as was either needed or possible. Again, even in its positive preaching of the following of Christ's example and purpose for the rest of my life, the Long Retreat fell flat. After all, what was I supposed to have been doing for the last fifteen years? This is no criticism of the *Exercises*, which have a unique role to play in the lives of people who need, and are prepared to face, a full-blown conversion in their way of life. But

I had no experience of being in such existential extremity, either before or in the novitiate or, even less, now. It was as if I was being asked to pose in artificially dramatic positions, or to work myself up into a state of religious enthusiasm or fervour that I had no reason to feel. I tried my best, of course. I performed the required midnight meditations, fasted a little, performed some penance, scrutinized my behaviour, examined my conscience, read Thomas à Kempis' *The Imitation of Christ*, kept total silence. Little, if anything, happened. I felt sated and bored with spiritual overkill. At least the Long Retreat in the novitiate had had the attraction of novelty; but by now I must have done well over a dozen annual eight-day retreats based on the *Exercises*, and even Ignatius' imaginative pedagogy had become jaded and largely ineffective. Later in the tertianship we all had to write up an eight-day retreat that we ourselves might give at some time in the future. I did mine carefully, and used it fairly often in the years to come. What it turned out to be, inevitably, was a well-crafted course in remedial theology, of little, or no directly, spiritual value. After a number of years I stopped giving retreats altogether, on the grounds that I needed a change from teaching theology all year round. I doubt if anyone was the loser.

When not engaged in other matters, Fr Stein lectured on the Society the whole year round, adequately and not uninterestingly. As the year went on, and thanks to the openness of our discussions, our interest veered towards the question of whether the Jesuits were still an effective vehicle for the work of the Holy Spirit in the Church. This rather basic question emerged because it turned out that it was a matter of genuine concern to a fair number of tertians who seem to have been sensing in themselves the kind of misgivings I shared. It was much to Fr Stein's credit, I think, that the matter was discussed frankly. The general conclusion was, rather surprisingly, negative. It was not felt that the Society, with its current system, was an effective organ in the Church. It was certainly felt that it still could be, as long as there was a considerable reform of its training and its operations. I felt relieved by this conclusion. I was obviously not alone in my doubts. It must seem odd that a whole year of tertians concluded that the religious order to which they were all about to commit themselves irrevocably was cripplingly defective. Of course, there was something academic and abstract both about the discussion and the conclusion, and in practice life went on as usual. But it all sounded a welcome note of honesty and clarity about the Jesuit system of those days, and the system, if there still is a system, has doubtlessly been much changed since.

It was with this note in my ears that I left the tertianship and Germany at the end of June 1964 and returned to England. I did not feel I had got all that much out of my year in Münster apart from some broadening of my still very narrow experience. I had met and worked with other people who, not altogether unlike myself, lived artificially bolstered and restricted lives; namely, military personnel. This encounter perhaps did me a limited amount of good; but I did not feel that I had done much good to them. I was never going to be a pastorally effective priest. I had all the theological and technical skills, of course, but I lacked basic human experience and the spontaneous understanding and the sympathetic and warm interest in other people's lives which a good priest should have. The years of serious academic study seemed to have drained the strength from such human feelings as I might have mustered. Far from reviving them, the tertianship did not even bring me back into contact with them. It was no *schola affectus* as far as I was concerned, either religiously or (to use a distinction I would not now make) humanly speaking. It had certainly not served to disperse the seeds of doubt I had been quietly nurturing about the Society. As yet another, and almost the last, stage in the imposition of Jesuitism I was pleased to put the tertianship firmly behind me. I would have to reconcile myself to becoming what I seemed to be destined to turn out – a teacher of academic theology. From Münster I travelled on to Preston, via Oxford and Heythrop, and began some background reading in early patristic theology, the field in which I hoped to jump the next, and last, hurdle – my doctorate.

⁊

I moved off by train to Rome in September 1964. I had not yet contracted the habit of flying. I travelled via Munich, an old haunt, and then straight on to Rome. This was new territory. I had never been to Italy before, and I spoke no Italian. I was trying to arrive in Rome before the Gregorian University opened in October, in order to pick up at least some of the language. In this I failed. Rome was simply not the place to do it. There were too many English-speakers around, mainly congenial Americans; and too many distractions for an old classicist. Again, it quickly became clear that Italian was scarcely necessary – a fatal discovery. For study purposes there was always Latin, and most Italians I met wanted to speak English anyway. I never learned to do more than stumble along in sub-standard Italian, and now I have forgotten even how to do that. I regret this very much.

My much-travelled trunk had gone on ahead and was waiting for me at the Collegio Bellarmino in the Via del Seminario, right in the heart of Rome, close to the Pantheon. The Bellarmino was the old Gregorian University, across from the Jesuit church of Sant'Ignazio. A gravelled quadrangle (in which we played volleyball) was surrounded by several floors of rooms and wide corridors. It was a prime site and a marvellous centre at which to live. It housed Jesuit postgraduates like myself from all over the world – about 120 of them, I would guess. Most of them were engaged in doctoral research prior to returning to their provinces, chiefly to take up university teaching posts. Some were doing a one-year sabbatical, updating themselves in their chosen fields. There were two main language groups, English and Spanish, and only a handful of Italians. The Rector was an amiable American, Frank Furlong, and among the older Jesuits retired there were distinguished Jesuit worthies like René Arnou and Paolo Dezza, fomerly professors at the Gregorian and authors of 'philosophy' textbooks of the severest Roman kind. It was a good community in which to live and work. The general tone was good. People were engaged on tasks which were personal to them, and they knew what they were supposed to be doing. They wanted to get their doctorates done with and go home and start work. But Rome itself is not, I am convinced, the best of all possible places for work. The research facilities, superb in some limited fields, are rather patchy and unreliable, and the distractions are potentially endless. What was indispensable, however, was the experience of coming into contact with the living Roman Church, however depressing the effect might turn out to be.

I found myself in a wide circle of good companions – Irish, Australian, American, one or two English. We enjoyed a weekly English-speaking Happy Hour, when we had cheap – very cheap – pre-dinner drinks. I learned to mix a large quantity of Manhattan cocktail in a plastic bucket – two bottles of red Vermouth to one bottle of Bourbon. I had no other means of getting the measurements right. I was also responsible for the supply of ice from the kitchen. Often we went on to a local tratto-ria for a pizza, or, if you were American, a steak. Later we would drink Italian or Spanish brandy – Cavallino Rosso or Fundador. None of this had any noticeable effect on anyone. If once a week we made life in Rome fun, it was because we needed to do so. Almost everyone one was working hard to a deadline when our several provinces wanted us back. The kind of individual research we were doing meant spending long hours on our own –

the real bane of doctoral research, until you adjust to it. With Clarence Gallagher, a long-standing friend from the English Province researching in Canon Law and already much at home in Rome, I visited one or two Italian cities. We had a memorable time in Florence, now my favourite city; and we saw Naples at Christmastime, assiduously visiting all the surrounding archaeological sites – Capri, Pompeii, Herculaneum, and the Campi Flegrei background to Virgil's *Aeneid VI*, which we had both studied at Oxford. Later I went to see the restored Monte Cassino and its awesome fields of war dead. From the social point of view, my time in Rome was a great success; but I was there to work.

And work I did. The Gregorian University, originally the Roman College, had been founded in the time of Ignatius Loyola, and was by now more than 400 years old. It was staffed and run by the Jesuits, and it was the leading institute for theology in Rome. I was entered for the 'biennium', a two-year set of postgraduate theology courses which included the submission of a doctoral thesis or dissertation of publishable quality written under the direction of one of the established Gregorian staff. The standards were rigorous and the drop-out rate quite high. A good number took longer than the initial two years to finish their thesis. With my background in classics, and in the hope of lighting on a well-defined topic which would enable me to finish off my already over-long education as quickly as possible, I chose to work in the field of patristics – the theology of the early Christian 'Fathers' and theologians. With this in mind I was accepted by Fr Antonio Orbe as his pupil. Orbe was a Spaniard, and arguably the world's top scholar in the strange but crucial field of early Gnosticism. He was shy, very retiring, rather deaf, charming and exigent. His knowledge was formidable, and he would have been far better known than he was had he not written his thick published volumes on Gnosticism in Spanish, not a language which is all that commonly used by the world's scholars. We got on well together. His direction was clear and tough, but he gave me my head when he thought I was on the right lines. His lectures on Irenaeus of Lyons, a *tour de force* delivered not from notes but simply from a large eighteen-century edition of this greatest of early theologians, with whose works Orbe was completely familiar, were the best thing I had heard since Oxford.

After busily fishing around in patristics for a while I hooked, with great luck, an excellent topic for my thesis – the short, well-known, but controversial text, probably of the third century and said to be the work of Hippolytus of Rome, the *Contra Noetum*. The sole eleventh-century Greek manuscript was in the Vatican Library, so I spent many weeks there, poring over my text in what must be the world's greatest collection of original materials, where the working conditions and the library services were excellent, and where some of the ceilings had been painted by Raphael. Daily I had the heavy, superbly bound codex, *Vaticanus Graecus 1431*, delivered to my desk. I handled it with all the care due to an object which was rightly described by an understandably anxious library as 'one of the monuments of Western civilization'. Full-size colour reproductions of the pages I required were provided free. At the adjoining desk worked Hubert Jedin, the great historian of the Council of Trent, working through rolls of original documents. For those in love with learning, surely this was very heaven. My luck held, and I was able to come up with a completely original proof that the short work I was studying was not, as scholars had long tended to assume, the end-fragment of a much longer work, but a small, complete, pamphlet-type theological diatribe of a well-known literary type. In the final stages of writing my thesis I returned to Oxford in order to have access to the Bodleian Library where I could work more quickly in familiar surroundings. My completed edition of the Greek text and the thesis which accompanied it was examined by Orbe and other experts. I passed *magna cum laude*. The work was rushed at the end and was not without its defects. I ducked the key question of authorship, though I am convinced the work is not by Hippolytus of Rome (allegedly the first anti-pope). He seems to me to be an early literary fabrication, largely concocted (not unlike the fake sixteenth-century statue of him which Pope John XXIII proudly placed in the entrance-hall of the Vatican Library) out of stray writings which happened to be in search of an author. I also steered well clear of adding more to what had already been written about the work's theology. My thesis, in fact, concentrated almost entirely on the text itself. It was eventually published and received decent reviews from knowledgeable people. But like all potentially upsetting findings in the scholarly and scientific worlds, it failed to make much of an impression. From time to time I am amused to spot my name and work quoted in obscure footnotes in esoteric monographs and journals, more often than not with approval, even if the writer has failed to take account of what I actually said. But recently I was immensely pleased to see that my little edition of the *Contra Noetum* has been canonized in the *Thesaurus Linguae Graecae*, an amazing CD-ROM collection, published by the University of California, of all extant ancient Greek texts from Homer in the eighth century BC to AD 600, in addition to further key texts which were written between then and the fall of Byzantium in 1453. I am happy to think it has found a good home. For me, the real value of my research lies in the lessons it taught me. I learned that the primary faculty employed in understanding anything, or in interpreting anything correctly, is imaginative insight. Without this even the splendid resources of the Vatican Library would have got me nowhere, and I would have had nothing worth writing about.

I say this, not because I happen to hold anybody's particular theory of the human understanding, but because I can vividly recall the actual experience which accompanied the exercise of my own imaginative insight into the structure of the text I was working on. I had been studying it closely for a year or more and with no striking results in immediate prospect. Then one afternoon at the Bellarmino, during siesta time (I was actually lying on my bed), the complex structuration of the text was suddenly, without warning and with complete clarity, 'revealed' – not a word to use lightly, but the right one in this case, the only word I can think of which is adequate to the experience. Of course, the 'revelation' did not come out of the blue: it was closely connected to the very considerable amount of serious work I had already put in over a long period. I knew the text very well; but the imaginative insight I suddenly acquired into how it worked as a text belonged to some different order of knowing. It was not the sort of thing that could have been acquired by the quantitative accumulation of any further 'factual' knowledge. It was much more than the sum of my research efforts. It was a brand new, fresh-created insight which stopped me in my research tracks. Without it I would have gone on compiling the all-too-familiar kind of worthy but pedestrian commentary on the text which would have won over the examiners by boring them into submission. The experience of having that insight – of the penny dropping – whilst it constitutes no proof that the insight is true, was well worth all the studying I had ever done. It told me that I was now capable of seeing things for myself and as the result of my own hard work. When I displayed my findings to Orbe, he was delighted and remarked, 'Abbiamo scoperta America' – 'we have discovered America'.

I think I only ever had one other similar experience. Some years later, I was supplying at Eastertime for Fr Bernard Basset in his tiny parish on the Isles of Scilly. For several weeks I had been poring over St Mark's Gospel, which I happened to be teaching as a Greek text at Heythrop, by then in the University of London. Every day I walked almost right round St Mary's along the seashore vaguely brooding on the structure and the meaning of the text. Once again, after quite a long time, but less dramatically than before, the penny dropped, and a surprisingly coherent plan of the structure of most of the Gospel (but not of the passion narrative) fell into place in my mind, again brand new and fresh-created. I later wrote it all up and expounded its meaning. When it was published, comments tended to be of the usual conde-scending kind, though another scholar kindly went on to apply my scheme to the whole Gospel. But I had had the same experi-ence of the sudden onset of imaginative insight as I did with my thesis, and I found it very exciting. One notable scholar, pre-committed in any case to the quirky view of the priority of St Matthew's Gospel, wrote to me: 'There is nothing in what you say except the power of your own mind.' I have never known quite what to make of this – on the face of it – rather offensive remark. But, oddly enough, I do not feel offended by it. It came from someone who had obviously never enjoyed the aesthetic and intellectual excitement caused by the kind of imaginative insight I have been vouchsafed. I am well aware of the dangers inherent in this apparently unmethodical approach to scholarship; but I do not see how method can be an end in itself. Method as such will get you nowhere without some measure of insight – a fact which is only too obvious from the shelves of second- and third-hand commentary to be found in our larger libraries. I would much rather reflect on the sheer pleasure afforded by my two-penn'orth of 'inspiration' than enjoy a scholarly reputation for having impeccably compiled mountains of alleged 'facts' and other people's opinions – which perhaps, yet again, may only go to show that, for all my love of learning, I was never to become what passes for a true scholar.

In the course of my second year in Rome, and in my eighteenth year in the Society, I pronounced my final vows. I had proved successful at my studies, and my religious observance and general behaviour had been declared unobjectionable. I was admitted into the top grade of 'solemnly professed' Jesuits – those who are allowed to take four vows, the three 'solemn' vows of religion – poverty, chastity and obedience – plus a special vow 'concerning missions', which in effect put the professed at the potential disposal of the Pope. In addition, the professed Jesuit makes five further 'simple' vows which bind him closely to his

Superiors. Although I was understandably very proud of my finally achieving full membership of the Society, I knew that the canonical complexities of different grades among the Jesuits meant little or nothing in practice. Not all the solemnly professed were high-flyers, and many of the most useful members belonged to the lower grades. I felt this to be especially true of the lay-brothers, or 'temporal coadjutors' as they were technically called. In their unappreciated ranks were some of the best Jesuits I ever met.

About twenty of us from all over the world took our final vows on 2 February 1966 at a concelebrated Mass in front of the tomb of Ignatius Loyola in the principal Jesuit church in Rome, the Gesù. The chief celebrant was the Jesuit Superior General, the remarkable Pedro Arrupe. It was a solemn and moving occasion which meant a great deal to me. It will have become clear that I am not a person of overt religious sensibility. I disliked, not to say suspected, the outward expression of religious feelings; and I had already begun, during my time in the Society, to have doubts about the effects of its spirituality. I had also detected traces of disillusionment deep within myself. Nonetheless, I pressed on with my final vows. I do not think I expected things to get better, or the Society suddenly to change. This, perhaps, was as good as it got. I took my final vows because I fully intended to persevere as a Jesuit. I thought I knew what I was in for, and I thought I could cope with what the future might bring.

If the experience of researching and living in Rome taught me valuable lessons about myself, other experiences taught me the same about the Roman Church. The times were favourable to this. During the periods when Vatican II was in session, ecclesiastical Rome was overrun with bishops and theologians of international standing. Thus I heard at first hand of the crafty deviousness of certain Cardinals of the Roman Curia in preventing prelates of whom they disapproved from putting their points of view to the Council. A prime example was Archbishop Thomas Roberts, an English Jesuit hero of mine and a man of radical integrity, who was simply never called on to speak. Then we naturally met some of the world's leading theologians – de Lubac, Karl Rahner, Hans Küng, Congar – and they had critical things to say about the way in which the Curia contrived to frustrate their efforts. I was able to pick up at first hand the clear impression that the Roman game has to do with power and control: control at all costs – control of the world's bishops, theologians, religious orders, the laity. Compared with the controlling exercise of sheer authoritative power, truth and justice seem to count for little. The Curia looked on itself as exercising a God-given role in the Church; and loyalty to an overwhelming sense of what they chose to see as their own pastoral responsibility, and an ingrained habit of being in charge, prevented them from welcoming the more enlightened ideas that an ecumenical Council suddenly imported into Rome. Some enlightened ideas perhaps forced themselves on the Roman consciousness, but it was not long before Rome was slipping back into its old ways.

This was very forcibly brought home to me in another Roman context. As someone who was supposedly proficient in German, I was one of a number of Jesuit postgraduates who were asked to help out on the secretarial side of the Papal Commission on Birth Control at the last of its plenary meetings before Pope Paul VI published his notorious encyclical letter *Humanae Vitae* in 1968. The Commission met in secrecy, of course, and all three of its sections were in attendance – the best Catholic experts worldwide on the theological, medical and demographic issues involved in birth control. It was a well balanced commission, fully representative of the wide spectrum of expert views held throughout the Church. All I had to do was to help others to translate and check the minutes of the theological section. This was a humble task, but I sat in on all the theological meetings, and was privy to all the arguments and conclusions reached. It was fascinating and deeply impressive. The world's greatest moral theologians – Fuchs and Zalba of the Gregorian, Ford from the United States, the admirable Redemptorist, Bernard Häring – debated and disagreed with vigour and urbanity. We were talked to – informally and intelligently – by Paul VI himself. In concert with the other sections, the theologians reached their conclusion – an overall majority in favour of a change in the Church's blanket condemnation of artificial birth control. None of the sections thought that the Vatican's current stance was either necessary or helpful. Hopes were raised that something, at last, would be done to help the married faithful in the running of their difficult lives. Very sadly, in the event nothing was done. The Pope dithered and simply followed the advice of a small conservative minority on the Commission who defended the *status quo*. He also took the line of his own Curia, who had not been officially involved in the Commission. The expert advice which he had asked for, and which had been generously given, was ignored. No explanations, of course, were felt necessary. At a final, embarrassing meeting, Paul VI thanked us all, gave us each a large flashy medal of his own pontificate, and invited us to visit the Vatican excavations under St Peter's – admittedly quite the best archaeological site in Rome. This was no compensation for the huge disappointment that most of the Commission – and most of the rest of the Catholic world – felt on the publication of his encyclical. My experience certainly fed and watered those seeds of disillusionment with the Church and its institutions which were already swelling within. I inevitably began to see the Roman exercise of authority as more than tinged with cynicism and, in its way, corrupt. The continuing exercise of power, not the honest pursuit of truth, was all that seemed to matter. But it must be remembered that I was a cradle Catholic of long standing; and I do not think that at the time I was either surprised or particularly scandalized by Roman behaviour. I do not think that many lifelong Catholics ever are. They are, more often than not, quite prepared to indulge their leaders and pardon even their obvious failings. In any case, I was now finished in Rome and I made my way back home in a positive frame of mind. At last I was about to start work. I first went up to Preston to begin preparations for teaching in September 1967. I had a good holiday touring Scotland with Barney McCann and Peter Whittall, a Jesuit on the College staff in Preston, a good friend. I was now supposed to be fully fledged as a Jesuit; but I was hardly prepared for the problems I might have to face when I tried to fly.

Chapter 6

Worlds in Conflict

The First Part of Goethe's *Faust* opens with Faust seated but restless at his desk in his high-vaulted, narrow, Gothic study. He complains, and I translate:

> Philosophy I've done, alas, along
> With casuistry and medicine,
> And, regrettably, theology as well
> – done them all, given them my passionate attention.
> I've got my Master's and my Doctorate,
> And for a good ten years I've led
> My pupils by the nose,
> First up, then down, across, awry
> – and realized there's nothing we can know.

It is as well that I did not realize, when I returned to teach at Heythrop, how apposite these words were going to be. Not literally veridical in my own case: I never studied medicine (though I had once intended to), and I never knowingly led my students astray; nor did I finish up convinced that there is nothing we can know. Yet Faust's words are broadly prophetic, if only because they point towards the struggle that awaits a thinking person who may well suppose that he has studied every relevant subject with the best of intentions, only to be suddenly stricken with the thought that he still does not know what it is all meant to mean. This was the realization that was going to overtake me, though not for a few years yet; and then I had the good fortune to be able to learn to cope with it over a mercifully prolonged period, during which I could keep on functioning satisfactorily enough at the tasks I had in hand. For me, entrance into what was going to turn into a purgatorial underworld lay through the portals of Theology – *und leider auch Theologie*. Not that I can truthfully say that I have ever regretted having studied and taught theology. In the first place, it happens to be a very interesting subject, and I enjoyed studying and teaching it at the time; secondly, I feel pleased to have survived the onset and the purgation of those particularly critical problems which are (and should be) naturally prompted by any serious theological study; and thirdly, almost any point of entry, whether through the arts or the sciences, which leads towards a life subject to the constant and critical examination of the quality of one's thinking and consciousness, and away from the *anexetastos bios* – the unexamined life – which Plato (*Apology* 38a5–6) thought no human being should be living, can be just as valid as any other.

But before I returned to Heythrop in 1967 to teach theology, I had not realized that I would not be stepping into the same river for a second time. Heythrop was now a much-changed place in a rapidly changing religious world. In the four years I had been away, the Catholic world, for far too long unused to change of any sort and neurotically suspicious of it, had at last begun to give a cautious welcome to change as a feature of church life. I suppose it must have been Vatican II's *Constitution on the Sacred Liturgy* which first showed Catholics that changes in approach and practice could be made without necessarily leading to the total abandonment of their faith. Not that all Catholics saw it that way. The laity, of course, cottoned on far more quickly and intelligently than did many of the clergy. Most of the former seemed, on the whole, pleased to be rid of Latin; but, more importantly, they felt led by the Council to suppose that their faith, despite an obvious setback like *Humanae Vitae*, might conceivably be meant to be meaningful and helpful to them in coping with their difficult lives. Above all, many of them wanted to get involved in the life of the Church. They were, after all, the Church, and the Church was theirs, and they had long felt excluded from it by the clergy. Many clergy, on the other hand, were more inclined to take fright, dig in their heels and make a heroic virtue out of resisting change in any shape or form. Around this time I was called on to undertake a few theological lectures and 'days of recollection' for the secular clergy round the country; and after my four years experience of contemporary continental Catholicism, I was struck by the lazy ignorance and arrogant resistance displayed by so many of the older priests at the very mention of any new idea. 'When I die, Pat, I don't want any of this new-fangled stuff – give me the old Latin Mass that the martyrs died for,' I heard one of them say. With the younger curates things were already somewhat different. But like Nicodemus, they felt able to come forward and speak only under cover of darkness, or at any rate when their parish priest was well out of earshot. But whether people liked it or not, the Church had moved into an era of change, and therewith of uncertainty; and people were going to stand or fall according to how they reacted to both.

Heythrop was now a newly established 'Pontifical Athenaeum', a comic title for any institution, given the English and Protestant environment into which it was introduced – a title which combined a pompous and sinister adjective with a noun which in English could only denote the top institution in London clubland. But then to most of our fellow-countrymen 'Heythrop' had only ever meant one of the country's snootier hunts. This whole Athenaeum phantasmagoria had been dreamt up since I had left, chiefly through John Carmel Heenan, the Archbishop of Westminster, in an attempt to open up what he supposed Heythrop could offer non-Jesuits, both religious and lay – a university education in Catholic theology and philosophy. It is, I find, difficult to imagine how this doomed project could ever have been taken seriously, let alone set in motion. Catholic universities may well have an important part to play in countries where Catholic higher education is not suspect, and where university education is not already easily accessible and publicly funded. Knowledge of the failure of an earlier project of Cardinal Manning's to set up a Catholic university in the 1870s in Kensington, where Catholics could get London University degrees – a far saner plan than the rural Heythrop Athenaeum – should have alerted those responsible for Heythrop to the inevitable shipwreck ahead. Heythrop, it must be remembered, was almost on the doorstep of the University of Oxford, with its distinguished Faculty of Theology and its already existing Catholic houses of study run by the Benedictines, the Dominicans, the Franciscans, and even by the Jesuits themselves.

I was no fan of the old Heythrop, and it was becoming clear that it would soon be moribund, whatever might be done to revive it. For one thing, the number of Jesuit vocations was dropping in the English Province, as almost everywhere else in the western world; and without the requirement that ecclesiastical studies need be pursued in Latin (although it was the genial Pope John XXIII, it must be remembered, who had tried hard to preserve the use of a dead language), fewer Jesuits might be expected to come from abroad to swell the number of students at Heythrop. Again, the Jesuit system of studies was happily being followed in more flexible ways, and the resources of existing universities were being regularly tapped, at least for research purposes. An exclusive dependence on Catholic institutions was on its way out. And as for the participation of lay people – were they likely to come in numbers, unfunded, into the wilds of North Oxfordshire? If they were not nuns, who would pay for them? And who would want Heythrop's Roman degrees anyway? A completely impractical triumphalism had possessed the founders of the Heythrop Pontifical Athenaeum, and I was glad not to have been involved in it.

But when I returned, there it was. Heenan was Chancellor, one or two already declining religious orders had been persuaded to build houses of residence in the capacious grounds, and there were a couple of untypical lay people who could afford to indulge their taste for theology and try for a degree which lacked the status and the standards guaranteed by a real university. I can see now, of course, that the Pontifical Athenaeum fiasco had much more to do with fond hopes of returning to a past now gone for good, and of counteracting change, than with serving the future. It sprang from minds still locked in the old-fashioned apologetics – the embattled defence of the faith against all-comers which had been the speciality of preachers like Heenan and others (many of them intelligent Jesuits) who had seemed to be so effective in the '40s and '50s, and for whom the eventual re-conversion of England to Catholicism still seemed a practical goal. In conscious, or perhaps unconscious and instinctive, opposition to the modernizing thrust of Vatican II, the Pontifical Athenaeum was part of a cracked vision in which the unchanging authority of Rome would come to be recognized in the religious and intellectual life of England. It was the measure of the extent to which leading elements in the English Catholic religious world lacked any true understanding of the realities of the ordinary world. It also displayed, to my mind, a profoundly unecumenical spirit. One of the achievements of which I shall always remain proudest was the active part I was soon able to play in the dismantling of the Heythrop Pontifical Athenaeum. Within three years of my return to teach there, it was dead in the water, though its empty hulk floated aimlessly around for a few years before it was towed off to the breaker's yard.

∞

But neither changes in my surroundings, nor any personal misgivings I may have been nurturing within, were what engrossed my attention on my return to Heythrop. I had been nineteen years in the Society by now and at last I had a job to do.

The older Heythrop staff made me welcome and proved pleasantly congenial colleagues. How many of them were happy with
the new Pontifical Athenaeum status and the consequent alterations to the work they were used to, it was difficult to tell. Most
of them were good, naturally conformist characters who went
along with what was required of them, and who, in any case,
were coming close to the end of their teaching lives. Some moved
off elsewhere to other jobs or into what counts as retirement for
Jesuits – working on some parish staff or doing pastoral chores.
But among the younger but already established staff a certain
disintegration immediately began to set in. Charles Davis was not
a Jesuit, but he had been seconded to the Pontifical Athenaeum
by Heenan. He was a very able man and the most influential
Catholic theologian in the country. Just as I returned, he left the
priesthood and got married – an event that was widely publi-
cized throughout the Church. It was just at this time, too, that
Francis Clark, a sound Jesuit theologian, did the same and
embarked on his successful career at the Open University.
Malcolm Clark, an excellent philosopher who had been a fellow-
novice of mine, also left. To judge from my conversations with
him, he was very seriously disillusioned. It was soon after this
that the peerless John Bligh walked out. But there were newer
arrivals, including myself, who seemed willing to try to make a
go of the new order of things, at least for the moment. I was
assigned the minor post of Vice-Dean of Theology, and the first
course I was given to teach was on predestination and freewill.
For all my lengthy and expensive training I had never entertained
a single original thought on this hoary theological topic. But since
there is no spur to learning a subject which can compare with
having to teach it, I decided to get down to some serious study.

I looked around at what staff were left for help and guidance,
and I was not encouraged by what seemed to be available –
except for one man, Fr Tom Gornall, a highly intelligent philosopher who had taught me fifteen years earlier. Tom, it has to be
said, had become increasingly reclusive with the passing years. A
Prestonian and an Oxford Greats man, he was an excellent writer
and teacher. His book *A Philosophy of God* (Darton, Longman and
Todd, 1962) is quite the most lucid and penetrating presentation I
know of scholastic Natural Theology. He was also a talented
musician, a fine classicist and, as his published work on Aquinas
and on John Henry Newman's letters and diaries show, a gifted
editor. I decided that I would ask him how to get started with
teaching predestination and free will. The trouble was that, as

Heythrop changed and staff departed, Tom had become intensely remote, rarely appearing in public, and hardly ever at meals – he seemed to live on bananas and on eggs boiled in a kettle – and for fresh air he worked, perhaps hopefully, at restoring the crumbling balustrades which surrounded Heythrop's formal lawns and Italian parterres. But I caught him one morning in the common room, reading the *Daily Telegraph*. I approached him cautiously and asked if he had any advice to give someone faced with my new task. He lowered the newspaper, looked into space and declared in his fluting voice: 'Two things – St Thomas, *Contra Gentiles*, 3.94; and [*crescendo*] never, *never*, NEVER, use the word "reconcile"'. He then raised his newspaper again – end of the first conversation we had had for almost a decade. But I could not have been given better or more practical advice. He had a rare gift for limpid brevity, and I had not expected much more than I got. (For some rather more extended remarks, see his important comments in 'A Note on Imagination and Thought about God' in *The Heythrop Journal* 4(1963) pp. 135-140). In easier days, when I was still at Oxford, he had given me a single quarto sheet of typed advice entitled 'How to make your Latin Prose sound like Cicero', a polished gem of distilled wisdom designed 'to make examiners purr', and unfortunately long mislaid. It is impossible not to think that Jesuitism did a truly talented person like Tom no good at all; and there was real sadness in what seemed to be his long decline. Perhaps some might argue, as I have heard it argued, that it is only under the dead weight of some system that certain peculiar talents are pressured into shape and action – think of that other sad Jesuit, Gerard Manley Hopkins, a man not unlike Tom in some ways. I find such arguments both dangerous and unconvincing. But at any rate, I remain grateful for Tom's advice and especially for his absolute veto on the theological use of the word 'reconcile'. At the time, of course, I was too stupid to realize the veto's full implications regarding the infinite irreconcilability, of 'God' and his creation; but it lay among the other seeds and time-bombs in my mind, and eventually they burst into life and produced results. I do not think I ever got to speak to Tom again.

So I began my teaching career. The course on predestination and free will was, I am sure, unmemorable, though I prepared my lectures meticulously and even almost rehearsed them before delivering them, a habit I never quite abandoned. I always felt safer and more in control that way. I wrote a naive little book, *The Theology of Creation*, and started to review serious theology for

The Heythrop Journal and other periodicals – another habit which I have maintained to this day. The fact was that I found that after all my training I did not have a great deal of teaching work to do. The old cycle of doctrinal treatises had been replaced by broader and more historically oriented courses for more general consumption. These suited my own inclinations, and they were easier to prepare. But I busily filled up my time with leading study-days elsewhere, giving retreats, lecturing on theology to adult groups, doing supply work on parishes, including what was now my family's home parish, St Catherine's, Farington, Leyland. While I was still in Rome, I had officiated at my sister Barbara's wedding to David Knight at St Wilfrid's, Preston, and soon I was to do the same at my brother Alan's wedding at St Catherine's itself. I gave a paper on my work on Hippolytus at the prestigious Oxford Patristic Conference. With Anthony Levi, by then a lecturer in French at Warwick University, I initiated an annual summer school in theology for the laity, quaintly called 'The Catholic Dogma Course', but wisely renamed after a year as 'Living Theology'. We got together a staff of ten or so of our most able Jesuit contemporaries and booked various annual venues – Beaumont College in Old Windsor, Coloma College in West Wickham in Kent, and Digby Stuart College in Roehampton. About a hundred residential participants came, and the original format was severely academic – just one-off lectures by competent individuals. There was nothing like it on the market at the time, and staff and students found it a generally enjoyable occasion. I planned and ran the courses for about five years, and then handed them over and they took on a different, less doctrinal coloration. I think they go on in some form or other to this day. One year I edited and published our lectures as *The Spirit in Action* (St Paul Publications, 1968). They give an authentic taste of our early efforts at educating the laity in theology.

But I would say that the most serious sideline I pursued in those days was the one-semester lectureship I took on at Lincoln Theological College. I became the first Roman Catholic ecumenical lecturer to be appointed in an Anglican institution for the training of clergy. This was due to the imaginative zeal of Alan Webster, later Dean of Norwich and then Dean of St Paul's. I lived in College at Lincoln during the week and returned at the weekend to Heythrop, where I had also been appointed Superior of the theologians' community, a job I performed badly. To make this and my other engagements possible I acquired a small car, and from this time onwards I was never without some form of personal transport; though I gave up the car when Heythrop moved to London and went back to the far more practical motor-bike. Lincoln, its staff and its students, I found congenial, and my lecturing and tutoring introduced me for the first time to a world of work outside the Roman and Jesuit fold. I was, in any case, beginning to meet many more ordinary people than I had ever done during the long years of study. About this time I went on holiday for the first time to the west of Ireland, and met Anthony and Fiona Simonds-Gooding at their family's home outside Glenbeigh on the Ring of Kerry. Within a few years I found myself going annually for a Kerry holiday in the mixed role of chaplain and *au pair* to their steadily growing family. It was my job to make the breakfasts, always starting with Flahavan's Process Oatlets, and to say Mass for all their many relatives who holidayed in the Dooks area. In many other contexts, too, thanks to my friendship with Kevin McHugh and my increasing employ-ment outside Heythrop, I met people who lay well outside my habitually confined social scope. I began, for the first time, to encounter women in open social situations, and I enjoyed their company. Above all, I began to learn to enjoy myself. All this proved to be an important psychological step towards what was to happen to me later. I began to realize that there was still an ordinary world, a life, and also work I could do, outside the confines of the Society, but still, of course, as a Jesuit. My reaction to the changed Heythrop situation might, I suppose, have taken other forms, and not least an increased concentration on research and writing. But I was, as I have said, not a natural scholar, but much given to the self-flattery involved in being ready to take on more or less any job that was offered. Things, it must be said, were not going well at the Pontifical Athenaeum, and I was glad to be away from Heythrop as often as possible. Student numbers were dropping steadily, key staff had left, the place and the whole hopeless project was proving predictably unappealing. This was no passing crisis, as some wishfully thought. A expen-sive new library was built, but it did little but serve as a symbol for those still determined to stay put. The Athenaeum's problems were terminal, and some younger members of staff, myself included, began to wonder about their futures. By the late '60s the time and the circumstances were right for a radical solution.

The Rector, William Maher – always known as Johnnie – had taught me at Preston when I was eleven years old. A man of instinctive intelligence and elemental energy, it was he who first aired the idea of closing down at Heythrop and moving the Athenaeum elsewhere. In the senior community there was considerable upset and consternation. The lid we had all been keeping on the problem brewing within the Athenaeum had been lifted, and it was never to be replaced. Factions immediately surfaced among the staff, and there was active lobbying for and against a closure. At least one of the older members, Freddie Copleston, the distinguished historian of philosophy, sided with the younger element, and this, I believe, proved decisive in the end.

But where would we land up? It was obvious that the survival of the Athenaeum project – or something like it – was going to depend on its being accommodated in an existing university context. But which one? The Rector encouraged the widest possible exploration of such possibilities as occurred to people, and he despatched carefully chosen delegations, always including himself, to a number of universities to take soundings of their administrations and their theological faculties. Would they welcome the arrival of our Jesuit faculties of philosophy and theology? Or perhaps of our desirable library? Or of an increased intake of students? Or would some carefully arranged ecumenical balances be upset? The outright closure of the Heythrop Pontifical Athenaeum was probably unthinkable, or at any rate politically rash in ecclesiastical terms, at the time. Heenan had only just, a year or two before, gone through the charade of a Solemn Opening ceremony at Heythrop, and an inaugural High Mass at Westminster Cathedral, packed with schoolchildren, supposedly the future beneficiaries of his enlightened foundation. Closure would have been by far the simpler, and probably the only, solution, but it would need to be arrived at (as it was) by means other than just shutting up shop. So we had to hawk the Athenaeum around the university scene. Oxford proved lukewarm, and it already housed sufficient religious houses of study. Bristol would have been too small, and we would have overwhelmed them. Manchester was a likelier bet – in the more Catholic North, with denominational colleges already attached to the Faculty of Theology, and a familiar Jesuit presence already there in its university chaplaincy and the Holy Name Church opposite the main university buildings. I went on the Manchester delegation, and at the time I considered Manchester the best option open to us. But by 1969 it had been decided that our future lay somewhere in the capacious arms of the University of London.

Heythrop was to become, after all due scrutiny, a non-grant-receiving School in the London Faculty of Theology. This had two immediate effects: by not closing the Pontifical Athenaeum its façade, and the Cardinal's public face, were saved; and Rome was craftily misled into thinking that its Pontifical Athenaeum was now part of a leading English university. But of course we never deceived London, who warmly welcomed Heythrop with its Jesuit staff and library, and rightly insisted that its courses would be taken only for London degrees. The Pontifical Athenaeum quietly became nothing more than an accommodation address at Mount Street W.1, quite distinct from Heythrop College (University of London) in Cavendish Square W.1. As late as 1976 I was sent to Rome to represent Heythrop at a prestigious Vatican conference on 'Universities and Faculties of Ecclesiastical Studies'. The participants were a mixture of Cardinals, Bishops and *Rectores Magnifici* from all round the world. I was simply a low-grade departmental head at Heythrop. The not-so-covert purpose of the conference was to enable the Vatican to assert its ultimate control over the running (and especially the staffing) of every Catholic teaching institution in the world. In the event the conference only revealed how completely out of touch the Vatican had become with the multitude of different forms which Catholic establishments had assumed over the years, and with the variety of staffing and working conditions that obtained in them. The Vatican still thought, for instance, that it could exercise a prior veto on any staff appointment anywhere, as if labour laws and trades unions and equal opportunities did not exist. The conference was a fiasco. Much to my private delight, when I checked in on the first morning, a natty little Monsignore, immaculately groomed for Vatican promotion and looking about twenty years old, looked at my papers, tried to fix me with a withering look and loudly declared: 'Heythrop – *fin-al*-MENTE!' At long last! But if Rome thought it was going to find out from me just what was happening to its Athenaeum in London, it was going to be disappointed.

In the summer of 1970 we had moved into the Cavendish Square premises of the graduate teacher training college of the Holy Child nuns, which was itself on the point of closing down. It accommodated our important library and had ample teaching space. Some newly built town houses in the mews were rented for the Jesuit staff. Our students, Jesuit and non-Jesuit alike, would now be reading for the London B.D. degree, a thoroughly respectable and rigorously academic qualification. Those destined for ordination could supplement this basic course with others which they were required to take. The B.A. in philosophy and theology was also offered, along with the Master's degree in theology. I would now be chiefly responsible for teaching the course on early Christian theology leading to 'Christian Doctrine II', a compulsory degree paper. I was also to be Head of the Christian Doctrine Department, and became a Recognized Teacher in the University. I also taught New Testament Greek, which was a compulsory requirement, and certain other theology courses as well. As far as outside engagements were concerned, I had to pull my horns in – at least until we got well established – but it felt good to have, at last, a responsible and settled job, and a clear mandate to do, in challenging surroundings, what I had been trained to do. I was to teach at Cavendish Square for the next ten years.

But the person who had made something of a false start at teaching at the Heythrop Athenaeum three years before was not quite the same person who now had to restart his teaching career at the new Heythrop. It is not easy to describe what happened without sounding melodramatic: but a few weeks before moving myself, my books and all my papers in a hired car from Lancashire down to London, I can only say that the bottom suddenly fell out of my understanding of what theology was supposed to be all about. Intellectually, I very nearly came to grief just when I was about to start the most serious teaching of theology I had undertaken to date. Since this event constitutes, to my mind, the most crucial juncture in my whole life; and because it led eventually to seriously radical changes in my general thinking and attitudes, and in fact to my leaving the Jesuits and adopting a completely new form of life, I must describe carefully and clearly just what happened. I was very badly thrown by this unwanted development at the time; and, in a sense, the rest of my life has been – and I expect always will be – a process of coming to terms with it.

In July 1970 I had left the old Heythrop in Oxfordshire, already sold to the National Westminster Bank as a staff training centre, with all my belongings in my ageing Triumph Herald, and I had headed home to do a summer stint in my home parish in Farington. I promptly sold the car for £25. In theory supply work gave me the opportunity to think and read and to write my lectures. Not, I think, that I ever did as much as I could have done. I was lazy, and I justified my laziness by the thought that at least I was exercising the priesthood, which for most of the time 'lodged with me useless'. But I would have been far better off buckling down to some decent study in a good library, and especially to some writing. I kept on writing, but chiefly articles and book reviews. If I failed to tackle anything bigger – and I made a number of false starts – it was probably because I did not yet feel I had anything worth saying. Again in hindsight, I can see that my feeling was correct, and I blush now to think of what I did write, and might have published. But just when I was looking forward to some years of decent employment as a university lecturer in London, one of those buried and unexploded time-bombs regarding the nature of theology and its language suddenly went off. As some measure of security was at last achieved in one area of my life, the underlying tectonic plates deep in the mind shifted and I found myself poised over an abyss, not only of intellectual, but also of moral uncertainty.

To reach for even more metaphors, I can best describe what happened by saying that I found I had 'gone critical' – gone critical, that is, somewhat in the sense that a pile of radioactive material, as I understand it, reacts by heating up internally when the leaden elements which have hitherto been used to control the radioactivity in the pile are withdrawn. The material begins to generate heat and energy that rise closer and closer to a dangerous 'critical' level. If left unchecked the material will explode with destructive violence, and radioactive fall-out from the explosion will affect everything far and wide. Whilst I was not overwhelmed by such an intellectual Chernobyl, I suddenly sensed the impending danger of one, if I did not do something about it. I was certainly not going to solve the intellectual and moral problem with which I found myself faced by playing with increasingly elaborate metaphors.

The issue presented itself as one of basic human honesty, moral as well as intellectual. Because its appearance was so important in my life, I shall describe the issue with all the honesty and clarity I can manage.

In the first place, as a Jesuit and a priest and a now a theology lecturer, I had contracted serious responsibilities towards the Church and the Catholic faithful, and towards my students in particular, regarding my handling of the truth and meaning of Catholic doctrinal and theological tradition. It was imperative that I understood that theology as profoundly as I could – that I realized in what sense it was true – that I understood how it made sense – that I understood its meaning – that I understood in what sense that meaning was true. If I did not measure up to these demands, I could hardly imagine that I was being a responsible theologian.

In the second place, the very raising of these questions indicated the type and depth of the crisis in which I found myself involved. Whilst I had the greatest historical respect for the Catholic doctrinal tradition, I still desperately needed to establish, insofar as I could, the precise sense in which the theological statements that went into the formation of that tradition meant what they said. Do they mean what they say in the same descriptive sense as the statements we habitually make about the ordinary world in which we live? Are they meant to be referring literally to another world which is real in the just same sense as the one we live in? Do we have to do with two equiliteral worlds, the ordinary one in which we now live, and another real world which is currently beyond our ken, but which is being accurately described to us in what theology tells us about it? The old Leyland situation where there was the ordinary world of Towngate and the other world of Leyland St Mary's beyond the Cross was back, and now as an problem in urgent need of treatment.

In the third place, I could be in no real doubt that the Catholic faithful considered that the Catholic doctrinal tradition, and the theologians and preachers who transmitted that tradition to them, meant what they said to be taken literally as a description of God's world and of God's dealings with them. The faithful would be scandalized to imagine otherwise. The life-and-death certainties which they derived from their faith would simply seem to evaporate.

In the fourth place, unless I could come to terms with my intellectual crisis, I would be at serious moral fault if I were to go on teaching and preaching without discovering the sense in which theological statements were actually meant, and how the Catholic doctrinal tradition contained the saving truth it claimed to express.

In the fifth place, if I could not achieve a satisfactory resolution of these issues (I do not say 'solve the problem' – I doubt if anyone has ever done that) I would have to take some drastic action, like resigning from the Jesuits and the priesthood. It would be irresponsible of me to go on, and sinful to hoodwink people deliberately.

I was in relatively serious trouble. There would have been no point in trying to suppress the issues that faced me. They were not superficial considerations about this or that Catholic doctrine.

Nor did they, at the other end of the scale, constitute Religious Doubt. Not for a moment did I think that Catholicism was called into doubt, or untrue, or meant nothing just because it had thrown up some radical problems regarding its interpretation. Serious and ill-timed as they were, the issues offered me a challenge I could have done without; but they also called for my close attention.

Now I knew that issues like these had long been dealt with by theologians. Theoretically there was nothing new about them. The stock answer to them was that theological statements were not meant literally but *analogically* – that is (as I understand it), the object of such statements could not be known directly but only indirectly, in ways proportionate to our thinking and our language. This is because God and his divine actions, by reason of his infinite transcendence of all created being, can never be directly described, and to suppose him to be directly describable is to commit idolatry, the reduction of God to the level at which we have to understand him. The trouble is, however, that in practice theologians – though not the best ones – habitually slip into the literalism which is technically forbidden to them. So do preachers, of course. That they should continually qualify their assertions about God and the world of the divine by saying that they are meant analogically would sound very strange in practice. It simply does not happen. But apart from that, I felt dissatisfied with 'the doctrine of analogy', not because I thought it was wrong, but because I could not see why theologians could not honestly admit that, when it came to God and his divine actions, they were simply speaking in metaphors. If 'analogy' is really telling us that theology works with metaphors, then I would agree with it; but if theological statements are metaphorical (as I happen to think they are), then it seems only honest and right to begin – at last – to say so, and to stop misleading people. None of this would lead to any denial of the ultimate mystery which experience tells us is involved in our human lives. But theologians and preachers do not like dealing in 'mystery' or metaphors, though they lie at the heart of religion, and certainly of Catholicism. They like to give the impression that they are 'in the know'. But there is no way in which we, with our tiny minds, can hope to know directly how the infinite and the finite can come to terms with one another – except when those terms consist of the metaphors to which all of us, theologians included, are restricted. (I shall have more to say on this topic later.)

I am now extremely glad that I began to realize, so early and so painfully, what was going to be involved in being a professional theologian. The questions that arose were intelligent questions, and I needed to find out just how intelligent they were, and if and how it was possible for a would-be professional theologian to live with them. Or perhaps it was the case that living with them was what being a professional theologian was going to be all about. There was very little to distract me in the parish. I was alone in the house, and I had to wrestle the matter out with the critical spirit which had suddenly invaded my private peace of mind and threatened to render my future work impossible.

At first I tried blaming myself for the onset of what struck me, not as just an academic question, but as a personal problem. Had I somehow failed to be true to 'my vocation'? Had I, in other words, become unfaithful in my observance of the duties of the religious life to which I had committed myself? Should I have been ignoring the questions as dangerous distractions, or quelling them in prayer? Was I simply losing my faith? In fact, I was living a busy and rather strict religious life, albeit with more outside contacts and relaxations than during the long years of training; and far from hankering, consciously or unconsciously, after a life outside the Jesuits, I doubt if I had ever been quite so happy with it, given the projected move of Heythrop into London and the new prospects it brought with it. So I could not see how I was to blame for a sudden rise in the critical level of my theological consciousness. The truth may be, I suppose, something like this: the sheer intensity and the length of my theological studies, playing on a mind that learnt and ruminated in a rather slow and reflective fashion, must have led to the shelving of certain issues – to the burying of intellectual time-bombs – which remained dormant until widening experience and deeper reading gradually and naturally removed whatever factors had been inhibiting their becoming critically active. But however I might speculate about the background to my suddenly going critical, and if I could not blame myself for it, the practical question remained: just what was I going to do about defusing the situation? I was due to start lecturing in London in a few weeks' time, and I needed to get my personal and intellectual act together, or at least to patch up the situation, and not to see it blown apart. Fortunately, I did not panic.

It might seem obvious that I should seek out someone – some fellow-Jesuit perhaps – with whom I might talk the problem out. I was, after all, in the privileged position of being surrounded at

Heythrop by able colleagues far more expert than myself, not least
in the kind of theological–philosophical issue with which I found
myself beset. The fact is, I am afraid, that it never once occurred to
me to turn to my fellow-Jesuits. This admission is bound to sound
strange, if not ungenerous; and I have to confess that it surprises me
now, as I mention it. But my problem struck me, as I have indicated,
not as merely abstract and intellectual, but as an intensely personal
and private crisis. Perhaps this lack of objectivity on my part was
actually part of the problem, and perhaps it made the problem more
intractable. Did I have to take it all so personally? I felt strongly that
I had to cope with the problem myself, to come to my own terms
with it. Again, my lack of consultation with fellow-Jesuits may have
to do with how I was now perceiving the quality of relationships in
the Society generally. We were not close to one another – indeed, we
were trained not to be. Where a certain warmth or closeness existed
between Jesuits, it did not follow that it was because they shared the
same interests or concerns, or that they were of the same intellectual
cast of mind. Outsiders would often say that they found that Jesuits
had a great deal in common with one another – that they 'all seemed
the same'. This was certainly not the view you would get from the
inside. To hazard a rather wild guess, I would be inclined to say that
most Jesuits had closer friends outside the Society than inside it –
not, of course, excluding their own families. Again, because I think
I was at least unconsciously afraid of the potential implications of
my kind of problem for my religious faith (a fear I now realize was
quite groundless), I was inclined to feel that it had its roots in some
moral failure, and I was naturally reluctant to confess it. In fact, to
put it briefly, taking my problem to a fellow-Jesuit would have been
much more like going to confession than having a discussion; and I
was clear both that I was not at fault and that I needed much more
help than some kind of genial absolution. I think I was also afraid of
being handed down some stock answer, some party line, derived
straight from the system; and of being patted on the head and
encouraged to relax or have a proper holiday or some time off. I
very badly needed to be taken seriously, and I could not see that my
fellow-Jesuits were likely to understand this. Of course, I can see
now that all these rationalizations tell their own tale: I was probably
already becoming dissociated from the Society and increasingly
determined to make my own way. My decision to go it alone over
the issues that confronted me should have alerted me to the degree
of my growing dissociation, but I was too preoccupied with the
problem of theology and metaphor to bother with that. All I knew
was that I needed some philosophical bomb disposal expert to help

me to defuse the dangerously explosive problem that was now ticking loudly and showing signs of overheating within.

It was fortunate that at this stage memories of the philosophy I had undervalued at Oxford began to stir. I had quite enjoyed Oxford philosophy, but, as I have explained, at the time I had neglected it in favour of the stronger attractions of ancient history. In the philosophy courses a certain name had occurred from time – the name of someone who was surely just the all-time bomb-disposal expert I was looking for. I knew a little about him, but obviously it was now time to look more seriously at the works of Ludwig Wittgenstein. Who better to consult in my intellectual crisis? I was not so philosophically naive as to suppose that I would turn up some handy solution in his difficult writings; but at least he, more than anyone else I could think of, would help to ensure that I was not just making my problem up, that there really was a problem with the meaning of religious and theological (or any other kind of) language and its proper interpretation, and that the problem, if it could not be licked, could at lest be licked into a tolerable shape. So then – I must get hold of what I could of Wittgenstein, and start reading. Preston was not a place where it was likely I would find his books, so one day I took a local train into Manchester, where I found a bookshop which had just one work of Wittgenstein in stock, *The Blue and Brown Books*. These preliminary studies for his masterpiece, the *Philosophical Investigations*, turned out to be exactly what I wanted and needed. I brought the book back to Farington, and perhaps without understanding all that much of it at first, I began to read it. I felt a little like Aeneas finding the magic golden bough which was to be his necessary passport and safe-conduct to the underworld:

> *corripit Aeneas extemplo avidusque refringit*
> *cunctantem, et vatis portat sub tecta Sibyllae.*

Aeneas quickly grabbed it, eagerly snapped it off when it resisted him, and carried it off to where the prophetic Sibyl dwelt.
(Virgil, *Aeneid* 6.210f.)

I was now irrevocably entering, though I could not realize it then, that dark and uncertain underworld of philosophical hermeneutics where my problem with the interpretation of theological language would be taken seriously and might be properly diagnosed and suitably treated – but where I might also come to such terms with it as might enable me to live and work with it. With

Wittgenstein as my guide – *tu sei lo mio maestro e 'l mio autore* – I
felt safe. I felt I could trust him, as I could not quite trust anyone
else, to be completely honest. In the years to come I was to find
what I can only call intellectual salvation and sanity with the help
of others besides him. But without the start provided by his later
view that the meaning of any proposition lies essentially in how
it is used in a particular language game, and that language games
correspond to certain forms of life, I would simply not have been
able to function as a teacher of that difficult language game,
theology. I also liked the stripped-out clarity of his style and his
amazing ability to be genuinely and intelligently puzzled. He
sounded like a man who had gone permanently critical at an
early age, and who had managed to maintain complete intellectual integrity along with a deep humanity. He had a gift for
making others think for themselves. I especially appreciated his
fine German – though some of his translators rather less. His
philosophical bent was pragmatic, and, very importantly, there
seemed to be nothing systematic or dogmatic or derivative about
his way of thinking. Most importantly, as I came to learn, he was,
in his own rather odd way, a profoundly religious man whose
tough views did not eliminate the possibility of religious faith or
theological discourse, but made the right kind of proper
allowance for them. These were the considerations which calmed
me down and soothed me, and began to defuse the explosively
critical problem lodged firmly inside me. Wittgenstein's writings
worked on me from the start like a first-rate intellectual therapy,
and he began to give me the confidence which I needed in order
to continue.

But *inde datum molitur iter* (ibid. 6.477) – 'It was from this point
that the required journey had to be undertaken'. I was still very
much at the start of facing my problem, and the first stage of
my journey through my personal and private underworld was
to take me more or less twenty years, in the course of which I
was to meet some other helpful heroes and one highly supportive friend. I also had to make some painfully public decisions.
I did much of the first stage of the journey alone. I did not –
chiefly perhaps because I could not – explain to others where I
stood, since my position was still being constantly worked out.
Most of all, though, I felt I did not want to upset anyone, so I
cultivated what I considered a thoroughly respectable kind of
theological 'reserve', keeping the still speculative consideration
of my problem strictly to myself whilst I got on efficiently with
my teaching and other occupations. I was, of course, very busy

in London from the start, and the consideration of my own problems was for long periods far from the front of my mind. I am
now very glad that I took so long over my journey. It was not
a personal journey that I could be expected to rush. Where all
this would leave the theological and metaphysical world of religion in which I had been living for so long would emerge only
in time.

෨

Most of the Jesuit staff who moved from the old Heythrop to
London threw themselves into the new situation with enthusiasm. Naturally there were some who had their doubts about the
wisdom of the move; but the whole staff pulled together well
enough under the College's new Principal, Freddie Copleston.
We organized our work into several Departments to fit the
London B.D. syllabus for which we now had to teach. This both
broadened and deepened our teaching, moving it away from
Roman obsessions with doctrinal and moral theology and giving
biblical studies a much larger share of our attention. Soon I was
able, as Head of Christian Doctrine, to get the syllabus extended
to include the more Catholic topics of ecclesiology and sacramen-
tal theology. Philosophy of religion and Christian ethics also
featured solidly on the teaching programme; and in some
subjects, like the study of non-Christian religions, we were happy
at first to depend on our colleagues at King's College in the
Strand. They were helpful and supportive in everything we did.
We also increased our staff with both Jesuits and non-Jesuits alike
to give ourselves more depth in certain subjects. All in all, the
way we tackled the move into London and its new demands was
very impressive. We had, of course, to prove ourselves, and we
taught our first year of undergraduates, a good mixture of religious and lay students, with some vigour. The degree results
were excellent from the start.

For me these were very busy times indeed. There were business
and other meetings to attend, documents to prepare, courses to
teach, tutorials to give. And that was just the academic side of
life. There were also Jesuit and religious duties to attend to. I
lived at Cavendish Square at the start, then for a year or two
I commuted daily from Osterley, and then, until I left Heythrop, I
lived at the Jesuit headquarters at Mount Street in Mayfair, a
short walk from the College. In all these places I was inevitably
involved in community affairs. I recently had occasion to list the
kind of extra-curricular jobs I found myself doing. Of course, I
cannot now imagine how – or in some cases, why – I did them. I

think I took most of them on because I felt it was important for the new Heythrop that someone from there should take on academic or other chores such as examining when asked; and I was also personally flattered at being asked to do so. Thus from the beginning I was, as a Recognized Teacher, a member of the Board of Studies in Theology in the University of London, and for a couple of years I served as its secretary. For seven years or more I was also a member of the Board of Examiners for the B.D. and for the B.A. in Philosophy and Theology, and chairman of the former for three years. For three years I also sat on the Board of Examiners in Theology at the University of London Institute of Education, and chaired it for two years. Over the same period I occasionally examined for higher and research degrees in the universities of London, Oxford and Nottingham.

On top of all this I also took on a great deal of work as an External Examiner in Theology. For five years I flew out annually in December to the University of Rhodesia/Zimbabwe, where I was met in Salisbury/Harare by many of my English Jesuit contemporaries and colleagues who worked out there. These were very dangerous transitional times for them, and much of the country was occupied by what were then considered rebel forces. A number of Jesuits – friends, contemporaries, even students of mine – were ruthlessly murdered as they worked on vulnerable missions in the bush. It was not even always clear which side had killed them. I like to think I cheered my fellow Jesuits up a little simply by being a regular visitor doing a routine job in such difficult times. They required very little of me, and apart from delivering items they had ordered from their contacts in London, I was expected to turn up with some good sherry, copies of the latest *Times* and *Daily Telegraph*, and a very large jar of Marmite. They gave me a royal welcome, and over the years I was escorted – with caution – quite widely around the country. I got to the Victoria Falls in the north and to the Great Zimbabwe ruins in the south, as well as out to Inyanga in the east, towards the border with Mozambique. The hospitality I received was memorable. Because of the political situation, I had often to fly to and from Zimbabwe via South Africa, and the Jesuits there also did me proud. I already knew most of them, and I spent very happy times in Johannesburg, in Durban (at the Cathedral), and in wonderful Cape Town. The more difficult side of South African life was fairly presented to me. I visited Soweto and the Cape Flats. I had taught Michael Lewis, a South African Jesuit and a keen, knowledgeable, and balanced enthusiast for his country, back at Heythrop; and it was with him that I saw Natal and its historic battlefields – Blood River, Spion Kop, Ladysmith, Rorke's Drift. On one occasion we took a group of his Zulu altar-boys to camp in a cave, high in the Drakensberg Mountains, with chattering baboons and growling leopards around us at night. I remain deeply grateful for all the kindness I was shown by Jesuits in Southern Africa whose lives, I fully realized, were much tougher than our own. The University of Zimbabwe provided each external examiner with a full-price air ticket, and I made great use of this every year by having it altered by the efficient Mrs Mills in Harare, the agent who coped with all Jesuit travel requirements, with the result that I could get round South Africa and to other places free. One year I even returned to England via Israel at no extra cost. This was my first of several visits to the Holy Land, a place I especially like.

There were other external jobs, too. I did a spell as Visiting Lecturer (on Christology) at St Patrick's College, Maynooth (National University of Ireland), followed by several more years of external examining there – a job I also did at the Jesuit house of studies in Dublin, Milltown Park. Then for three years I was External Examiner in the Faculty of Theology at the University of Manchester. Just as I enjoyed umpiring at cricket and refereeing at soccer more than actually playing either game, I also enjoyed external examining, and I think I gave satisfaction in all these places. It was thought that my general academic judgement was sound; and with my long Jesuit training and my Oxford classics behind me, I found I had a wider acquaintance with broader theological and historical topics than some of the rather over-specialized local staff. I also enjoyed the travelling involved, as well as all the generous hospitality that was offered.

Back in London I also undertook the more formal work of representing the Faculty of Theology on the Academic Council Standing Sub-committee for Theology, Arts and Music, eventually becoming its representative member on the Academic Council and on the Senate of the University of London. In 1981 I was elected Dean of the Faculty of Theology, but other developments prevented me from taking up office. At any rate I think it can be said that I dived head-first into our new London situation at the deep end. But I did not neglect requests from church sources either. I joined a team who did important work in the Archdiocese of Westminster for adult religious education, and many of my evenings were spent in some parish or other giving talks and answering the questions which intelligent laity had begun to raise. I thought this work was very rewarding, and I did it for years. Sometimes I gave more formal lectures, both at theological conferences and for lay audiences. I took part in some broadcasts for BBC Radio 3. I preached fairly often, including a course of sermons at Farm Street. Throughout all this I wrote a good number of articles and numerous book reviews for journals and newspapers, both Catholic and non-Catholic. I even got round to publishing my doctoral thesis. I still did my parish supply work annually, though with diminishing interest. In all this I do not think I was consciously out to prove anything just for myself. What, if anything, I wanted to prove was that the new Heythrop was viable in the ordinary world of academic theology, and that what it had to offer was an important contribution both to learning and to the Catholic Church. In any case, I was far from being the only one working as hard as this: many others on the staff were doing better and more distinguished work than I, and on many, more difficult fronts. It is my view that for the first few years the new Heythrop was a great success. The staff, especially the Jesuits, were enthusiastic and very effective; and it soon became deservedly recognized in the United Kingdom as a centre of excellence which was a credit to the Society. I was proud to be on the staff.

❧

Beneath all this, however, my personal problem with the nature and meaning of theological language persisted, indeed developed. During one of my Easter supplies on the Isles of Scilly I read nothing for three weeks apart from Wittgenstein's *Philosophical Investigations*, and walked round and round St Mary's almost every day ruminating (as I had done in another year on St Mark's Gospel) on its applicability to my case. I came to see that what Wittgenstein was providing me with was the equipment and the method I was going to need if I was to sort myself out. I would need ideas such as language games, forms of life, the use a word has in the language. But what I could not expect to derive from him (or at least not from the *Philosophical Investigations*) was much that had to do with the specific content of my problem – the precise nature of theology and the meaning of its language. I was going to need more help with this, and, very fortunately, I did not have far to look. I was asked to review for *The Tablet* Hans-Georg Gadamer's masterpiece *Truth and Method*. Here was just what I was looking for – the link between a philosophy like Wittgenstein's and the central role of interpretation (hermeneutics) and tradition in human understanding. I was beginning to be able to see what theology actually was, and how it worked – it was essentially a matter of using religious language to interpret a special kind of experience in a meaningful way. It was, above all else, the imaginative creation of metaphors. And more: it produced a set of interpretative understandings which could – indeed, if it was to survive the vicissitudes of history, which had to – develop itself into a tradition, an evolving history of transmissible ways of understanding and interpreting the basic experience. I was beginning to come to terms (terms derived from Wittgenstein and Gadamer) with the problem I had with the subject I was busily teaching. In one other thing I was also very fortunate: I was lecturing chiefly on the history of early Christian doctrinal theology, following the development of the Church's earliest efforts at formulating its ways of interpreting and understanding the religious insight which its Founder had handed on to his disciples, and I could understand this history in terms of what I was learning about the nature of theology. I was also becoming familiar with the often acute controversies occasioned by the variety of views held by different theological factions and 'Fathers' in the Church. So I could feel at home with a Church in which there was, as a normal fact of life, a range of divergent theological interpretations even of the most central Christian doctrines, the Incarnation and the Trinity. I was also well aware of the role played by the Church's earliest ecumenical councils in engineering and asserting credal compromise between incompatible interpretations. So I was in a good position to appreciate that Catholic theology was a matter of participating in a very specific language game in which words derived what meaning they had from the way they were employed to interpret a foundational religious insight, in order to try to ensure that the crucial insight, and what it was believed to entail theologically, was effectively handed on down the generations of believers to help them sustain a certain specific form of life and faith. In this way I felt I was perhaps getting closer to a manageable approach to the problem of the nature of theology and its language. All this was going on in my private intellectual underworld, while for most of my time I was busy with all the jobs I kept taking on in my public life. I do not know if my uncertainties ever showed; but I do know that no one at Heythrop seemed in the least interested.

చ

From the start the students were a stimulating bunch, and they were well motivated to work hard. They wanted Heythrop to succeed as much as the staff did. There were a number of able

Jesuit scholastics among them, but also a new breed of student who would never have been attracted to the old Heythrop in its rural and pontifical phase. These were intelligent lay folk who wanted to read for a degree in theology in an accessible Catholic setting, and with the help of a local authority grant which would enable them to do this at a English university. This was just the type of student that it had been hoped would come to Heythrop. Among them, in our very first year, was Barbara George, married (but not happily) with two children, and determined to make herself well qualified in theology, independent, and employed in some Catholic field. It was no more than a matter of months before we became friends, and found we had much in common. From the start I had the impression that here was someone I could talk to, and who would instinctively understand the kind of personal intellectual problem under which I was privately labouring. We must, I suppose, have talked about my views, though I cannot remember just when we did so. But the important thing was that she was there. I make particular mention of her friendship because it became, early on at Cavendish Square, another material factor in my situation. In addition to my obvious work-load, I now had not only my private intellectual problem, but also some close personal support to help me see it through.

Of course, it is bound to have been said by those with closed clerical minds, especially in view of the distant fact that Barbara and I finally married some twenty years later, that I was indiscreet, or that she lured me away from my religious vocation with her womanly wiles. I find both of these suggestions wholly fatuous. I left the Jesuits and the priesthood, as I shall explain, because, after some twenty years of careful thought, I found my position personally and intellectually untenable. And even then I did not leave to get married – marriage was only a very happy afterthought. Barbara did more than anyone to keep me in the Society for so long, even perhaps for too long. Our relationship strengthened me immeasurably. It helped me to sustain whatever tension there was between my busy life and my personal uncertainties. The relationship was certainly no guilty secret, involving as it did both our families and our friends from the start, and we behaved, of course, very properly. It also has to be said that after the inculpable breakdown of her first marriage, Barbara was far from interested in entering into another marriage, least of all with as dodgy a prospect as myself. She was eventually divorced and then she had her marriage annulled by the Church. If I appear to dwell on this friendship, it is because I am keen to counter the

smug clerical jibe that in all cases where a man leaves the priesthood the only explanation that needs to be sought is *cherchez la
femme*. Not only is this evidently untrue in all cases, even though
it may be true in some, but it serves the world of celibate clerics in
particularly nasty ways: it totally exonerates them from any
responsibility in the departure of one of their colleagues; it glori-
fies celibacy – a mere matter of ecclesiastical discipline, after all,
endowed with religious value simply in the interests of economy
and control – to the extent that any decline from it can only be a
matter of personally sinful folly; and, worst of all, it lays much of
the blame for any difficulty men may have with celibacy squarely
on women. It is time the self-flattering attitude that many clerics
show towards their own celibacy gave way to something
approaching human maturity and balance. In any case, as far as I
was concerned, old Fr Henry Davis' dictum was beginning to
come true: I was not getting support from anyone in the Society.

Meanwhile by the late '70s all was not well with the staff at
Heythrop. Even I, an enthusiast for the place, had become slightly
restless and bored. I found myself looking every week through
the newspapers at the advertisements in the higher education
supplements, searching for university lectureships I might possibly ask permission to apply for. It may have amounted to nothing
more than wishful thinking on my part. But if there was a serious
fault-line in the Cavendish Square set-up, it had to do with the
way the College was funded. Heythrop was a non-grant-receiving School in the Faculty of Theology – it received no share in the
grant made by the government to the universities, though its
students were eligible for local authority grants. It was, in other
words, privately funded in the main, and generously so, by Jesuit
money lodged in a charitable trust. The Jesuits were its
'Providing Body'. From the start all staff had been given contracts
of employment with full tenure. Jesuits like myself who had been
appointed to the staff had such contracts but did not, of course,
receive salaries, so our services came free. Other non-Jesuit religious had contracts but were paid a modest honorarium.
Contracted non-religious would have to be paid salaries at the
going rate. Money was tight, and it was important to keep salary
costs to a minimum. All went well enough until a couple of
contracted staff formally left the priesthood to live in the lay state,
and so had now to be paid full salaries. This put a heavy strain on
the College's limited resources, but their contracts gave them
tenure, and they refused to resign. The rest of the staff then

divided into two factions. On the right there was a feeling of
outrage that the defectors did not have the decency to see the religious and financial embarrassment they were causing and withdraw from the College; and on the left there was a feeling that
they had the legal right, firmly based on their tenured contracts,
to keep their jobs. The split became obvious, and it was known
whose side everyone was on.

It was a situation which was far from easy to judge. The right
wing, the Jesuit Providing Body in league with the Visitor of the
College, Cardinal Heenan, felt that the defectors had to be got rid
of. It was thought that their continuing employment militated
against the Catholic character and interests of Heythrop, and that
their salaries were not covered by the legally defined purposes of
the trust which provided Heythrop's money. The left wing
stressed that, whatever the status of the defectors, they had valid
contracts of employment with tenure, and they were entitled to
stay and to be paid the proper salary, even if it bankrupted the
Providing Body and closed the College down. The right was
convinced that Catholic institutions did not exist to employ ex-
priests. There was some intemperate use of the *cherchez la femme*
ploy. Heenan had only recently had similar problems with his
institute for catechetics, Corpus Christi. Neither support nor
respect, let alone employment, could be seen to be given to those
who abandoned the priesthood. The left, on the other hand, realized that they had been handed a great opportunity of embarrassing ecclesiastical authority and getting back at them. The
university teachers' union became involved, and legal advice was
sought by both sides. Should the College Governors simply sack
the ex-priests? Such a dismissal would be vigorously contested
by the union in court. Staff relations were thoroughly soured. The
right wing postured away, and the left wing sat tight. Heythrop
had quickly turned into an unhappy ship with a deeply divided
crew.

Running parallel to these sad developments was the process of
appointing a new Principal of the College. I was approached by
the Providing Body and the Governors with a view to becoming
Principal. I was flattered as usual, of course, and I agreed to be
put forward for election. I thereby automatically aligned myself
with the right-wing position regarding the staff problem. On
entirely pragmatic grounds my view was that, given the pecu-
liarly vulnerable status of Heythrop as dependent on a charitable
trust, those who were causing the problem should do the decent
thing and resign. If the worst came to the worst and the existence

of Heythrop became threatened, they should, regrettably, be sacked. What I did not know when I was unanimously chosen by the Governors as the new Principal was that the College Charter gave the Governors no powers of dismissal. This, to my mind, rendered my new post untenable, and I declined to take it up.

Understandably, these were not the best of times either at Heythrop or among the Jesuits. Factions, obfuscations, recriminations, wild uncharitable judgements were all too frequent. Supposed friendships evaporated, a few others strengthened. Heythrop was not popular at the Vatican, still sore about the fate of its Pontifical Athenaeum, and the problems that beset the College were welcomed by powerful figures in Rome and London as a sign that it was time to close it down. There were strong, confusing disagreements between Jesuit Superiors. But I refrain from writing about these matters in further detail. Too many of those involved are either still alive; or, as they say, I know too much about where the bodies are buried. I am pleased that Heythrop has survived and has gone on to flourish. I would not have been the Principal it needed at that time. I shall simply blame myself for ever allowing my name to go forward as a candidate for the post. No bones were broken, no one is ever indispensable, and the upshot of my inevitable departure from Heythrop was that it was eventually easier for me to leave the Jesuits, though I did not take that step for almost another decade. I consider that the whole Principalship episode did me a great favour – and that I did the College a great favour in refusing to take on the role. With my problems regarding the nature and function of theology and my steadily growing disillusionment with the Society, I was hardly the right man for the job. I often take solace from a remark made by Maude Petre, the doughty supporter and close friend of George Tyrrell: 'If I am wrong, then I am so deeply, fundamentally wrong, that only God can prove it to me. If I am right, then he will make good to me what I have forfeited before men.'

⁂

Obviously I had no future at Heythrop, and I would just have to look around for work elsewhere. The Jesuit authorities would not help: they simply considered that I had got myself into a mess and I could get myself out of it or stew in my own juice. One or two loyal Jesuit friends, for whom I retain great respect – not least the late Michael Kyne, one of the most impressive Jesuits of my generation – encouraged me in taking the only course of action open to me: that of working out my own salvation. I had to move

on. By great good fortune I at last discovered the kind of adver-
tisement I had been seeking for some time. Ironically, it had been
pinned on the noticeboard at Heythrop, presumably for the attention of a graduate student. It advertized for applicants for the
post of Head of Religious Studies at the Roehampton Institute of
Higher Education. With the permission of the Provincial – as far
as he was concerned, it was a handy way of shunting me into a
convenient siding – I sent in my application to Roehampton, and
in Spring 1981 I was shortlisted with five other candidates. We
were all interviewed and closely scrutinized over a period of two
days, first by the Principals of the four colleges in the federation
which formed the Institute, then by the staff of the department,
and finally by the formal, and very large, panel of interviewers.
The whole business turned into quite an ordeal. I had never
before put myself out, so to speak, to public tender, and I had
never had to face external competition for any post I had filled.
When I returned to Mount Street after the first day I was no
longer sure that I wanted to continue. But Clarence Gallagher, by
this time the Assistant Provincial, wisely cheered me on. I slept
well, and I returned the next day for the formal interview, back in
fighting form. My references were good, especially the one I had
from Alan Webster, now the Dean of St Paul's. I knew I was justified in considering myself a strong candidate – a good academic
record, wide administrative, teaching and examining experience,
and only recently elected to a College Principalship. I thought I
dealt with the interview panel in perhaps too debonair a fashion,
but later that evening I was telephoned at Mount Street and asked
if I would accept the job. I readily did so, and confirmed my decision by letter. I was pleased to note that the ordinary world
showed itself more accommodating that the world of my fellow-
religious.

I moved from Mount Street at the beginning of September 1981,
to live in an old cottage in Roehampton Lane which belonged to
Digby Stuart College, the Catholic component of the Institute. It
was doomed to be demolished in a couple of years' time, and I
lived there free and alone to stop vandals or squatters taking it
over. For my work I was assigned to the Froebel Institute College,
the only non-denominational member of the Roehampton
quartet. I fancy this was a move which was meant to preserve my
neutrality within a Department of Religious Studies whose staff
and students were spread over all four colleges. I was the first
Head of Religious Studies ever appointed at Roehampton, and
the post was highly sensitive. To have a Roman Catholic priest

and a Jesuit in charge of a Religious Studies Department could easily have been seen as a threat to the interests of Whitelands, the Anglican foundation, and perhaps more particularly to Southlands, the Methodist component with its strong commitment to religious education. It would have been tactless to be too closely connected with Catholic Digby Stuart. I was fully aware that a rather raw situation needed careful handling, and I managed, I think, to do nothing that would alarm either the colleges or my own department. Such changes as were necessary I made very circumspectly. I was to be Head of Department for almost ten years, and though not everything went smoothly, I managed to keep the department running and performing comparatively well against a background of quite severe reductions in staff and funding, and in line with all the changes of syllabus and regulations which the Institute required in its long – and eventually successful – bid to incorporate itself into the University of Surrey. What is more, I grew fond of my staff, and I liked being at Roehampton.

On my arrival the Roehampton Institute was still at an early stage of its development. It had been conceived and planned some five or six years previously by the Principals and Governors of its four colleges, two on the Roehampton side of Wimbledon Common, and two on the other. Previously teacher training establishments, the colleges had been encouraged by the government to diversify into other, more academic areas of work, and to prepare their students for university degrees. This they had done, offering degrees validated by the University of London Institute of Education. It was as an examiner in Religious Studies there that I had first come across Roehampton Institute students and staff. The formation of the Roehampton Institute struck me as a very worthy aim, though when I got there I thought its unification still needed strengthening, and that too much emphasis and play was still being given to its separate colleges. Their rather bullish Principals were inclined to view the Institute as a means of guaranteeing that the colleges would continue to live in the style to which they had become accustomed; and the individual colleges were over-represented in the Institute's governing structure. Perhaps all this was understandable in the Institute's early days, but the tensions between the colleges and their Institute could endanger the proper development of the whole. I had to be, of course, on the side of the Institute to which I had been formally appointed – I had been assigned only for practical purposes to a college.

The same tension affected the work of my department. My staff had all been appointed originally to what were still independent colleges and not to the Institute as such. They had never had an Institute appointee as Head of Department. I had to move with caution. The widely spread location of their offices and of the courses they taught did not make it easy for me to deal with them and their ingrained habits of work, their loyalties, and, in one or two cases, their accustomed idleness. Only a few stalwarts among them seemed convinced by the idea of the Institute. A few others disliked change or disturbance or the need to work out new and better courses. They were insecure and very watchful of developments that might imperil their jobs. Most of them had been recycled once, when degree courses were first introduced; and they did not now like being recycled again into a larger department. Apart from two or three who were academically excellent, they were modestly qualified professionally and academically. Most read and studied little, and researched hardly at all; and so they did not have the confidence and ease that comes with being in command of their subjects. The students were normally – but by no means always – of an academic standard which did not challenge their capacity to teach them. But I quickly learnt to live with limitations such as these, and I believe that in my time at Roehampton I made the best of things. My relations with my staff were, except in the case of one able but entrenched opponent, friendly, and I could well understand their misgivings and their insecurities in a rapidly changing Institute which a number of them had perhaps never really wanted. When I began, the recently combined department was overstaffed for what it was prepared to do. But the staff soon thinned itself out, as I began to make it clear that I expected people to work; and before financial considerations really began, late in the 1980s, to dictate what was possible, I was able to make two or three good appointments, all of them young, bright, well-qualified women. I came to like the Roehampton students very much. For all their lack of academic strength, they were fresh, varied, sensible and interesting people in themselves. Many suffered much more from poor schooling than from lack of ability. They deserved the best the department was capable of, and it was gratifying to see the progress they could make. The student numbers remained fairly buoyant throughout, and I thought we did a respectable job with them on the whole. We were, I think, the largest Religious Studies Department in the country, and, despite our shortcomings, acknowledged to be one of the best in the Institute.

Over my stay at Roehampton I gave a number of very different courses in biblical studies, early Christian theology and philosophy of religion, and I tutored students in these subjects. Very early on, in 1982, we had to prepare to move from London-validated degrees to degrees of a new format validated by the University of Surrey down the A3 in Guildford. This was the first big organizational job I had to undertake for my department, and I did it almost single-handedly. I aimed to ensure that each member of staff could stick to teaching his or her preferred subject. I imagined this might lead to increased personal specialization and research without making staff feel insecure. I am afraid this approach did not always work, since many took it as an excuse for falling back on what they thought they knew already. Another misjudgement of mine was in not engaging more of the staff in the framing of the completely new courses. As long as I did all the work, most of them seemed content to pour their old wine into whatever new bottle I provided for them – wine, in some cases, that would not have burst a paper bag. There were exceptions, however. I was fortunate, for instance, in having Cyril Rodd of Southlands as, so to speak, the *doyen* of the department – a Methodist clergyman of the highest ability, extremely hard-working, worthy of a professorial chair in any British university, editor of the learned *Expository Times*. In asking Cyril to stick to teaching Old Testament studies and his uniquely computerized Hebrew, I knew that he would immerse himself in the subject and produce results, and he did. I also enjoyed solid support from Janet Dyson, later the Vice-Principal of Southlands, and a reliable teacher of New Testament studies. But larger issues like the composing of the whole rationale for the 'new' courses and the presentation of them to the Surrey Validation Panel I had to undertake on my own. I was delighted and relieved when the Panel raised no serious difficulties with my new scheme, and the Department was edged a little further forward towards academic respectability. I think that I was touching on one of the defining differences between the universities and the old institutes of higher education. In a university setting new opportunities such as the move to Surrey degrees might have caused some excitement or interest among the staff, and perhaps new ideas might have been generated. At Roehampton my staff, for the most part, wanted to be left alone. I took account of this, insofar as I had to, but I felt it was ultimately unfair on the students, who were not unresponsive to stimulating teaching and certainly deserved the best.

My ten years at Roehampton turned into a bonus in human living that I could not have expected. It was a truly formative and useful experience. It sprang me out of the Heythrop trap I had fallen into, and gave me a new lease not only of academic life but, far more importantly, of life in the ordinary world inhabited by real people. I was surprised, for instance, to find that so many Institute staff could do excellent work with a commitment and motivation that did not need the support of a religious system. Roehampton also confirmed me in my ability to live alone and make a life for myself. After the old cottage was demolished I moved into a flat in Digby Stuart, paying rent and doing everything for myself. I did all my own shopping, cooking, washing, and, for much of the time, cleaning. These I consider basic life-skills which should be within the scope of any grown-up person. Cooking I took up with enthusiasm, and I made myself a reliable and even creative caterer. I reckon cookery, along with gardening, to be one of the best of stimulants to the intelligence and the imagination. I entertained select friends in my flat from time to time, and it was good to be able to repay at least some of the hospitality which had been lavished on me in the days when I had no facilities with which to pay my social debts. I love good food and drink; and I count myself fortunate in the fact that alcohol generally makes me feel ill long before it might make me drunk. I continued to see a range of friends, and Barbara was, as ever, supportive. At some time in the mid-1980s she gave me a kitten, a coal-black creature with large golden eyes called Nero. I recall very clearly the first night I had him in my flat. For peace and quiet I shut him, tiny as he was, in the living room, and went off into my bedroom. I could hear him scratching at the intervening door to come and join me. The revelatory thought came over me: 'I am in my mid-50s, and this is the first creature to be entirely dependent on me, the first being for whom I am wholly responsible. There must be something wrong with my life.' Nero and I got on very well, and he proved to be just the company I needed. He grew into a big long-haired fellow who roamed over the roofs, fought with the Hoover and ate potato peelings and Twiglets. When he was killed by a car during one of his stays at Barbara's, I was more distressed that I had ever been over any human death so far; and along with Sebastian, the very dear but grumpy old cat that Barbara and I later had for a long time, I still miss him daily. I have learnt far more about many of the important things in life from animals than I ever did from Jesuitism.

It will be obvious that the atrophy of my connection with the

Jesuits was set to accelerate as the years went by. I now saw very little of them, and I was plainly not being encouraged to maintain contact with them over and above the bare essentials. I had been dumped. Lack of contact meant that Superiors could avoid, as they always tried to do, confronting the issues that had arisen. My guess is that Superiors were trusting to their time-honoured formula of letting someone they regarded as a miscreant fend for himself – he has made his own bed and he must lie on it. I recall how George Tyrrell's Superiors, almost a century before, quite expressly decided to leave him to his own devices. I wonder if this was meant to bring me to me senses, see the error of my ways, ask to return to the fold, and so on. If so, I can only say that it showed a seriously faulty appreciation of how much I was enjoying my demanding work and my new independence down in Roehampton. I was earning a considerable salary – a professorial one by the time I retired – and the arrangement with the Jesuits was that I would take my living expenses out of it and send the residue on to Mount Street. This I continued to do very dutifully to the end. My expenses were not high: I had to run a small car to get me round the colleges, down to university meetings at Guildford, and so on; I had to pay rent for the flat; and then I had my very modest living and leisure expenses. Apart from this I spent virtually nothing, and the Jesuits did very well out of what was left of my salary. More or less monthly I sent them a large cheque. I would reckon that over the years I easily paid the Jesuits back for everything they had ever spent on me, and more. I am glad I did, if only because it ensured that I had even less reason to feel ungrateful to them when we finally parted.

In 1983 I was called on to deliver my Inaugural Lecture as Head of the Religious Studies Department. I entitled it: *Poetry, Prophecy – and Prospects? Religious Studies at Roehampton*. I did not want to bore a large audience with a lecture on some theological topic, so I chose to base my material locally, in late-nineteenth-century Manresa House, the Jesuit novitiate down in Roehampton village, a place which I had known well, now owned by the Borough of Wandsworth and used for further education. To illustrate my theme I chose two Jesuits who were both at Manresa in the same year, 1881–2, though in different communities: the poet Gerard Manley Hopkins in the tertianship, and the prophet George Tyrrell in the novitiate. On to what turned out to be an entertaining account of what I called 'two matching, middle-aged, marvellous Jesuit misfits, a major poet

and a major prophet' I added some pertinent reflections on how
I saw religion as a mixture of poetry and prophecy, and on how
I thought Religious Studies should develop at the Institute. The
lecture was declared a success, and I got a great deal out of
writing it. But two great benefits I derived from it were, first, to
re-assess Hopkins as a man who was seriously harmed by the
Jesuit system (his latest biographers bear this out); and second,
to re-acquaint myself with George Tyrrell. I hardly need to point
out that here was a troublesome Jesuit, certainly 'un peu difficile', with whom it was only too easy for me to identify. I had
taken some interest in him before; but like Wittgenstein, he had
lain dormant in my mind until it was time for him to rise up
and come to my aid. Just as he had been rusticated to Richmond
in Yorkshire by his outraged Jesuit Superiors, for instance, so
had I been virtually abandoned in Roehampton by mine. I am
not suggesting more than the most superficial comparison
between us, because Tyrrell was, I am convinced, something of
a religious genius. But in Tyrrell I found someone whose outspoken attitudes to institutional authority I could now readily
appreciate, and I admired the way in which he was prepared to
take on what he called (in another –ism) Medievalism, the
systematic embodiment of Catholicism as he found it in the
Roman Church.

Serious theological research was ruled out at Roehampton by
the inadequacy of the Institute's libraries. But Roman Catholic
Modernism was a more accessible topic, and I pitched into the
study of it. I edited some of Tyrrell's letters to his Jesuit colleague
and friend Herbert Thurston and published them with a running
commentary in a sub-standard booklet. I attended a summer
conference on Modernism, and joined the working party on the
subject which was affiliated to the American Academy of
Religion. Tyrrell once defined his aim as being 'to elaborate a
modus vivendi for liberal Catholics in an illiberal Church'; and this
was in line with what I believe to have been the general aim of
Modernism, namely to make Catholicism more credible. This, I
fancy, was what really outraged the Roman authorities who saw
it as solely their business to declare what was, or was not,
Catholicism. But as my study of Tyrrell proceeded I found that I
was less attracted to his Catholic liberalism (an attitude I have
never found congenial), and more specifically interested in the
nature of Catholic believing and its function with regard to
Catholic faith. What I had begun to look for was what I would
call 'a *modus vivendi* for radical Catholics in a radically revised

Church'. I am not by nature a liberal person, except in the obvious sense that I try hard to be tolerant of others.

I like to think my own way towards radical precision; and my approach to Modernism led me to want to know the answer to a radical question: just what is happening when a person who shares the Catholic faith says: 'I *believe* in X, Y or Z', as he or she recites the Creed? This seemed to me to lie at the heart of being able to understand and interpret Catholicism, rather than moves made towards some necessarily vague 'liberalization' of it. Be a Catholic believer by all means, but precisely what are you *doing* when you declare that you 'believe', say, in the Trinity? And just what have your Catholic *beliefs* got to do with your Christian *faith*? Tyrrell sensed the importance of these questions, and he once remarked that what really needed elucidating was the word *Credo*, but I did not find any satisfactory treatment of it in his writings. John Henry Newman's *A Grammar of Assent* was much closer to what I was looking for, but in the end I felt I was going to have to look for answers on my own. I found that I was becoming quite well equipped to do so. Wittgenstein had helped me to come to terms with religious and theological language and how it might mean what it was trying to say. Gadamer had helped me to come to terms with the traditional and interpretative nature of the theology I was teaching. Tyrrell showed me that I would, in the end, have to come to radical terms with my Catholic faith as a system of beliefs authoritatively required by the Roman Church. At Roehampton I had time to work out a crude synthesis of my own which drew heavily on these three masters and covered the area of the concerns I had been nurturing for almost twenty years.

I still functioned daily as a priest, of course, saying Mass in the College when requested (there was a College chaplain who dealt with the religious life of Digby Stuart and its students), hearing confessions in the local convent, preaching chiefly ecumenical sermons in surrounding churches, doing parish supply-work in the vacations and at weekends, giving evening talks to Catholic adult education groups, and so on. I was always happy to do so, and I enjoyed meeting the wide range of people these activities involved. I cannot think I was much good at them, but neither do I think I did any harm. What I did was generously appreciated. I visited Barbara and her two children. Michael went to Stonyhurst and then followed in his mother's footsteps through R.A.D.A. Sarah married an American Air Force sergeant and found herself stationed in Hawaii with a daughter. I also continued to see my family quite often. My sister Barbara lived in the wide open spaces of Norfolk, and my brother Alan, by now a successful full-time artist, remained settled in Leyland, where my Mother still lived in a flat which had a spare bedroom, and I stayed with her from time to time. Barney McCann had moved from Preston on the death of his father, and now lived and worked in the North-East. We still met either in the north or the south fairly regularly. Other friends in Weybridge and Walton-on-Thames I saw quite often. I had contrived to make a useful life for myself at Roehampton – still the religious life of a Jesuit, but greatly enriched by the supportive contacts I maintained with my family and my friends. The Jesuits themselves played a rapidly dimin-ishing part in it all. By the late '80s it had become obvious that my situation, tolerable enough as I had made it, could not go on much longer.

I felt that there was nothing more to gain from remaining a Jesuit, and that there was nothing I would miss in leaving the Society; though I would regret not seeing some few individuals. I felt, frankly, as if I had grown out of a marriage that had turned sour and died. I did not even feel strongly about the whole busi-ness. Only in a distant and vicarious way could I share, for instance, in the *saeva indignatio* which George Tyrrell shared with his fellow-Dubliner, Jonathan Swift, and which burst out to such splendid effect in the long, searing letter he wrote to the Jesuit General (the decidedly weird Luis Martín) from his Richmond rustication before leaving the Jesuits (M.D. Petre, *Autobiography and Life of George Tyrrell*, vol. II, pp. 459-499, at p. 498f.):

> It seems to me, in conclusion, that I have not altogether run in vain, or wasted my life, if I have done no more than win to my present clearness of moral conviction through many tribulations, strug-gling free from the briars and brambles of a false system in which my feet were early ensnared. It is a good life's work to have arrived by personal experience and reflection at the solution of so plausible and complicated a fallacy as that of Jesuitism.

Not for nothing does Tyrrell still command an entry in *The Oxford Companion to English Literature* (1985). His *Medievalism* (1908, republished by Burns & Oates, 1994) remains a highly relevant masterpiece of well-aimed religious invective. But I cannot recall feeling quite so strongly about my inevitable divorce from the Jesuits.

Again, life and work at Roehampton were becoming more diffi-cult. Like all establishments of higher learning, it was coming under savagely increasing financial pressure. Money came to dominate the running of the place. All courses had to be 'costed' – a fatuous exercise. Much-needed staff appointments were ruled out as too expensive and we had to make do with visiting lecturers who were unavailable for the usual chores involved in teaching students and attending meetings; work-loads (at least for the willing) increased; morale became difficult to maintain; endless changes to teaching methods were required in response to government demands, a complete system of course-units had suddenly to be imposed on the syllabus validated by the University of Surrey, familiar and reassuring figures began to tiptoe away from the Institute into retirement to be replaced by more expensive accountants. Work went on in the department (now renamed by me as the Department of Theology and Religious Studies), and staff did their best to cope with all the chop-and-change we underwent. One of my excellent secretaries (Janet White) was succeeded by another (Jane Basso), and now the latter saved us all from foundering as paper proliferated and had to be pushed around the Institute ceaselessly. There was now little room left for any academically-based judgements regarding the work of the department. A system of Faculties with their Deans was imposed in an attempt to give the Institute what were hoped would be the beginnings of a university structure that could be built on (as they have been) later. I am not at all opposed to change, and indeed I could have suggested far-reaching changes of more practical value that the ones we had to suffer. Undoubtedly there was a measure of slack and waste at Roehampton, as there always is in any institution, and it needed to be corrected. What was becoming uncongenial to me was that all the corrections applied were cost-cutting exercises based on financial, and not on academic, grounds. I had simply not been brought up that way in my academic life. How much longer did I want to go on trying to keep my little show on the road against unstoppably increasing odds? By 1988-9, interiorly and exteriorly, I was under pressure to do something about my personal position and my future, both regarding the Jesuits and regarding Roehampton.

ℛ

I decided to tackle the problem with the Jesuits first. By now it was clear that we would have to part. This was a sad conclusion to come to, but as I looked ahead to the future and to my eventual retirement from Roehampton, parting seemed inevitable. I was not keen on it. I had no other plans. I was not interested in leaving them and staying in the priesthood, as I was in fact invited to do, since the priesthood had only ever been part of being a Jesuit as far as I was concerned. I might feel as if I were losing a certain status, perhaps, but it was no longer a status for which I had much respect, and Roehampton had shown that I was reasonably viable in the ordinary world – and what was pragmatically far more important, Roehampton would also provide me with a pension. I had, with Jesuit permission, enhanced my contributions to my occupational pension, and I reckoned I would possibly have just about enough to live on if I retired. Perhaps the Jesuits had let me increase my pension contributions because they guessed, accurately, that I was sure to leave sooner or later anyway. So the future seemed to lie open, and there was no need to feel caught in what had turned out to be a bad marriage. Another reason for making a move to leave the Jesuits was that I could not now envisage ever going back to live in a Jesuit house. I was once – only once, I think – invited by a new Provincial to supper back at the Mount Street Jesuit HQ, and the house, where I had been content to live for some years, now struck me as a place inhabited by alienated characters, all the stranger for being once familiar to me. I have a still vivid memory of pulling out of Mount Street into Park Lane, and then rounding Hyde Park Corner in my red Volkswagen Golf on the way back to Roehampton, and feeling downright guilty that I was so lucky and happy to be out on my own. Again, leaving the Jesuits and the priesthood was, as they say, 'no big deal' any longer. I knew plenty of ex-colleagues who had done it; and it seemed to me a matter of personal honesty to get out rather than to do what I had seen too many do: dissociate internally and hang on in the Society, sometimes turning sour and cynical, a drag on the institution. It was not always their fault, of course, since most simply had nowhere to go. But I could have somewhere to go, though I did not yet know where.

I made my decision to leave as I lay in the Princess Grace Hospital at the start of 1988 recovering from an operation on my back, quite seriously damaged by over-enthusiastic exercise. The hospital was close to Mount Street, but I was relieved that only Francis Walker, who had taken over Heythrop when I left, came to see me. Conversations with him helped to convince me I was doing the right thing. On 17 January 1988 I wrote to another new Provincial, Michael Campbell-Johnston:

After many years of careful study and reflection ... I have finally decided to resign from the Society. I can no longer say that I personally accept its principles or its discipline. This is no easy move to make at my age; but it would be obviously wrong to mislead myself and others in so important a matter. Conscience has its rights, and what is called the salvation of souls, including my own, comes into question ... Hence I shall be asking you to effect my release as quickly and as amicably as possible.

On 2 February Francis and the Provincial and I met for a quick lunch in a small West End restaurant, and I confirmed my decision. After that there was no further live contact whatever between myself and my Jesuit Superiors. There was never any discussion of my reasons for wanting to leave, and, of course, no attempt to persuade me to stay. Not that there would have been any point in it anyway. I had, I suddenly realized, taken almost twenty years to come to my decision; and the Jesuits had probably been waiting about eight years for me finally to go. After a full biblical forty years in the Society, the process of separation and divorce was slow and very cold. All further proceedings were conducted by post.

Veteran observer of ecclesiastical folly as I had become, I have to say I was amazed at the incompetence with which the English Jesuits handled the business – it was as if no one had ever left the Society before. At first, in a typically ecclesiastical move, it was thought best to search around for, and if necessary to fabricate, legal reasons to 'dismiss' me from the Society – 'dismiss' being the infelicitous translation of the Latin *dimittere,* which simply means 'release', though 'dismiss', I am sure, was preferred since it connotes the use of a certain imperious authority. This was the attitude taken by the Jesuits at the start – an instinctive, face-saving ploy which has the happy effect of keeping them in the right while putting the individual firmly in the wrong. They were simply doing what Rome instinctively does: ensuring that you are in 'bad faith'. But I did not care what attitude they took as long as they got on with proceedings. But then it appears that they tumbled to the fact that there were no reasons, legal or otherwise, for 'dismissing' me, since I had done nothing reprehensible – unless, of course, thinking my own thoughts was reprehensible. I was guilty of nothing but applying to resign. It eventually occurred to them that the 'dismissal' of someone who was only asking to leave anyway was a nonsense which was likely to make them look stupid; and that always having to put people in the wrong so that you yourself can claim to be right is silly, not to say very unjust. Thankfully, after many months of delay the Roman Jesuit authorities stepped in and recommended a new approach.

I was to be asked to write a letter, formally addressed to the Pope, requesting dispensation from my religious vows and all the obligations of the priesthood – with the exception of celibacy.

If I had misgivings about being expected to remain celibate, they were allayed by two considerations: first, I had in fact no prospects of getting married; and second, a covering letter from a Jesuit canon lawyer in Rome assured me – with all the exquisite casuistry of double negatives – that 'this request [the letter to the Pope, agreeing to remain celibate] does not imply that a man is not thinking of marrying at some time in the future'. So the position, as I saw it, in this delicate matter now amounted to this: I would be released from all my Jesuit vows, including the vow of chastity, as well as from all my priestly obligations, but not from the law of celibacy which the Roman Church imposes on its priests – though, as it happens, not on all of them. If, for instance, you happen to be a married ex-Anglican vicar who converts to Rome and becomes a priest, celibacy is rightly not required. Now, it appeared, Rome was also insisting on celibacy for those who are effectively its ex-priests. It was further explained to me that if I was willing to accept the imposition of celibacy for the time being, I would be free in all other respects; and if I ever wanted to get married, I could ask again for the imposition of celibacy to be lifted. I am too old, and too ingrained a Catholic, to bother taking issue with what most sane folk would take to be time-wasting nonsense which insults the intellectual and moral standards of the people it is meant to impress. I felt embarrassed for the Church, rather than angry with it. I felt a crude trap was being set for me: the bait of freedom from all my other obligations was being dangled over the pit of continuing – though not necessarily lengthy – celibacy. I was being caught up in a silly game: either they expected me to take the bait and remain steadfastly celibate, or they were inviting me to see through their cynicism, to go ahead and get married if ever I should want to, to face Rome with a *fait accompli*, and then ask on bended knee, of course, to be granted a condescending dispensation. Heads, Rome wins: tails, Rome wins. Rome can only be in the right. The law of celibacy must remain intact. In both cases the customer loses. But Rome's real aim would have been achieved – to put anyone who disagrees with Rome in 'bad faith'. I decided there was only one possible attitude to take towards this pettifogging chicanery – to treat it with the utter contempt it merited. I could not believe that Rome was seriously claiming the right to transfer its ex-priests automatically into a new Order of Lay Eunuchs.

It was in this spirit that I wrote my humble request to the Pope, sticking strictly to the suggested terminology and format:

Holy Father,
I, R.B., a religious priest professed of solemn vows in the Society of Jesus, request from your Holiness the favour of loss of the clerical status, with dispensation from all obligations of the clerical state and religious life, with the exception of the law of priestly celibacy. My serious reasons for making this request are the following:

1) After many years of study and careful deliberation, I have decided that my personal salvation is no longer promoted by continuing to live in accordance with the principles and discipline of the Society of Jesus. I cannot, therefore, in conscience remain a member of the Society, bound by the obligations of vows and religious life.

2) Since I have never, in practice, considered my priestly ordination as other than a necessary part of my vocation to the Society of Jesus, the discontinuance of the latter entails a request for release from the obligations arising from the former. I have, consequently, no wish to remain a priest or to exercise the ministerial priesthood.

3) My present wish is to live as a single layman in the Church.

The date of this letter was 23 August 1989. The perfunctory Roman reply, from some indecipherable Vatican archiepiscopal lackey, was dated 23 May 1990, nine months later. My request was granted *firma manente obligatione sacri coelibatus* – 'the obligation of sacred celibacy remaining firmly in place'. So ended my life in the religious world, and my return from that desert detour to the ordinary world. There would be re-entry problems, naturally, as there are for astronauts who return from the weightlessness and artificial support systems required for life in space away from our ordinary world to the gravity and the atmosphere in which normal mortals have to live and work. My feelings about the preceding twenty years were twofold: on the one hand, I was glad I had continued to function effectively and satisfyingly as a Jesuit priest and academic throughout, and I had done my best, as I saw it, at every turn. I had at least avoided doing anyone harm. It had been interesting and enlightening to experience rejection by the Jesuits. I realized that what I had done was to trigger their built-in auto-immune system which was programmed to whip up antibodies so that they mindlessly rejected those considered to be an alien virus still in their midst. This kind of immature allergic reaction was part of a problem they still had within their own religious system, and really had

little to do with me. On the other hand, I felt that whilst I had
been through a long period of internal strife, at least I had not
hesitated to plunge into what I had seen as the underworld of
uncertainties. There I had been greatly helped by my chosen
guides, and I had come to realize that what I had passed through
was nothing more than a return to the ordinary world of people
who intend to be serious about their human lot. I felt I needed to
reject the artificial Jesuitism which I had had transplanted into
me, and to get my native Catholicism back. I felt I no longer
needed the Jesuit superstructural system to support my life in the
ordinary world. The other metaphysical world of religion was
now redundant – was dead. I wanted to persevere in becoming a
serious human being.

Even before the reply came from Rome, I had moved out of the
flat in Digby Stuart. I felt that, kind as the College had been, it
might be embarrassed by my presence. I moved into Barbara's
house as a lodger. Her family had flown the nest, and there was
plenty room for both of us to live our separate lives. She was
newly retired from her job as Head of Religious Education at her
old convent school in Isleworth – a job in which she had distinguished herself. I continued to work at the Roehampton Institute,
commuting from Uxbridge, where I now lived. In November 1991
Barbara and I surprised ourselves – but perhaps not many others
– by getting married. We married, in the presence of close family
and friends, in the ancient local Anglican Church of St Lawrence
Cowley. The officiating minister was Fr Tony Eagles, a long-
standing friend of both of us, and an Anglican priest of distinction. We would have preferred to marry in the Catholic Church,
but I saw no point whatever in asking Rome for permission to be
released from my bogus obligation to celibacy. I consider I had
been automatically released by the evident nonsense I had experienced in our previous dealings. My view is solidly based on the
theology I had once imbibed at the old Heythrop: in any Church
man and wife marry one another before God – the Church does
not marry them, but acts as no more than a witness; and in that
case, it seems to me to matter little which Church is involved. In
any case, we both still count ourselves very happily married
Roman Catholics.

In the course of 1991 the Roehampton Institute, in pursuance of
its drive for economy on staff, offered everyone over the age of
fifty-five the option of early retirement. I discussed the matter
with Barbara, and we decided that we could live well enough on
our twin pensions. I was now in my sixty-first year, and, like

many older staff members, I was growing intolerably frustrated by the money-led thinking which the Institute was forced to adopt by the government. So I snapped up the offer of early retirement. I was asked to reconsider and to stay on as Head of Department for a while, but I declined to do so. On 31 December 1991 I formally retired, and the next day, free at last and happily married, I began to emerge and face life in the ordinary world of human uncertainties.

Chapter 7

Re-entry into the Real World

Having known one another and our respective families for almost twenty years, Barbara and I rapidly became a happily married retired couple. We had both earned adequate professional pensions – adequate, that is, for a life together of modest scope and reasonable comfort. This had come about in my case by luck. When I left them, the Jesuits gave me, 'in full and final settlement', a lump sum which may have looked generous enough to them, but which was in fact considerably less than one year's salary at Roehampton. They had the grace to throw in my ageing car. I do not think they intended to be mean; but considering that I had spent forty years with them, was by now moving into my sixties with sharply diminishing prospects, had no property or savings, and over the last ten years had dutifully contributed to them from my Roehampton salary a sum well in excess of what they were prepared to pay out, I think it is fair to say that they were being economical with their not inconsiderable resources. Of course, I could have worked on at Roehampton for another five years until retirement age; but this, as I have explained, would have become increasingly stressful and distasteful as the standards I thought appropriate to higher education rapidly declined across the nation. If I had not had my small pension entitlement, and been dependent only on the Jesuit pay-off and perhaps some casual employment, I could soon have found myself in difficulties – a consideration which, as I know, can weigh on some who might otherwise happily quit the religious life. I must add that I was being dealt with more generously than other ex-Jesuits and other ex-religious whose circumstances I happen to know. Provision for retirement naturally plays little part in clerical thinking, because eventual retirement from the clerical state is ruled out. Popes themselves continue to give dubious example by hanging on to their office until they drop. Refusal to retire is considered a virtue, and retirement counts as some sort of moral defeat. The people who suffer most from all this are, of course, the Catholic faithful.

I worked for a couple of terms as a visiting lecturer in my old department at Roehampton, but then I was happy to withdraw completely into retirement. I felt that retirement might prove a waste of the brief and very valuable time left after my long detour through religious life if I did not use it to the full to face up to the problems of who and what I was and how I was really meant to live. Two ancient Greek mottoes imposed themselves: 'Know yourself' and 'How should one live?' To respond adequately to them I decided it would be best to clear the clerical decks and get back to personal basics; and in particular, to depend no longer on my status or my job, or on leftover bits of my job, for such feelings of self-worth as I had. I was surprised to discover how dependent I had become on having been in charge of a department for almost a quarter of a century, telling people what I wanted done, keeping the show on the road, sitting on committees, chairing and attending meetings, representing the interests of other parts of the establishment and other members of staff – in general, on just being responsible. I had always identified closely with the jobs I had done, and I had been trained to derive most of the personal worth I thought I had from doing them properly. My personal worth to the Jesuits had proved to be nothing more than my willingness and ability to function. Gone now was the protective social and personal carapace provided by my being a Jesuit and an academic. Gone, too, were all the mindless but consoling certainties about life which I had derived from supposing that long religious commitment and serious theological study automatically afforded privileged access to wisdom and goodness. Above all, I felt I stood in urgent need of 'salvation' – for goodness and wisdom, for some kind of 'holiness'. The spiritual aspirations, such as they were, with which I had set out in my 'teens were still there unfulfilled, and it was clear to me that they were not going to be satisfied by any religious system, Jesuit or Catholic. I had heard others say that they had left religious life for the very same reasons for which they had originally embraced it, and I could now see how this might be true. But I was still convinced that somehow Catholicism, properly understood, would fulfil my needs. I was also convinced that now my detour into religious life was finished, and I was back on life's highway, my route to 'salvation' lay through marriage. But as I started out, I felt exposed and vulnerable; though I realized that I ought to be glad that I was free of all that had been buttressing and protecting what I could now only view as my bogus identity – though I must admit that there were times when I felt bereft of the comforts of the old façade.

Fortunately I now had a wise and good and loving wife and some real domestic responsibilities to bring me down to earth. It took me some time to realize it, but I had already cracked my re-entry problems in principle, and partly in practice also, simply by getting married. I was no longer on my own, and what might otherwise have been an intolerable vacuum had been instantly filled with all the delights and demands of married life. There were new friends and new family relatives to get to know and visit and entertain. There was a house to be run, and a hum-drum domestic life to be led with enthusiasm and attention – shopping, cooking, cleaning, gardening, minor maintenance, putting out the bins, taking holidays, walks, outings, dinner parties – all shared activities done now with and for one another. There was step-parental care to be exercised over Michael and Sarah as they confronted the difficulties of early adult life. After displaying much talent and promise at R.A.D.A., Michael had the misfortune to be waylaid by schizophrenia, and he was to spend more than a decade in care. Then, just when the excellent treatment he was given by the N.H.S. had proved successful, and he was established in his own flat in Camden, he died, very suddenly, of a pulmonary embolus in February 2002. Sarah's marriage had broken down, and she remained with her delightful daughter Jeni in Honolulu and worked as a paramedic. We were far from immune from family traumas, but we had one another, and, whilst we gave Michael and Sarah all the care and support they needed, we had time for the ceaseless attentions and adjustments that a married couple who are in love demand and give to one another. Whatever else I was going to make of life in the new world of retirement, I had firm foundations to build on and the best of all possible starts for working at its further construction.

I had made the radical exchange of the systematically remote religious world for the immediate world of human persons and their needs. What mattered now was no longer simply how I was functioning, but who I might be becoming. I recalled a phrase from (I think) Ignatius Loyola's *Constitutions*, in which the Jesuit is described as an *instrumentum divinitati conjunctum* – 'an instrument (or tool) conjoined to the Godhead'. It expresses accurately, but with chilling impersonality, the functional ideal which had been meant to be the inspiration of my Jesuit years. Nothing could be further from the world of marriage, where the core relationship was not some functionally operative link with God, but the entirely personal union in mutual love of a man and a woman – a union which validates the personhood of both, and provides both with the opportunity and the help they need to grow into mature and serious and happy human beings. The achievement of this degree of union demands close attention and hard work. I found I needed to learn to love and – what I found far more difficult – to be loved. I was humanly rusty, and I could sense that my personal feelings and reactions lacked warmth and spontaneity and took time to creak into action. Barbara dealt with my failings patiently and wisely. No doubt I still have a very long way to go.

We were both people who were inclined to keep ourselves occupied, and this we did in our different ways. Barbara has filled her years of retirement in a number of imaginative ways: a university diploma in psychology, a successful foray into sculpture, the creation of a beautiful small garden which remains a constant joy, a keen interest in local history, and, currently, intense research into family genealogy. We both use the Internet regularly. I am, I suppose, less widely spread in my interests and less enterprising. I studied painting for a few years, enjoyed it greatly, but did not really have the talent to improve, though I was good enough to want to take it up again, when I have time. Books and learning have remained my greatest interest, and immediately on retirement I gave up theology and went back to the study of classics, and especially to following Dr Johnson's famous advice: 'Greek, Sir,…is like lace; every man gets as much of it as he can' (Boswell's *Life of Johnson*, The World's Classics, p. 1081). I was well equipped with the latest and largest Liddell and Scott lexicon, several venerable grammars, and J.D. Denniston's indispensable *The Greek Particles* (Oxford 1950). I was equally well equipped for nostalgic visits to Latin literature, but these came later. I carefully read, and made notes on, many of Plato's dialogues, revisiting *The Republic* at length, and dwelling on the *Phaedrus*, the *Theaetetus*, and, with E.R. Dodds' commentary, the *Gorgias*. The steely lace of Plato's prose – surely the finest ever written – I found entrancing. A retired colleague from Roehampton asked me to help him with the Greek he had very effectively taught himself, and we still meet on a monthly Monday morning at 7.30 to pick and chat our way through a long session on some Greek text, usually Plato. To facilitate our passage through the *Symposium*, I recently completed a full translation. I discovered that in the thirty years I had been away from classics, a whole crop of new commentaries on Greek and Latin texts, some written by familiar scholars and some by a newer breed, had sprung up and were now ripe for harvesting: Dover, Mynors, Barrett, Burnyeat, Henderson, Garvie, Dawe, Easterling, Dunbar, and many others, all of whom I found both entertaining and instructive. One Christmas Barbara bought me the three volumes of Eduard Fraenkel's master-class on Aeschylus' *Agamemnon* – like his *Horace*, the work of one of the last century's most learned classicists, and a book which offers a classical education in itself. I compared it closely and at length with Denniston and Page's elegant and complementary treatment of the same play, a much more 'British' achievement. I loved the heavy learning, the meticulous accuracy and the linguistic and literary minutiae displayed in the commentaries, along with the inventive subtleties of the textual apparatus; and fortunately I was still handy enough both at Greek and Latin to follow most of the arguments, and even to disagree with them when I saw fit. I learned to work on the computer with the excellent American Perseus Project – 'Interactive Sources and Studies on Ancient Greece' – and with the huge *Thesaurus Linguae Graecae.*

For some years I turned to the challenge of accurate translation. I translated the trilogy of the *Oresteia*, and other plays, too: Sophocles' *Oedipus Rex*, Euripides' *Hippolytus* (with the help of Barrett's outstanding commentary), and, for sheer pleasure, Aristophanes' *Birds*, *Frogs*, and *Women in the Assembly*. I had long had an intense dislike of those readily available 'translations' of Greek plays which, at the onset of any difficulty or in the interests of modern theatricality or some other irrelevant fad, presume to leave the Greek text to its own devices and seek refuge in a fanciful, pseudo-lyrical verbiage which is as profoundly un-Greek as it could be, and must only mislead the reader. I found it more fitting to translate the dialogue of Greek plays into simple verse, and the lyric choruses, oddly enough, into strong English prose. Greek choruses are sung or recited words that accompany a group dance. They are exquisitely and tautly structured in strictly metrical units, *strophes* and *antistrophes*, which exactly correspond with one another and accompany the to-and-fro movements of the dancers in the *orchestra*, the stage on which they dance. Of the musical accompaniment and the choreography and the overall effect we know next to nothing. All we really have are the words. These, to my mind are characteristically strong and sinewy in their expression. There are no superfluities and none of the flaccid verbal tissue with which third-rate English lyricists love to pad out their affected versions of them. So to translate them into well-measured prose seems to me preferable. But in fact I believe that the whole idea of trying to translate poetry into 'poetry' is, in any case, nonsense – a useful definition of poetry itself being, as they say, precisely 'what gets lost in translation'. I have no doubt the poetry gets lost in my hum-drum efforts. One consolation in retirement afforded by translating Greek is that I will never run out of texts calling for attention. I have even begun to make my own translation of St Paul's letters. I do not think mine can be any more or less theologically biassed than the rest that are on general offer. I would argue that there are certain key elements in Paul's thought which are missed in the translations known to me. Of course I am conscious that, despite the late efforts I still expend on Greek and Latin, I shall never really become more than fairly competent at them; but the efforts, and sometimes the results, bring their own reward.

But neither Barbara nor I are inclined to keep too busy, either. I think we both find it helpful in retirement always to have some 'work' or other on the stocks. But we take great pleasure in going on as many holidays as we can afford, to prepare for winter in the autumn and to shorten the winter in February or March. Summer we can cope with easily, given the garden and fair weather. Both of us had travelled long distances in the past: Barbara to the Far East and East Africa during an early spell as a top B.O.A.C. stewardess in the leisurely pre-jet age, and I myself, as I have already explained, to Southern Africa and South America. Now we concentrated more on Europe, with parts of which I was already familiar. For winter sunshine we went to the South of Spain, to Egypt, Tunisia, a few Greek islands, Madeira and the Canaries, and for shorter breaks to Italy, and, most delightfully, to Florence. An extended tour of Greece gave my Greek studies a useful stimulus. Malta provided great Easter consolation after Michael's death, and Barcelona proved a revelation. Not that we neglected England, Wales or Ireland. But one year we decided to go right round the world before we got too old to do so. We took just over an effortless month over it and had a wonderful time: Hong Kong, Beijing, Hawaii (where Sarah lives, of course), San Francisco and New York. Neither of us would care to pick out a preferred location, though Hawaii had both its obvious and its special attractions, and New York was surprising fun. We flew for about 41 hours in all and covered 21,000 miles. Since then we have calmed down a little, but we still pursue as happy a mix of work and holidays as we can devise. So, for the moment, life in retirement goes on, unspectacular in the main, underpinned by convenient routines which are occasionally broken by some welcome variation. We are generally busy. Time passes ever more quickly. Every other day, I am convinced, is Friday.

સ્જ

But with whatever happened to be occupying me, from time to time one particular project kept on competing for my attention. I would fall to wondering if I ought to conduct some sort of personal review of Catholicism, now the dust had settled on my long years in the Jesuits. After all, my long experience of the latter was more than matched by my longer experience of the former, and both displayed points of close comparison. I could easily read out of my Jesuit experience much that fitted Catholicism at large. Again, I still had an unusually comprehensive knowledge and experience of Catholicism. I had lived under six Popes, and for much of that time I had been a cleric whose daily life was closely controlled by ecclesiastical authority. I had also spent two or three years living in Rome itself. But far from feeling less a Catholic after my lengthy and not altogether happy experiences, I began to feel rather more of one as my humanity revived in the new life I was now leading. I occasionally began to see more in Catholicism than had ever met the eye, and it was positively helping me to live in the ordinary world more effectively and more happily than it had ever helped me to live in religious life, where it simply dominated and demanded conformity. I suppose I am conservative at heart, though intellectually fairly radical. I have never been inclined to sweep away the past. It always struck me as extremely implausible to argue that all the intelligent and wise and holy people who worked at the establishment of so durable and impressive a religious tradition as Catholicism could have been plain wrong. On the other hand, I was quite prepared to maintain that what they had established might be overdue for further development or revision or even radical reinterpretation. I had never felt it necessary to reject any part of my Catholic faith, and I had been careful to observe what had been happening to my understanding and appreciation of it over a long period – and how other people's Catholicism had appeared to function in their case, too. In the light of this rare personal experience, it might be understandable – it might be necessary – to want to see what I thought Catholicism now amounted to, and where I now stood as a Catholic. In particular I wanted to know what had been going wrong with it after all the promise of Vatican II, and why the Church's pastoral efforts, instead of promoting Catholicism, were still so far from having their effect.

Some might say that I could have claimed by now to have had an overload of Catholicism – that I might be a burnt-out case; and that it would be best if I just left it alone and got on with my various happy avocations. But still I felt I had much to get out of it. Of the Church's over-centralization and its over-intrusive outreach, its sclerotic systems, its unacceptable metaphysics, its bully-boy wielding of authority and power, its pretentious hierarchical structure, the dominance of an all-male clergy, the habitual oppression of the laity – of these I had certainly had more than enough. But then these undesirable qualities belonged not to Catholicism as such – they merely represent the upshot of the ways in which the institutional Church had, over the centuries, thought best to promote it. Far from being qualities that afflicted Catholicism as a religion, they sprang simply from the serious human failings of its ecclesiastical purveyors. What I still felt in need of was precisely the *religion* of Catholicism – the spiritual life, the life of its Founder's spirit, which was supposed to enhance ordinary life more abundantly, to endow it with that life-giving, death-and-sin defeating quality so boldly manifested in the Founder's resurrection. Why was I still in so much need of the wisdom, the goodness, the holiness which Catholicism surely, somehow, had to offer? Paradoxically, a lifelong commitment to Catholicism, much of it spent in the professed religious state, had left what spiritual life I could still claim to have as an oddly dry, independent set of practices applicable to a world distinct from the one I was now living in. I had become retarded, atrophied, in my religious and spiritual development. Marriage and life in the ordinary world highlighted my deficiencies. I would certainly not exempt myself from blame for this outcome, though I had been faithful enough to the system's demands. Well, the system had not worked for me, and I wanted to know why it had not.

So what kind of Catholicism was I now looking for? Might it not be at least interesting to try and work out a practical way of understanding, of interpreting, Catholicism in ways that would release its religious and spiritual potential from the dead hand of system and the power of ecclesiastical authority? My interest was less in structural, and therefore superficial, Church reform than in the radical recycling of those elements which I considered as constituting the mind and heart of Catholicism – the mainline doctrines that made up its religious tradition. But this, I quickly realized, was not only profoundly unfashionable (does the Church still even *know* its own doctrinal tradition?) but also too large a project for me to handle – though I did occasionally work at it. My interests were more pragmatic At what points did I actually find that the shoe had pinched and, so to speak, stopped the circulation of the spirit of the Founder? Different people will answer this question differently – or, of course, repudiate it altogether. Speaking only for myself, I would say that there were three points at which I thought that Catholicism had failed to provide me with the support I needed for my religious and spiritual life, and which I was convinced that it might have provided had I been allowed freer access to the riches of its tradition than its system and its compulsion to control were prepared to offer.

In the first place, Catholicism had failed to give proper emphasis to the salvific function of the ordinary humanity of Jesus. I say 'Jesus' deliberately, and not 'Christ', because the latter is already a theologically loaded title. I mean Jesus the human being of thoroughly Catholic orthodoxy, who was everything being human meant 'for us and for our salvation'. Further, the particular human characteristic of Jesus that gave his humanity its saving power had long been ignored.

In the second place, Catholicism was wildly over-invested in metaphysics, and it had rendered its saving truth dependent on the existence of two worlds – a religious world and an ordinary world, as they had been perceived in the Leyland of my childhood. It taught its belief-system, its creeds and doctrines, and practised its prayer and worship, as referring to another existent world beyond and above this present, ordinary world. This other world, understood literally and not metaphorically as befits anything metaphysical, became in due course 'the next world', and Catholicism became obsessed with it as the place where human beings really came alive – after their deaths. This move had reduced this ordinary world to a mere training ground for the 'next' – an obstacle course, a boot camp to be survived, before entrance to the really real, everlasting world of eternity (all concepts I found seriously lacking in any literal sense) could be achieved. Far from fostering the religious and spiritual potential of living human beings, this approach simply expected Catholics to live, so to speak, with one foot on the ground (or in the grave) and the other already planted elsewhere. The religious and spiritual thrust of Catholicism had been diverted towards anticipating, as much as possible, the possession of life after death. I needed to get this supernumerary world off my back. Metaphysics may have its place in philosophy, but in religion it cannot aspire to more than an elucidatory role.

In passing, I would add the following: the position I was adopting had nothing to do with a flat denial of 'life after death', but it has everything to do with how that phrase is understood. I am more than willing to accept that those articles of Catholic belief which seem to imply human 'life after death' are religiously useful and meaningful, as long as they are not literally or descriptively meant – which is, after all, to say no more than that, despite our understandable curiosity, we simply do not (and cannot) directly know or say what actually happens to people when they die; but we very properly hope – and pray – that through and in death they achieve their personal fulfilment and their complete happiness in whatever way the final, definitive encounter in death with the ultimate mystery discerned in human life, and which we address as 'God', happens to occur. It is not reasonable to expect a literally descriptive account of what 'happens' or 'goes on' at or after death. We just cannot have a literal, blow-by-blow, slow-motion, action-replay of whatever it is. It was Wittgenstein who reminded us that death is not an event in life. Intellectually, the only proper position to take up is agnostic, simply not-knowing. Montaigne once spoke wisely of 'the right not to know what we do not know' – a right that Catholicism needs to reclaim for its followers.

In the third place, Catholicism had a problem with the Church – the institutional Church centred on Rome. Catholicism is not simply identifiable with this Church. The Church as we know it is, however lofty its origins and its theological dimensions, an organization that exists only to preserve and promote the religion and spirituality of Catholicism, and if it is seen to be obstructing the fulfilment of this mission, then the Church must be changed, scaled down, downsized, until it ceases to be an obstacle and becomes a clear-running channel for the spirit of Catholicism's Founder. There can, I think, be no doubt that for many well-intentioned Catholics, it is at this third point – the problem with the Church – that the shoe pinches most.

These three issues I identified, in a very rough fashion, as the ones I wanted to address, and to see what extent a revised Catholicism might possibly begin to emerge from some consideration of them. It would be quite beyond me, I thought, to mount a full-scale make-over, let alone a reconstruction, of Catholicism. For one thing, I had lost my taste for theology; and for another, I was reluctant to leave off my other studies. But from time to time I broke off from Greek and made a number of clumsy attempts at saying what I thought needed to be said. One by one they too sank into the theological sand which had silted up my mind over the years. As Wallace Stevens memorably declares: 'Theology after breakfast sticks to the eye' (*Les Plus Belles Pages*). The upshot was that my years of retirement became littered with half-written, half-thought-out presentations of Catholicism as I thought I understood it. Perhaps the attempts were worth making, but none of them gave me the satisfaction I was looking for, and I aborted and abandoned all of them at various stages of incompletion. From them, however, there has begun to emerge a broad, but still unfinished, picture of how I would now like to see Catholicism develop.

I found that in trying to think through the emerging views of my native Catholicism a powerful image continually imposed itself. It must have been first impressed on me when I saw our old house, Holyoake in Towngate in Leyland for the last time. The developers – to give them a name they hardly deserve – had removed the roof, and had dismantled the old chimney-pots and taken down the heavy slates. Like hyenas round a dead wilde-beest, they had clawed and eaten their way into the flanks of the old house, and had opened up the upstairs and downstairs rooms in which we had once lived, where my mother had died, and where I had been born. Streamers of long-superseded wallpaper were hanging in ribbons from the interior walls. Savagely chopped pipes and wires had been left hanging. Brick and plaster debris covered the ground floor. I pushed through the old back gate through which we had access to the car park where, half a century before, my brother Harry and I and our approved friends had played our games. More recent inhabitants had changed the house only superficially. Our big, black-leaded, coal-fired kitchen range over which my Grandma had presided was long gone, of course. So was the big flat stone sink (the 'slopstone') in what had been our back kitchen. So was the heavy, cool, stone shelf in what had been our pantry. So was our big toy cupboard. Other solid and familiar features were missing, too: the shiny banister-rail and the carved and polished newel-post on the stairs – gone along with the whole staircase and all the tall sash windows and the front door with its stained glass. Gone, too, the picture-rails and the skirting-boards – gone along with the floorboards. And the polished and panelled doors – gone along with their frames. Only a few days more and entire house would be gone.

But then it was with relief that I realized that these potentially valuable items had not been ruthlessly destroyed – they had all been clinically removed, judiciously stripped out, to be sold off and recycled, to begin functioning all over again, but somewhere else, in a fresh setting, on new foundations, in another, better house. So I found myself imaginatively designing a new house to accommodate them – a house I would feel at home in it, surrounded by the old features newly arranged, still fulfilling their functions in a new design that would bring out their serviceable qualities with a new emphasis and give them renewed importance in the overall plan.

The image of the old half-demolished house and the recycling of its valuable elements began to take over and control the way in which I thought Catholicism might be revised. Some work went ahead fitfully, as I said. Plato and Sophocles were far more congenial. Before any rebuilding of Catholicism could take place, and even before it would be possible to offer an 'architect's impression' of what my finished reconstruction would look like, a considerable amount of intellectual ground had to be cleared. The theological sand had to be dug out. I needed to sink some shafts and get down to some rock. I had to agree with myself about the basic ground rules I would need to establish and put into practice in any eventual revision. Until I had worked them out to my satisfaction, no recycling could be undertaken. The valuable elements I had managed to salvage from my old Catholicism would have to be put in storage. Rebuilding must wait, too, until I was more sure of my foundations.

Hence I can only conclude this book with what I currently regard as some (but surely not all) of the fundamental rules for the revision of Catholicism which my experience of the kind of religious life I have led has imposed upon me. They represent for me the essential preliminaries ('propaedeutics', as they are sometimes called) to the constructive work needed in the reclamation of Catholicism's saving truth. Of course my rules for revision are bound to seem idiosyncratic; and I openly confess that they are. They roughly cover the three issues I mentioned above. They are inadequately refined and crudely expressed. I like to think they have an air and a feel of imaginative DIY thinking about them – which is what I intend. I would expect few to agree with them, though some may be challenged to try a similar exercise and concoct some propaedeutic rules for themselves. They are not meant to mark the first move down the slippery slope towards demolishing what people see as their Catholicism. *Au contraire* – my purpose is simply to work towards making Catholicism a more effective and credible spiritual religion, and less of a materialized and materialistic system. After my forty desert years under the ecclesiastical and Jesuit systems, I can no longer even imagine how any religious system as such could mediate the human kind of salvation which I still need and want; and yet I think Catholicism, duly understood, can still offer it.

There will be those who will instantly see any attempt to frame a personal interpretation of Catholicism as intolerable arrogance. Among those who consider themselves pastorally responsible for the Catholic faithful – and consequently among the faithful themselves – insistence on the literal and unexamined meaning (and, even more importantly, on the absolute certainty) of every aspect of the Catholic system has long been prized as possessing a religious and devotional value in itself. Sound Catholicism, literalism and complete certainty have long been virtually synonymous. But the serious reservations I developed over the years regarding the literal truth of much that is peddled as literally true and certain in the name of Catholicism are likely, as far as I can see, to remain permanently valid; and in extenuation of my apparent arrogance I can only suggest a careful reading of St Paul's largely ignored call in 1 Corinthians 2 and 3 regarding a spiritual, as opposed to a 'fleshly', understanding of God's mysterious wisdom in accordance with the mind of Christ – a call away from being milk-fed 'infants in Christ' who are still immature, to eating solid food fit for grown-ups. It has been obvious to me for some considerable time that I had to wean myself off what amounts to the theological apologetics for Catholicism (in effect a more sophisticated version of 'The Penny Catechism') on to the critically-based diet that I can actually stomach; not, I like to think, through some upstart intellectual arrogance, but through some correlative personal and spiritual growth in myself. In this regard the author of the letter *To the Hebrews* pulls no punches: 'everyone who lives on milk, being still an infant, is unskilled in the word of righteousness. But solid food is for the mature, for those whose faculties have been trained by practice to distinguish good from evil' (5.13–14 NRSV).

☙

The first rule I would adopt is this: any proper revision or rediscovery of Catholicism as a religion must, before all else, be regrounded absolutely, as on its sole foundation, in the man Jesus. The spirit of the Founder, as revealed in all we can know of his humanity, alone provides the basic law and principle of his religion – I mean the human spirit of the Founder, his faith and his imaginative expression of it. I am not talking abstractly of Jesus' humanity as one of the elements in his theological make-up – as one of his two 'natures' that 'concur' in his 'person'. Theology, and the christological doctrines it has elaborated, retain all the importance which is their due (as we shall see); but as centuries-later interpretations they cannot possibly bear the weight that has to be put on the sure foundation which a religion like Catholicism needs from the start. True, the New Testament, and not least the Gospels, present us with a Jesus already theologically interpreted, but I doubt if many sane scholars would declare him completely inaccessible as a human being. Certainly the theological pantomime horse somehow compounded of divinity and humanity which has so fascinated generations of theologians provides no real religious basis for Catholicism, however theologically orthodox it may be thought to be. It does not do justice to the religious and spiritual importance of the fact that in the beginning was the man. I no longer want to play the barren games of theologians. If Catholicism is going to offer the way a serious human being can come to know and to share the saving mystery ('God') which surrounds our being human – that saves us precisely as the human beings we are – then it must start (and finish) with a real man and his actual experiences. We cannot be saved by a theological fiction. We need to seek out, as much as we can, the sheer humanity of Jesus *in its own right* – a wholly orthodox notion anyway, and the most obvious point from which to access the religion of Jesus on which the religion of Catholicism claims to be built.

It is important not to put the cart of theological interpretation before the horse that alone can provide the religious pulling power, so to speak, of Catholicism. This power we find in the real Jesus who is a unique, individual, historical man, the man who is the subject of the later theological interpretations of Paul, of the evangelists, of the other New Testament writers, of the Fathers and Councils of the Church, of the great Christian theologians. The divinity of Jesus, rightly ascribed to him by those who were moved to see 'God', humanity's ultimate mystery, present and at work in this man, is already, of course, a later product of religion, a theological construction put on him, and so it cannot serve as that religion's foundation. Divinity cannot be the reason why Jesus must be the absolute ground and sole foundation of Catholicism – that reason resides in his real and unique humanity with all its openness to, and union with, the saving mystery of 'God'. In other words, theology and all the constructions it has put on Jesus and on his essential function as our 'Saviour' (another necessary but secondary theological construction) must step down from the overpowering role they have come to play in

Catholicism and, at least at the start of the drama, leave the stage to the real man Jesus. I know about the problems involved in discovering this real man; but few, I think, would deny that beneath the interpretations there lies a man who is human in the same sense as we are all human beings. He is everything, neither more nor less, that we mean by 'a human being'. We must not let theology and later doctrines, however devoutly held, distract us from this fact. If Jesus is not human, he cannot possibly be the source of the kind of 'salvation' which the religion of Catholicism offers. The Church knew this from the start, and it condemned as heretical those who denied it.

As I write I can sense that many good Catholics are reaching for their dogmatic revolvers. I am aware that this approach of mine may scandalize and upset Catholics, who have been heavily conditioned – in school, in church, and not least in the seminary – to practise their faith in denial or at least in grave distortion of the completely common humanity of Jesus, prefer- ring to live on some higher theological ground and seek their consolations in what they have been told are the more impor- tant 'facts' about Jesus. I can hardly hope to be able to counter all their prejudices, but I am irresistibly reminded of the Case of the Nappies. I am told that some years ago, at Leyland St Mary's, it was decided to invite the primary school children to decorate the Christmas Crib. This they did with enthusiasm. To some the real presence of a human baby in the stable meant one thing – nappies (diapers) hanging out to dry on a clothes-line slung between convenient trees. But this was more than certain devout parishioners could stand, and the parish priest was formally requested to have the offending nappies taken down. This he sadly (and heretically) agreed to do. I often used this episode as a serious test case in my lectures on the history of early Christology. Do you really accept that Jesus was human just as we are? It was surprising how uncomfortable the ques- tion made even intelligent Catholics. Surely the sheer humanity of Jesus cannot be as definitively important as all that? Surely what really makes him our Saviour is that he is divine, with his – and incidentally, our – humanity, so to speak, in tow? (The theological cart, as usual, trying to pull the horse.) The low valu- ation put on Jesus' humanity was perhaps reflecting the low valuation their Catholicism had taught people to place on their own. They had been led to accept the kind of 'docetic' Jesus – an ideal being who simply posed as human – popular among the gullible in early Catholicism and never satisfactorily expelled. 'Swaddling-clothes' might be tolerated, but nappies were out.

Just to try to reassure the doubters, I will confess that during my years of academic teaching I developed a soft spot for the Fourth Ecumenical Council of the Church, held at Chalcedon (near Istanbul) in 451 AD. Not only did the assembled fathers re-issue and endorse the all-important creeds of the earlier Councils of Nicaea (325) and Constantinople (381) and other canonical texts from churches of the West and the East; they also drafted a masterly and definitive summary of the Catholic doctrine of the Incarnation. Acute controversy over the correct theological inter-pretation of Jesus had dogged the Church's thought and mission from the start. The Council of Chalcedon hoped to bring the controversy to an end – the kind of hope that no Church Council ever sees fulfilled – by devising a formulary that would satisfy the disputants once and for all. The operative summary which the Council agreed and issued is arguably the prime artefact of Catholic theology. I make no apology for presenting this tough text which, as I see it, is absolutely fundamental to Catholicism:

> Following then the holy Fathers, we confess that our Lord Jesus Christ is a single identical ['one and the same'] Son, and all of us agree with one another in teaching that he is complete in divinity and that he is complete in humanity; truly God and truly a human being; that he has a rational soul and a body; that in his divinity he is of the same being as the Father, and that in his humanity he is of the same being as we are, in every way like us except for sin [Hebrews 4.15]; that before the ages he was begotten in his divinity from the Father; but that in the last days, for us and for our salva-tion, in his humanity from Mary the Virgin Mother of God – a single identical Christ, Son, Lord, Only-begotten, acknowledged as being in two natures with no confusion, change, distinction or divi-sion; that at no point has the difference between the natures been destroyed through the union, but the characteristics of each nature are all the better preserved and meet up in a single person and a single reality; that he is not parted or divided into two persons, but that there is a single identical Son and Only-begotten God, Word, Lord, Jesus Christ, just as the prophets and the Lord Jesus Christ himself taught us concerning him, and the creed of the Fathers handed it down to us.
> (The translation of the Greek text in Denzinger-Schoenmetzer, *Enchiridion Symbolorum*, ##301–2, is mine.)

Commentary and reflection on this brilliantly balanced theologi-cal collage has filled volumes. It represents Catholicism's supreme effort at getting its collective believing mind round its Founder, Jesus of Nazareth. It is worthwhile seeing how this basic text tries to do it. It has to approach Jesus in a theologically analytical pincer movement, from the side of 'divinity' and from the side of 'humanity'. But in doing this the text, unless we watch it very carefully, is in danger of misleading us into thinking that divinity and humanity are qualities that share the same level of reality – that they are somehow real in the same way. But of course they are not. We can understand, come to terms with, Jesus' humanity, because it is exactly the same as our own; but we cannot understand, come to the same kind of terms with, divinity, because it is clearly beyond us. We cannot know what it means to be God in the way that we can know what it means to be human. If we thought we did comprehend divinity, we would be no more than idolaters – reducing God to our own terms and categories, making God in our own image and likeness. This is an abomination that Chalcedon never commits. The text moves on two quite clearly distinct levels which the Council, wisely, never attempts to 'reconcile'. On the first, concrete level Jesus remains solidly the individual, real man of Nazareth who once lived like each of us in his own time and space. On a secondary, analytical level, Jesus is said to be 'in two natures' – to have everything it takes to be both divine and human, without in the slightest compromising either. In fact, it seems that in him both divinity and his humanity mutually enhance one another. And note, too, that because personal sinfulness is no defining part of being human (none of us *has* to commit sin in order to be human!) Jesus' sinlessness makes him all the more, not less, a true human being. It is at the first, concrete level that the real Jesus confronts us as the source of our Catholic religion. It is at the secondary, theologically analytical, level that we find expressed the humanly formulated beliefs which are necessary if we are to understand Jesus in the orthodox fashion as the person whose spirit of faith we are to share, if we are to be 'saved'. (I have more to say about faith and beliefs below.)

The impression that Catholics have been given that their salvation or redemption is effected by some form of metaphysical transaction between Jesus' divinity and his humanity, with divinity having an active role and humanity being largely passive, simply will not do. We cannot be saved by theological analysis. As Chalcedon, and other creeds, declare: what worked 'for us and for our salvation' was Jesus, born a real man from Mary, a man who lived, suffered and died like the rest of us. This is the kind of salvation which is distinctive of Catholicism. Hence the urgent need to relegate theology (without at all dismissing it), and to salvage from the old Catholicism its supreme religious possession – the actual, human Jesus – and to recycle him as the new foundation of our rediscovered religion.

Following this rule should have absolute priority, and I would hope that it might determine the whole form of my revised Catholicism, and explain the order in which I would place the rest of my rules for revision.

෨

The second rule would be to establish that particular human attitude or quality which is centrally defining to Jesus the man, and to which we, if we share in it, can look for our 'salvation'. What is the human factor in Jesus that makes him effective 'for us and for our salvation'? If this factor can be identified, it will give my revision of Catholicism both a firm foundation and a clear direction. Catholicism will become the religion which aims at imparting this saving attitude or quality to its adherents, at getting them to share in it and thus be saved. To find it, we obviously have to look to the way in which Jesus experienced his world, his life in it, and his departure from it. Here there are difficulties, greater for some than for others, regarding the reliability of the Gospel evidence, but they are not insuperable. It would not be impossible to agree on a broad-brush picture of Jesus and his relations with the people he found himself among, and of how he faced the circumstances in which his brief life was situated. The relevant texts would need to be collected and critically assessed, but the attitude in Jesus which I found richly evidenced in the New Testament writings, once my reading of them had become attuned to it, was nothing other than his human faith in God – his commitment to the transcendent mystery he discerned in his experience of being human, of his own humanity. By this I mean a comprehensive attitude involving profound commitment, love, obedience, and especially trust. In my reconstruction of Catholicism (were I ever to undertake it) I would, I believe, have no difficulty in showing, for example, how in translations of the Pauline letters, 'faith *in* Christ' has, out of theological prejudice, at times ousted the equally plausible 'faith *of* Christ'. The Greek grammar involved is often completely open to either translation – it is the minds of Pauline scholars that remain closed.

Once again, I sense dogmatic revolvers being drawn; because it is a sadly common position among Catholic theologians that Jesus could not possibly have had a human faith in God, for the simple reason that he was personally divine and did not need it. Once again we are faced with an example of how the theological cart has been put before the real horse. An entirely proper but abstract theological construction (divinity) has been crudely bolted on to a real concrete human being (Jesus), and has rendered him, at a stroke, essentially inhuman. In the interests of devotional overkill we are expected to accept a fatally diminished Jesus, deprived of the whole range of precisely that basic human experience (religious faith) which best qualifies him to be the potential source of our actual salvation. Just as there are no new sins, there are no new heresies; and the Church thought it had dealt with the view that Jesus was so divine that he did not need an ordinary human mind or all the attitudes that went with it, as long ago as the fourth century (Apollinarianism). But I would guess that there is no heresy – except perhaps the docetism I mentioned above – that continued, after its formal condemnation, to remain more widespread or more virulent among Catholic believers. It effectively denies that Jesus was a real man.

As a real man, and as a religious Jew of his day, Jesus of Nazareth had a thoroughly human faith in God. The Gospels present, it seems to me, beneath the overlay of their characteristic interpretations of Jesus, a man whose Jewish faith was in severe crisis – or as I would prefer to put it, a man who was finding that his faith in God, intensely personal as it was, was no longer getting the religious support and expression that it needed from his Jewish beliefs and practices. His experience of life – whether in the long years at home or in some brief episode in the desert, we cannot know – brought him to a point where he found himself possessed of a radically new imaginative insight into his own native religious tradition, the Judaism of his day. I do not think it would be going too far to say that this experience involved him in giving a whole new meaning to his inherited idea of 'God'. The novelty of Jesus' new interpretation of Judaism must have been radically and offensively different enough to explain how the challenge it offered to the establishment occasioned his death. It created tensions with his co-religionists which proved his undoing – yet at the same time it was convincing enough to encourage and license the few followers who had gathered around him – and not least women among them – to distance themselves from their own religion and gradually form their own sect and attract others to it. In this inchoate way, Catholicism began to be grounded on the faith of Jesus.

Jesus' radically imaginative insight, I would say, consisted in a reinterpretation of what he saw as the meaning of the Jewish religious tradition as a whole from its beginnings in Abraham, the model man of faith not only for Judaism but also for Islam, and still for Catholicism, where he is honoured at Mass as 'Abraham, our father in faith'. Abraham was a man involved in a divine encounter in which he received the promise from God on which his whole future existence, and the way he would face it, depended:

> I will make of you a great nation, and I will bless you, and make your name great, so that you will be a blessing. I will bless those who bless you, and the one who curses you I will curse; and in you all the families of the earth shall bless themselves.
>
> (Genesis 12.2–3 NRSV)

To this promise, and to subsequent demands made of Abraham, God required from him a completely positive and self-sacrificial response. This response was *faith*, a deeply existential stance which displayed Abraham's utter confidence in his encounter with the transcendent mystery involved in being human (God), and his conviction that the divine promise, despite all appearances to the contrary, would be fulfilled, along with his determination that he would obey God's demands at all costs to himself. Abraham thereby accepted the power and will of God to fulfil his promises, declared his trust in God, and committed himself and his family to God as being utterly sure and dependable. Abraham's faith-response to his God was religiously paradigmatic for the three different religions which look back to him as their starting-point. It was to the maintenance and fostering of this foundational faith that Judaism was meant to look. Jews were to replicate in themselves, nationally and individually, the faith of Abraham in God. If Judaism fell into decline, it was because the pristine faith-response of Abraham towards God was not being maintained, but was being overlaid by other distracting and trivializing considerations.

This seems to be how Jesus viewed the religious system of his native Judaism. It had become contaminated by attitudes and practices which not only had little to do with the faith-religion of Abraham, but which also actively frustrated its human salvific effectiveness. The prophets, in their different ways, had held the same view. But Jesus was more than just another religious revivalist – he was a radical religious innovator, calling for a whole new way of interpreting the religion of Israel. He was out to re-imagine what Judaism as a whole, Abraham included, was supposed to be about; to re-interpret Judaism's meaning in the dashing metaphors and parables of his teaching and in the symbolic actions of his miracles; and when those failed to get his point across, in the supreme tragedy of his own cruel death. True to his own Jewish faith, he saw it all in a vivid and original light, and he exercised his lively mind and imagination on re-expressing a novel understanding of what he saw as his sadly distorted religion. In Jesus a unique religious genius was at work, re-interpreting for his followers, not only in his teachings and his miracles but also in his own personal approach to his life and notably to his death, saving truths about the human condition that had long ago been implied in Judaism's founding story of Abraham's faith-response to the promise and the demands of God, but which no others had yet fully understood and expounded in a graspable fashion to their fellow human beings. This is why Jesus did not see his teaching and his activities as subversive of the Jewish tradition, but as the completion, the final and proper 'fulfilment', for which that tradition had been waiting over the centuries: 'Do not think that I have come to abolish the law and the prophets; I have come not to abolish but to fulfil' (Matthew 5.17 NRSV).

The insight which Jesus' faith had prompted in him was into the ultimate mystery of his own human condition – an insight which evoked in him an imaginative vision of how reality actually was for human beings, a vision that called for theological expression in man-made beliefs. He saw that religion could not be meant to be a matter of overloading human beings with such systems of beliefs and regulations and practices, but a matter of evoking the response of faith, of spiritual insight and vision. Jesus' attitude to his own Judaism could well serve as a paradigm for what our own attitude should be – when and as appropriate – to Catholicism as we know it. The real meaning and purpose of the original religion of Abraham was to relate to the human experience of existing as a human being and to meet the needs that arose from the experience. Jesus' ground-breaking insight, I think, had its source in, and got its authority from, Jesus' own unique individual experience of how, on the one hand, being fully human meant encountering the demanding mystery of his own human existence with which he found himself confronted, the mystery he lovingly addressed as 'Father'; and how, on the other hand, Jesus himself could no longer find this interpretation of 'God' operative in contemporary Judaism.

It was Jesus' personal faith that drove him to get back to the original meaning of 'God' as the mystery which 'saves' human existence from itself, from its own enslaving limitations and chronic waywardness – a meaning signalled by the great myths of Jewish history. 'God' and the religion built around him were meant to set people free from the enslaving oppression of the human condition by enabling them to accept and face the inexorable demands of human existence which belonged to their full humanity; to lead people back from the exile of their own self-alienation to the promised homeland of their own true selves; to establish people once and for all under the rule or kingdom of their 'God' where they could live at peace with themselves and in justice with others, seeking together to respond fully to the common necessities which are imposed on all by their own acknowledged humanity. The religion of Judaism, as Jesus saw it, was effecting little or none of this. If anything, it served to exacerbate the difficulties involved in being human. But in confronting, through his own exemplary faith, the mystery implicated in his own humanity, Jesus discerned the need and the possibility of a radical reinterpretation of the faith-response of Abraham as a example of the faith-response that was demanded of all human beings. It would take a new religion to preserve and promote this faith-insight of Jesus, and to share it with mankind – a new religion that would in time become Catholicism. It is in that sense that my revised Catholicism would be grounded in the faith of Jesus, and it would only be by sharing his faith – *sola fide* – that we might be saved.

The third rule I would follow in my revision of Catholicism would be to make sure that it accommodated that sense of human mystery which belongs to the faith of Jesus which Catholics are called on to share, and which promises to lead them to their fulfilment – in theological terms, to 'save' them. To make room for this sense, and to provide it with the spacious conditions it needs for its nurture and development, adjustments will need to be made to Catholicism as we have come to know it. This sense calls for close and lengthy attention from the human mind and spirit and imagination; and these cannot usefully function in an ambience where religion is reduced to the literal acceptance of dogmatic and moral certainties, to sticking rigidly to the system, to unquestioning and uncritical obedience to rules and regulations and to the authorities who have invented them – in other words, where the sense of mystery essential to the religion of Catholicism cannot flourish in the kind of religious system that Jesus found unacceptable in his native Judaism. If, as I have suggested, our

'salvation' lies in our personal appropriation of the faith and
mind-set of Jesus and is the effect of our sharing his spirit, then
Catholicism must have built into it the right spiritual opportunities to facilitate this appropriation, and must encourage its adherents to make full use of them. Of course, it would be true to say
that spiritual opportunities have long been there in Catholicism –
for example, perhaps in the contemplative orders – but they have
been on offer only to the very few, and under the strictest supervision. In a revision and rebuilding of Catholicism it would be
imperative to make such opportunities into prominent and accessible features of the new construction. But if this is ever to
happen, some of the currently dominant features of Catholicism
have got to give way to make room for them. Certain leading
features of current Catholicism will have to be, not removed, but
firmly relegated to their secondary and supporting functions. It is
a matter of defining and sustaining the right religious and spiritual priorities.

The most dominant feature of familiar Catholicism which, in
the interests of a more spiritual religion, must be duly relegated
to its important supporting role is a belief-system which demands
a literal understanding. I yield to no one in my admiration for
Catholicism's system of beliefs, its credal and doctrinal tradition,
its dogmas and its definitions. Nor in my estimation of their
importance. In them Catholicism possesses one of the supreme
artefacts of the human mind and imagination. It has long been the
boast of Catholics that they know just what they believe in. Its
comprehensive and authoritative deliverances have attracted
many converts. Sadly, proud boasts in the Catholic belief-system
seems not to be matched by much intelligent knowledge or critical understanding of it. In fact, nowadays it does not appear to be
taught to young Catholics, and to be largely ignored, or at any
rate little known, even among the clergy. Yet it remains norma-
tive for any understanding of Catholicism. But however norma-
tive the belief-system may be, it is not the 'stuff' of faith. I have
suggested that for Catholics the 'stuff' of faith is their personal
participation in the faith of Jesus. The belief-system, I would say,
articulates, supports and guarantees the shape of the religious
vision of reality which that faith entails. In other words, the
belief-system (like all theology) is essential but secondary, and
would need to be relegated to its proper place in my revised
Catholicism. This move is no dismissal of dogma. It is a call for
dogma to make room for saving faith. Merely accepting beliefs
and dogmas will never save us.

So I would maintain a clear distinction between Catholic faith and Catholic beliefs. The former I take to be the wholehearted share of the Catholic individual and community in the faith of Jesus, and their personal commitment to the imaginative vision of reality which belongs to that foundational, saving faith. The latter I take to be the subsequent construction put on that vision in order to articulate it and to give it imaginatively intelligible expression. Thus the doctrines of creation, original sin, the incarnation, the Trinity, the Last Judgement serve to give graphic and articulated expression to the vision that rests on faith. They are not *prima facie* literal descriptions of actual states of affairs, the obedient acceptance of which will guarantee 'salvation'.

This distinction and its consequences are important enough to merit fuller treatment. Long before I retired, my attention had been caught by an intriguingly obscure passage in St Paul's *Letter to the Romans*:

> Moses writes concerning the righteousness that comes from the law, that 'the person who does these things will live by them.' But the righteousness that comes from faith says, 'Do not say in your heart, "Who will ascend into heaven?" (that is, to bring Christ down) or "Who will descend into the abyss?"' (that is, to bring Christ up from the dead). But what does it say?
> 'The word is near you,
> on your lips and in your heart'
> (that is, the word of faith which we proclaim); because if you confess with your lips that Jesus is Lord and believe in your heart that God raised him from the dead, you will be saved. For one believes with the heart and so is justified, and one confesses with the mouth and so is saved. The scripture says, 'No one who believes in him will be put to shame.' (10.5–11, NRSV)

This looked to me like an attempt on Paul's part to indulge in some stylish embroidery on the 'faith v. works of the Law' distinction familiar to recipients of some of his other letters. Paul, it is insufficiently recognized, was an accomplished practitioner of the rhetoric of his day, not least of that used by popular philosophers, the style misleadingly called 'diatribe'. Writing to Rome, he may have been out to impress, and the intricacy of the passage may reflect this. Still, he also appears to be giving his readers an elaborate analysis of what is involved in the act of faith itself. I fancy the Romans must have been as baffled by it as many of Paul's commentators, who carefully avoid (as biblical commentators tend to do) committing themselves to any clear interpretation of the passage. At any rate, in my perfunctory searches I was never able to find any useful or convincing account of the passage's meaning.

The best I have been able to do for myself is to suppose that Paul is proposing his version of the distinction between faith and beliefs. Obviously he has in mind a passage from Deuteronomy (30.11–14) in which Moses is depicted as stressing the basic connaturality, the inwardness and ease, of the law he is imposing on Israel. It is not a matter of outlandish demand. It does not come down from heaven or from across the sea: 'No, the word is very near to you; it is in your mouth and in your heart for you to observe' (30.14 NRSV). But Paul is insisting on some difference between heart and lips, and on how they perform different functions in those whose righteousness is based on faith as opposed to law. Lips confess beliefs, hearts have faith. Lips are used to utter certain belief-statements, such as that which is commonly taken to be the earliest form of the Christian creed: 'Jesus is Lord'. But at the same time, hearts have a different function: they have faith that God raised him from the dead – in the faith they share with Jesus they accept God as the mysterious power which overcomes death (10.9). If the heart does its job, a man is justified; and if the lips do theirs as well, he is saved (10.10). I do not know whether this is what Paul means; but in the absence of any scholarly guidance which has ever convinced me otherwise, I have long taken it to be the case that belief-statements – simple as they were in Paul's time, before they became the formalized theological propositions enshrined in the creeds and definitions that now belong to the Church's doctrinal tradition – are to be treated, not as objects in which we put our faith (it is not in them that we directly have faith), but as necessary contextual supports for that attitude of faith which is really what we need if we are to become what Paul calls, in more theological metaphors, both justified and saved.

Consistency in making such a distinction between beliefs and faith seems to me essential if we are to avoid supposing that we can be 'saved' simply by believing in, holding on to, what are at root no more than *theologoumena*, theological propositions, essentially imaginative fictions created to form part of the construction of the world of Catholic beliefs which expresses and sustains our Catholic faith-vision of reality, our faith-perception of how reality is – our personal and communal Catholic faith which has the power to 'save' our human lives by discounting and defeating the negative power which death (and sin) inevitably exercises over us, and which enables us to live our human lives to the full. The

Catholic sees that it takes the faith of Jesus and his religious vision of reality to bring this about in us. It is not possible to see how believing in credal propositions as such could do this.

Yet the 'confession' of credal propositions – later, the recital of the so-called Apostles' Creed or of the Nicene Creed – has always been required of Catholics ever since the days when, as St Paul indicated, 'Jesus is Lord' was the simple belief-statement to be uttered by the lips. Not even infants at their baptism, we should remember, are excused from reciting the creed, even though adults have to recite it on their behalf. This fact alone, it seems to me, makes the Catholic meaning of 'belief' and 'believing' quite different from the ordinary usage of these common words, and something quite peculiar to Catholicism. I know that 'belief' and its justification is a well-worn topic among professional philosophers, but I have derived little help from them when it comes to any specifically religious usage. Theologians, on the other hand, take believing for granted, and are more interested in analysing faith as a literal 'gift of God' which then presents them, in their muddled way, with the man-made problem of 'reconciling' God's gift with the human freedom to receive or reject it. None of this I find enlightening when it comes to saying what the words 'I believe' mean with regard to the traditional Catholic system of beliefs and doctrines. I remain convinced that we are faced with a distinctive and quite specific religious use and meaning.

Just what this meaning is, is not easy to say. One way of trying to find out would be to go back to the meaning of 'I believe' (*pisteuo-pistis*) in New Testament Greek, and beyond that to its meaning in the Hebrew *'aman* in its various forms. The trouble with this methodical approach is that none of the myriad references is likely to cast any direct light on a specific matter which largely post-dates them all. All the same, it might be possible to pick up clues as to what 'I believe' (*Credo*) actually means for the Catholic. The general meaning at the root of the biblical data appears to be linked with somebody or something being accepted as firm, solid, trustworthy. It rarely has to do with an intellectual grasp of truth. 'I believe' seems to be more like a positive affirmation of lasting trust and confidence on the part of the 'believer' in the person who is being addressed or faced, or in whatever is being proposed for acceptance. To put it crudely, in Catholicism 'believing' should be a matter of 'putting your money where your mouth is'. The believer makes a self-investment, so to speak – invests himself in what his lips are led to assert: the formulated beliefs and doctrines which articulate

(hence some of them are called 'articles' of the Creed) and serve
to express the saving faith-vision of reality the Catholic claims
to share with Jesus.

Interesting support for making a clear distinction between faith
and beliefs might be discerned in those many people whose
admirable lives often show that they share much of the positively
death-and-sin-defeating attitude of Catholic faith, but find themselves unable to hold the beliefs which (as I am claiming) are
meant to function as faith's support and expression. I found that
Wittgenstein is an instructive example of this type of serious
person. In his *Culture and Value* (in fact the translation of a selection of his *Vermischte Bemerkungen* [Miscellaneous Remarks],
Blackwell, 1980), he often refers to Christianity in ways that show
his sympathetic understanding of it, and his abiding interest in it.
But it is clear that the systematic beliefs and doctrines of
Catholicism simply did not work for him – that is, they did not
contribute to an attitude of Catholic faith. I translate an extract
written in 1937:

> In religion it has got to be the case that to each stage of religious-
> ness there should correspond a sort of expression which makes no
> sense at a lower stage. This doctrine [Wittgenstein is thinking of
> predestination] which is meaningful at a higher stage, is null and
> void for a man who is at present standing on a lower stage – it *can*
> be understood only *wrongly*, and so these words have *no* validity
> for this person.
>
> For example, Paul's doctrine of predestination is, at my stage,
> irreligiousness – hateful nonsense. So it is no good for me, because
> I can make only a wrong use of the picture it offers me. If the
> picture is to be pious and good, then that is so at a completely
> different stage, at which it has to be made use of in life completely
> differently from the way I could use it. (p. 32, his italics)

Wittgenstein appears to be saying, among other things, that the
meaning of systematic beliefs and doctrines depends on, and
corresponds to, the level of religious development or maturity a
person has attained in his life; that maturity has to do with not
having to take beliefs and doctrines literally; that taken literally
(as they must be by someone who can know no better), they can
be irreligious nonsense. There would be a great deal to be learnt
from this and other remarks of Wittgenstein on religious belief.
He treats religious believing seriously as an activity that deserves
attention in its own right, and he sees the problem of both the
distinction and the connection between holding beliefs and

having faith. But I translate only one more remark of his that ties up, incidentally, with our problematic passage from *Romans*:

> I read: 'no one can say "Jesus is Lord" except by the Holy Spirit' (1 Corinthians 12.3 NRSV). And it is true: I cannot call him *Lord*, because that says absolutely nothing to me. I could call him 'the Exemplar', even 'God'– or actually I can understand, when he is given such names. But the word 'Lord' I cannot pronounce with meaning. *Because I do not believe* that he will come to judge me – because *that* says nothing to me. And it could say something to me, if I lived *entirely* differently. (p. 33, his italics)

Whether belief statements like 'Jesus is Lord', or doctrines like the Judgement make sense and are of any use, or can be meaningfully affirmed, ultimately depends, in other words, on the spiritual quality of the life one is prepared to live. It is only a life lived with the faith-vision of Jesus that validates the beliefs of the Catholic tradition which have been framed to support and express it. Faith and beliefs are distinct but related factors in Catholicism.

⊗

At this point a fourth rule would need to be brought into play. This rule would require me to take an honest look at the beliefs of Catholicism and seriously question how they are meant to be understood. Are they to be taken as literally true? Or true in some other way? These are awkward questions, not normally asked; but they have been evaded for long enough, and failure to address them can grossly mislead those who are expected to subscribe to the beliefs in question. It also sets up a false opposition between religious beliefs and the findings of science. I cannot see that the truth of Catholic beliefs can be other than metaphorical, or that they originate from a source other than the human imagination. In my revised Catholicism they would have to be treated openly as metaphorical and imaginative constructions or fictions. This drastic view sounds disastrous – as if there were no longer reasons for taking them seriously, or as if beliefs could no longer provide the support which faith depends on, as I have tried to explain. But this reaction comes from their having been presented consistently as direct, literal descriptions of some other, different, metaphysical world or reality; and believers have become habituated to depending on, and finding consolation in, their literal truth; and once this kind of truth is denied them, they understandably feel, not only that they have been cruelly misled, but that they might just as well abandon their Catholic beliefs as no longer useful or relevant to them. This reaction would in fact be quite unjustified, because with regard to the faith we are speaking of – our share in the saving faith and vision of Jesus – it is not only historically verifiable that the beliefs and doctrines of Catholicism were produced by the imaginative efforts of theologians (sometimes at Church Councils), but it is also impossible to suggest a human source for beliefs other than the operation of their theological imaginations and their skill with religious metaphors.

Talk about metaphor and the imagination raises problems chiefly, I think, because of its unfamiliarity in the context of religious believing. It gives the impression that there is some intention of undermining the truth of beliefs. In fact, the kind of statement a belief is needs to be determined before it becomes possible to say in what sense it is meant to be true. Again, to speak of metaphors and the imagination seems to undermine that much over-prized quality of beliefs, their certainty. But if we have no critical control over the way belief-statements are meant, we cannot say how they are true; and if we cannot say how they are true, then their certainty can hardly be an issue. To think of metaphors and the imagination as somehow belonging to a secondary class of discourse, inferior to literally meant statements and to the truths and certainties attainable by human reason betrays a faulty appreciation of how human beings most frequently, and most vividly, manage to express themselves and run their complex lives. I shall deal first with metaphor.

I am aware of some of the barren philosophical discussions which the notion of 'metaphor' has occasioned, and I am keen to avoid them by opting for a loose and general sense of the word. By 'metaphor' I mean no more than what the word says: namely, that such meaning as a metaphorical word or expression possesses is given to it – is 'transferred' to it – from the use and meaning the word has elsewhere, in another field. When I have recourse to metaphor, I am extending my range of meaning by saying how something is true in terms of something else. George Eliot put my point perfectly:

> O Aristotle! If you had had the advantage of being 'the freshest modern' instead of the greatest ancient, would you not have mingled your praise of metaphorical speech as a sign of high intelligence, with a lamentation that intelligence rarely shows itself in speech without metaphor, – that we can seldom declare what a thing is, except by saying that it is something else?
>   (*The Mill on the Floss*, Book 2, chap. 1 (epigraph))

Aristotle's 'praise of metaphorical speech' (*Poetics*, chap. XXII, 1459a5–8) occurs in his discussion of stylistic devices in Greek tragedy. He notes how important a matter it is that their use of such devices should be appropriate. I translate:

> ... but much the greatest thing is the metaphorical; for this alone cannot be got from someone else, and is a sign of native talent; because using metaphor well is a matter of observing resemblance.

Metaphor is a verbal device, a figure of speech or writing, by which we aim at 'getting across' some new kind of understanding. This we do by spotting that an already familiar word or expression has the kind of resemblance or similarity to what we want to say or mean which will enable it to serve as a carrier or bearer for the new understanding we wish to promote. We take the familiar word or expression away from its normal or common use and use it in a transferred, 'metaphorized', non-literal sense. 'We can so seldom declare what a thing is, except by saying it is something else,' said George Eliot, but she may be exaggerating, if only slightly. We do not appear to be using metaphor, for instance, when we are pointing out the ordinary contents of our world: hammer, nails, cat, Melissa, and so on. Our verbal intercourse with one another can get along at this wooden, literal level for some time. But then we find it helpful to shift verbal gear, so to speak, when we need to promote, not just basic acts of recognition, but the understanding of certain meanings which we have in mind, and which we want to 'get across' to someone else. To create this effect, we take words and employ them fictionally. We make metaphors of them.

This is a thoroughly creative activity, and one that appears to come entirely naturally to us, though some people are better at it than others, and our native facility with metaphors can be practised and improved. The words we choose to make metaphors of need to be words already in use: that is, they already have a meaning for the hearer, or can quickly acquire one, in a language already known. The speaker (I could just as well say 'writer') plays on the word's familiarity – perhaps what Aristotle meant by 'observing resemblance' or similarity. For what is already familiar he creates a new setting, a new field of significance. The speaker's words could now, it would seem, be referring to a whole new world, though that world remains no more than the creation of the mind of the speaker, who is trying to get his hearer to take a fresh look at the ordinary world he is living in, or to turn his attention to its wider implications, and to do it in the light of the new world of meaning which the speaker is metaphorically creating. Through his artfully transferred use of familiar words, the speaker is suggesting – in fact, 'revealing' is probably the *mot juste* in this regard – what might be taken for another world altogether. But the speaker is not asserting the literal existence of some alternative reality. For reasons he has in mind, he is trying to enlarge and enhance – to transform, transfigure – the hearer's existing perception of his own ordinary world, or at least the scope of his attention to the world he lives in. The hearer can now see his ordinary world in the light of the speaker's newly revealed one, in the light of a new world of meaning. The speaker has revealed that the hearer's ordinary world has a new, hitherto unfamiliar, unsuspected meaning. He has said what one world 'really' is by creatively – imaginatively – poetically – endowing it with the fictional context of another world. This comes close to solving my problem with supposedly 'equiliteral' worlds. There is only one, ordinary world, but it takes the invention of another metaphorical, religious world (the world of the Catholic belief-system) to locate its truth and its importance in the vision of reality that belongs to the faith we share with Jesus.

The process of using metaphors is complicated only when it has to be spelled out. Everybody uses metaphors naturally and unconsciously every day. We are most conscious of the metaphorical process when we meet it in the high arts of poetry and rhetoric, when a speaker or writer (or politician) is out to persuade and convince others to adopt a certain point of view, a certain way of seeing things, a new approach to their world, a new way of 'coming to terms' – imported, metaphorical terms – with the world in which they live. 'Look at it this way ...' Rhetoric and poetry work, more or less subtly, by suggestion, by persuasion, by putting an imaginative construction on things, in order to produce whatever effect they desire. They suggest, in all kinds of ways, newly imported verbal terms in which they want their audience and readers to revise or enlarge their perception of the world. They aim at recommending the adoption of those terms. The ways employed might include arguments of more or less logical rigour, illustrations, stories, individual analogies; and in poetry the subtler collocation of the sound and sense of the words themselves to help to evoke the desired perception. What is happening in the use of metaphorical language is that the speaker or writer is introducing people, not directly to new information, or to new literal 'facts', or to some different and distinct world as such. Rather, he is revealing a fresh way of understanding the ordinary world in which the hearer or reader happens to be living.

Such is the process which I describe as 'metaphor'. Metaphor belongs to, and indeed may be said to characterize, our human language capability. We would be lost without it. Without it, for instance, we could not say 'the sun rises' – which, literally speaking, it does not do, of course. But what happens is that the mundane act of our own getting up in the morning is imaginatively observed as having a resemblance to the appearance of the sun over the horizon; and merely by that transference of terms from ourselves to the sun, we are invited to see the world we inhabit in a new, positive and rather flattering way as the centre of our solar system. We willingly accept the invitation, non-factual, non-literal, pre-Copernican as it is. We give ourselves an enhanced and enlarged status – as if we were the sole focus of the sun's daytime attentions. But, literally speaking, the sun stays where it is, and we stick to revolving on our old orbit around it. This may be a trivial example, but in its minor way it shows the power of a simple metaphor to suggest and reveal a fresh and enlivening perception of ourselves and the world we live in.

But whilst we all have easy and habitual recourse to metaphor in much of our discourse, there are those who are especially gifted in its use. According to the field in which they employ their gift, they are writers, philosophers, prophets, poets, politicians – and, because they are faced with the more difficult task of expressing what they imaginatively discern in the mystery of God, the founders of religions. Whatever they may claim about the source of their gift for metaphor, or even about the provenance of the metaphors themselves, the effectiveness of their use of metaphor will, in human terms, directly depend on the degree of imagination with which founders of religion can express themselves, and so communicate whatever their particular message happens to be. Their gift for metaphor is, in the last analysis, a personal gift. This rule applies to the human imagination of Jesus just as much as to any other 'inspired' founder. As Aristotle says, 'This alone cannot be got from someone else, and is a sign of native talent.'

Driven, inspired, by his personal insights, Jesus proved himself supremely capable of making metaphors out of his experience of our common world, and of interpreting – making us understand – our common world in ways that enlarge and transfigure its meaning. Of course, the sheer vividness and force of their imaginations will sometimes make religious geniuses sound as if they had personal access to another, distinct realm of reality and truth. The power of their metaphors can be such that they seem to be describing another world entirely: to be giving a factual, literal account of a reality beyond the ordinary reality we have to live in. But the fact is that they live in the same old worlds as we all do; and it is their imaginative vision of the meaning, the significance, of our ordinary, common worlds that they are seeking to express. No doubt gifted visionaries of every kind have, in their zeal for over-investing in their own metaphors, managed to delude themselves into supposing that they are actually in direct contact with a reality other than this one. We have to be very careful not to follow them in their delusion. But this critical caution does not entail, even despite the obviously crazy claims of some of them, rejecting out of hand what others might be trying to say about the meaning of the ordinary world we live in.

So my revision of Catholicism would have to emphasize the metaphorical nature of the religious language which its Founder – and all those later, far inferior theologians – had to use. There are other ways of looking at both the result and the process of using metaphors, and I am aware that there are differences between them. As I have said, traditional theologians have long favoured the use of 'analogy' to describe the mental shift which they say must be brought into play in their discourse about the transcendent realm of God and his actions. But I find 'analogy' obscure as a description of the *process* involved in 'doing theology'; and as a description of the *result* of the process I find it ambiguous. It is too easy to think that analogy does give limited access to some other, further, rather less literal world, a world whose literalism has only been, so to speak, diluted. In any case, most theologians, having sworn mental allegiance to the analogical method, tend to ignore it in practice and fall straight back into the comfortably literal, deceiving both themselves and others. 'Myth', too, is a fashionable term for the description of the world of religious and theological discourse. But whilst it may describe the *result* which religious thought and language achieve, it fails to account for the *process* involved in the production of myths and the reasons for it. Hence 'myth' is almost too bald a description, and, for many people, too like 'fairy-tale', for what theological and religious language is about. Again, 'symbol' is another way of saying what the *result* of such language usage is, but it is difficult to envisage the *process* whereby it comes about. But 'symbol' I find too polyvalent and slippery a term to use with any confidence. All these terms – analogy, myth, symbol – no doubt have their uses in the right hands, but I prefer to stick with the literary and verbal term 'metaphor' as an account of the *process* which takes place when we have recourse to religious and theological language; and as a description of the imaginative *result* obtained.

When it comes to the particular power or faculty of the human mind which creates the constructions and fictions of metaphor in order to enable us to express such understanding as we can have of what we find a mystery, I can see no alternative to turning to the imagination – the basic human ability to create and employ images when faced with what is unknowable directly or what is only sensed. We have an innate gift for creating images and functioning through images – to use our imaginations where we cannot simply use our reasoning minds to gain insight into what we do not and cannot know. The handiest account of what I mean by imagination I find in the following description given by that wild and wonderful English genius, Samuel Taylor Coleridge – the kind of imagination he calls 'secondary' (*Biographia Literaria*, chap. X). He went on to describe it, and to distinguish it sharply from the uncreative 'fancy' (*ibid.* chap. XIII):

> The imagination ... I consider either as primary, or secondary. The primary imagination I hold to be the living power and prime agent of all human perception, and as a repetition in the finite mind of the eternal act of creation in the infinite I AM. The secondary I consider as an echo of the former, coexisting with the conscious will, yet still as identical with the primary in the kind of its agency, and differing only in degree, and in the mode of its operation. It dissolves, diffuses, dissipates, in order to re-create; or where this process is rendered impossible, yet still at all events it struggles to idealize and to unify. It is essentially vital ...
>
> Fancy, on the contrary, has no other counters to play with, but fixities and definites. The fancy is indeed no other than a mode of memory emancipated from the order of time and space ...

I take this to mean that the primary imagination is what Coleridge calls the human mind's power to receive sense-impressions from the world about us, and out of them to create perceived images, or perceptions, from which the rational mind can then proceed to its typical work of understanding. As the old adage had it: *Nihil in intellectu, nisi prius in sensu* – 'nothing reaches the understanding without first coming through the senses'. But it is Coleridge's secondary imagination that exercises the imaginative creativity which produces the metaphors which

constitute our religious beliefs. Significantly, its purpose is to 're-
create' our world in terms of something else. With Coleridge's
fancy we have nothing to do; although I cannot resist remarking
that what he says of the products of the fancy could pass for a
description of a great deal of the theology I have encountered,
and may explain why it appeared so dead. But it is to the secondary, creative imagination that human beings must turn to provide
them with the appropriate kind of intelligible insight when they
confront the saving mystery of God: when the human mind has
reached the end of its strictly reasoning tether, and still needs to
come to terms – imaginative terms – with the mystery which
alone can offer it the promise of fulfilment. For the kind of imagination required Coleridge coined his own strange adjective:
'esemplastic' – meaning 'moulding into a unity', creating a world
or a limited whole. This seems to me to be what the imagination
does in the formation of the beliefs which express the vision of
reality evoked by faith.

  Yet in all this it must be remembered that necessary as the
elevation of the imagination to a leading role in the revision of
Catholicism certainly is, it is by no means sufficient. In the case of
Catholicism recourse must be had to an entirely specific – in fact
uniquely individual – set of imaginative insights into the mystery
of God which provide Catholicism with its very foundation.
These insights came to their first expression in the creative imagination of Jesus as expressions of his vision of reality in the light
of his personal faith in the mystery of God. Jesus, as a fully
human being, also needed to come to terms with the mystery that
confronted his, and everyone's, humanity – a mystery of which
his experience of human living and facing death made him
supremely conscious. The exemplary human faith of Jesus also
needed to be supported and expressed in and by his beliefs –
beliefs which were based on material available in the tradition of
his native Judaism, but 'metaphorized' in his imagination to give
the kind of novel meaning which his co-religionists found so
offensive, but which his disciples were prepared to adopt. Jesus'
faith involved a new vision of the saving mystery of God beyond
that afforded by Judaism as he experienced it – or, as Jesus' first
interpreter Paul preferred to put it, opposed to that on offer
through the observance, or works, of the Law.

  I have stressed the importance of metaphor and the human
imagination, and their employment by Jesus because I deem it
important to incorporate two key values in my revision of
Catholicism. In the first place, I would wish to eliminate the need

and the possibility of bogus appeals to the literal 'Beyond' or to the merely theological as the source from which the religion and spirituality of Catholicism derive their meaning and their value; or as the theatre in which Catholicism really operates – where 'the action' really is. There exists the mystery of being human (which we call God), and there exists humanity in the here-and-now. Catholicism finds the meaning of both of these in the humanity Jesus shares with us; and it is the purpose of the religion and the spirituality of Catholicism to bring the two into spiritual contact 'for us and for our salvation'. We do not need a literal 'Beyond', and we should not fall for the temptation to run to it for intellectual and moral cover – a move well described by Tom Gornall in another of his memorable early warnings as 'Dialling 999' – and to seek explanations of the puzzles with which life confronts us in ready-made theological concepts like 'revelation', 'the incarnation', and so forth. In the second place, in my revision of Catholicism I want to 'push' the sheer humanity of Jesus and all that is entailed in it (his salvific faith, religious vision, insight, mind, imagination), because in so doing I would be 'pushing' the humanity which the whole of mankind shares with him, and Catholicism might then be discerned as the one, true humanism.

∽

A fifth and final rule would have to determine the place and function of the institutional Church in the religion and spirituality of my revised Catholicism. The Church had exercised a dominant influence over long stretches of my life, and I was far from ungrateful for the benefits I had derived from the privileged roles I had been called on to play in its service. Perhaps above all, the Church had given me a sense of belonging, and the Jesuits had endowed this sense of belonging with a determinate identity. In this way they had, insofar as they could, supplied deficiencies in me. I suppose I had needed to belong and was still in search of a secure identity when I was still in my teens. But there is more to real human living than having your identity and your personal worth affirmed by strangers. Neither the Church nor the Jesuits – so I had come to think – were able to put me on the road to the fully human 'salvation', the personal and spiritual fulfilment involved in coming to terms with the real, ordinary world, the fulfilment, which as I saw it, the religion of Catholicism was supposed to offer. This had to come to me from God, the mystery which defined my being human, through my sharing the faith of Jesus by my following the religion of Catholicism. Where Catholicism promised that faith shared with Jesus would vouchsafe transforming insights into the human condition and its remarkable potential for an ever fuller, more open human life lived in an ordinary world imaginatively construed in terms of Catholic beliefs, my long experience of the Church and the Jesuits had found that all this had been predetermined, foreclosed, functionalized, reduced to formulas and practices – in a word, discounted in favour of an impersonal religious system which would be all you would need to carry you through this vale of tears into some fictional world beyond. The mystery and the potential involved in being human had been pre-empted and, so to speak, drained out of it. In effect, there was little room for religion and personal spirituality, since they were not needed, and might distract you from the demands of the system. In my own case, after many years of cooperation, disillusionment had set in, and I found that what the Church and the Jesuits offered was not the life-enhancing and death-confronting approach to life that characterized the faith of Jesus. In fact the institutional Church, in some of its aspects and functions, I found inimical to the religion and spirituality of the Catholicism which it was meant to preserve, promote and represent. But there is nothing in this commonplace criticism of the Church that has not already been better expressed – and at much greater length than I could express it; so I shall not pursue that matter here.

My fifth rule has a more positive purpose, which is to put the institutional Church in its place – the place it must have in any revised Catholicism. All of my rules for some eventual revision of Catholicism – it will have been noticed – have advocated either the salvaging and elevation of neglected features in Catholicism to their proper prominence, or the relegation of hitherto over-prominent elements to their proper places. Thus the humanity of Jesus and his human faith and the religious function of metaphor and the imagination have been brought to the fore; whereas theology and the Catholic system of doctrines and beliefs has been assigned its proper supporting role. In this necessary re-prioritization nothing need be lost, but some hitherto prominent features of Catholicism will find themselves recycled and duly demoted, and among them is the institutional Church which has its centre in Rome and exercises its authority over the whole spread of Roman Catholicism.

When Catholics declare in the creed that 'we believe in one, holy, catholic and apostolic Church', they are, according to the view of religious belief-statements I have adopted above, not referring directly to the institutional Church as we know it. Not only is there no point in religious belief in the obvious case of what John Henry Newman called 'a fact in the world's history'; but not even the most ardent Catholic would suppose that the Church as we know it is complete in its unity, its holiness or its universality or indeed in its conformity with the inchoate religion of the apostolic community who knew Jesus. Rather, when Catholics formally declare that they believe in 'the Church', they are employing a theological metaphor (transferring the meaning from other gatherings or assemblies) to give expression to what they see as a key component in their faith-induced vision of reality – the ultimate gathering of all human kind into the 'salvation' offered by Jesus. In fact, it seems to me (though this is fanciful rather than imaginative) that the metaphor might have its origins in the highly figurative context in which Jesus himself solemnly declared: 'you are Peter, and on this rock I will build my church, and the gates of Hades will not prevail against it' (Matthew 16.18 NRSV). In a text that has been avidly appropriated of the Roman Church, 'church' does not, of course, refer to an actual Church whose institutional reality in Rome Jesus somehow foresaw, but – if indeed the remark came from Jesus at all – must represent Jesus' imaginative way of speaking about his hopes for a united community of followers under the initial leadership of Simon Peter. It is in this metaphorical sense that Catholic belief in the Church appears in the earliest extant creeds (from the second century), and in the creeds still used today.

It has been a standing temptation for the institutional Roman Church to be carried away on the wings of the grand theological metaphors which the body (another metaphor) of believers created for itself in the course of its long history. Such products of the theological imagination (*theologoumena*) as understand the world community of Catholic believers in terms of 'the people of God', the assembly (*ekklesia*), or 'church' of those who share the Spirit of Christ and constitute his 'Mystical Body' in which the wide variety of its members are 'incorporated' – these are respectable and helpful efforts at the metaphorical understanding of the communal effect of participating in the salvation which Catholicism has to offer. But they are not be taken literally as descriptions of the actual, existing, institutional Roman Church, which, at least from time to time, has been only too willing to claim, or suggest, that they are precisely that. They represent expressions of belief and call for careful understanding as ways in which the community of believers sees itself in the vision of reality afforded by sharing the faith of Jesus. We have to beware of their being hi-jacked as literal descriptions of the Church as we know it.

By hi-jacking theological and metaphorical expressions and ascribing them literally to itself, the institutional Church long ago inaugurated a programme of self-aggrandizement which has led to its regarding itself as the actual object in which Catholics must formally declare they believe in their creed. It is this deeply entrenched attitude on the part of Rome, along with all the ceaseless propaganda that supports it, that urgently requires that the institutional Church be severely relegated in any revision of the religion of Catholicism. The institutional Church has promoted itself, over the centuries, to the virtual status of an end-in-itself, whereas it cannot possibly be more than the means of preaching and practising the religion of Catholicism, and promoting the salvation it exists to serve. To serve those who make up the Church is what it exists to do, not to rule. It might not be too much to say that the institutional Church has contrived to take over, to displace, the religion of Catholicism and has effectively reduced it to a religious system of its own devising, leaving little room for the personal and spiritual development of its members, and being suspicious of any such development, should it occur without due permission. In fact, this is much the same kind of systematic distortion of religious and spiritual values as I considered I had discovered on my long detour among the Jesuits.

Hence, in my revision of Catholicism, I would seek to relocate and refashion the Church in a less overpowering and intrusive form. I would want to reduce the overall influence of Rome and to lower its profile, to decentralize its government, to return the Pope to his role as the Bishop of Rome, from where he can exhibit his infallible leadership to the rest of the Church, to make the Church far more local, to give bishops back their proper status, to educate intelligent men and women to serve as clergy, married or celibate, according to their wishes, to let local churches forge suitably ecumenical links with other churches, and so forth. But these I count as no more than fairly superficial reforms, endlessly discussed but, in my opinion, hardly likely to be put into effect until there occurs a far more serious attempt to subject the religion and spirituality of Catholicism to the kind of radical revision along the lines of the rules I have tried to draft.

I have stressed what I see as the distinctiveness of Catholicism as evidenced in the form of salvation it claims to offer – by my account a radically humanistic affair consisting in the spiritual sharing of a faith-vision with Catholicism's Founder which, given imaginative shape and content by Catholicism's belief-system, serves to enable a Catholic to make the most of the one life we have in this one world, and to face that life's crises, the weakness of sin, the sufferings, the illnesses, and eventually death itself – and even the unknowable consequences of death for ourselves and for those we love. How other religions, even how other Christian Churches, see all this I have not ventured to discuss. As I said from the start, I do not have either the experience or the knowledge to deal with these matters. All I know is that there is a clear distinctiveness about Catholicism as a religion and as a spirituality, and it was this I found it necessary to try and rediscover by initiating a process of revising it. But there is nothing exclusive, or unecumenical, in labouring the distinctiveness of Catholicism, if only because what is distinctive about it is that it is all-inclusive; and my rules are, *mutatis mutandis*, all applicable to any religion or Church. As I see it, Catholicism, duly understood, cannot be limited to – and still less identified with – a particular Church, however dominant, precisely because it is, I believe, the religion and the spirituality of humanity as such. By this I do not mean that other religions and other Christian Churches need conform to it, but that they should see whether their own religious systems do not also call for a revision which ensures the salvation of our humanity, in the manner in which Catholicism is meant to do. Do they work 'for us and for our salvation'? No doubt other religions have Founders whose salvific insights have been overlaid by later distortions; and no doubt other Christian Churches have inspired origins which have come to be neglected. It strikes me as being thoroughly ecumenical to raise what must be a basic issue for any religion.

Of course, all I have so roughly said still requires careful formulation and precise documentation; and, in a way, all I have done so far is to apply to Catholicism as a whole those precepts which the Church laid down at Vatican II for 'the appropriate renewal of religious life' in its own religious communities, and which I quoted in part in chapter 3. Renewal is said to involve two simultaneous processes: '(1) a continuous return to the sources of all Christian life and to the original inspiration behind a given community and (2) an adjustment of the community to the changed conditions of the times' (*Perfectae Caritatis*, 2). What I have called for is an adjustment on the part of Catholicism which cannot be effected by any amount of ecclesiastical tinkering, but which is far more radical, and which involves not only a renewed intimacy with the spirit of Catholicism's one foundation, but also much serious critical thinking about the end and the means of religion. No one who observes our world can deny the many oppressive, explosive and destructive forces that drive what still passes for religion. Catholicism, as a religious humanism, could serve as an example of what true religion might bring about.

❧

Meanwhile my life goes on in my ordinary world and I have much personal progress still to make. My native Catholicism, now revised and better understood, will continue to give me the religious support I need as I have to make my way through whatever remains of life, my detour over. Whilst I feel I have enjoyed a privileged, even somewhat pampered, existence, and whilst I am no longer alone but happily married, there are still uncertainties, the trials that beset old age, and death to be faced. I hope I have at least picked up something of what John Keats famously defined as 'Negative Capability, that is when a man is capable of being in uncertainties, Mysteries, doubts, without any irritable reaching after fact and reason'. Even more, I hope I have acquired some share in that positive human faith which is, as I have suggested, fundamentally characteristic of Catholicism.

I sometimes ask myself what it now feels like to have come to the conclusions to which my life has directed me. To answer such a question is the job of a poet, and I am not a poet. But I know a poet who gets very close to expressing what I feel. Without an explicit reference to religion, this poem by Wallace Stevens – *The Latest Freed Man* (Parts of a World, 1937) – gets the feel of things as they are:

> Tired of the old descriptions of the world,
> The latest freed man rose at six and sat
> On the edge of his bed. He said, 'I suppose there is
> A doctrine to this landscape. Yet, having just
> Escaped from the truth, the morning is color and mist,
> Which is enough: the moment's rain and sea,
> The moment's sun (the strong man vaguely seen),
> Overtaking the doctrine of this landscape. Of him
> And of his works, I am sure. He bathes in the mist
> Like a man without a doctrine. The light he gives –
> It is how he gives his light. It is how he shines,
> Rising upon the doctors in their beds
> And on their beds ...'
> And so the freed man said.
> It was how the sun came shining into his room:
> To be without a description of to be,

For a moment on rising, at the edge of the bed, to be,
To have the ant of the self changed into an ox
With its organic boomings, to be changed
From a doctor into an ox, before standing up,
To know that the change and that the ox-like struggle
Come from the strength that is the strength of the sun,
Whether it comes directly or from the sun.
It was how he was free. It was how his freedom came.
It was being without description, being an ox.
It was the importance of the trees outdoors,
The freshness of the oak-leaves, not so much
That they were oak-leaves, as the way they looked.
It was everything being more real, himself
At the centre of reality, seeing it.
It was everything bulging and blazing and big in itself,
The blue of the rug, the portrait of Vidal,
Qui fait fi des joliesses banales, the chairs.

Printed in the United Kingdom
by Lightning Source UK Ltd.
105111UKS00001B/43-240

9 780852 446362